Bias in
Psychiatric
Diagnosis

Bias in Psychiatric Diagnosis

Edited by Paula J. Caplan and Lisa Cosgrove

A project of the Association for Women in Psychology

JASON ARONSON
Lanham • Boulder • New York • Toronto • Oxford

Published in the United States of America
by Jason Aronson
An imprint of Rowman & Littlefield Publishers, Inc.

A wholly owned subsidary of
The Rowman & Littlefield Publishing Group, Inc.
4501 Forbes Boulevard, Suite 200, Lanham, Maryland 20706
www.rowmanlittlefield.com

PO Box 317
Oxford
OX2 9RU, UK

British Library Cataloguing in Publication Information Available

Library of Congress Cataloging-in-Publication Data

Bias in psychiatric diagnosis / edited by Paula J. Caplan and Lisa Cosgrove.
     p. cm.
   Includes bibliographical references and index.
   ISBN 0-7657-0375-0 (hardback : alk. paper) — ISBN 0-7657-0001-8 (pbk. : alk.
paper)
    1. Mental illness—Diagnosis—Social aspects. 2. Psychodiagnostics—Validity. 3.
Discrimination. I. Caplan, Paula J. II. Cosgrove, Lisa.
   RC469.B52 2004
   616.89'075—dc22   2004005939

Printed in the United States of America

♾️™ The paper used in this publication meets the minimum requirements of American
National Standard for Information Sciences—Permanence of Paper for Printed Library
Materials, ANSI/NISO Z39.48-1992.

To the memory of Paul Gladstone, his radiance
—Paula J. Caplan

To Ellin Ellett Cosgrove, in memory of Robert Cosgrove,
who taught by example, and to Kelly, Brendan, and Abby
for making the world a better place
—Lisa Cosgrove

Only with radical social changes leading to a just society will there be a reduction in the incidence of emotional problems.

—Psychologist George Albee

Contents

Foreword by *Maureen McHugh*   xiii

Acknowledgments   xvii

Is This Really Necessary?   xix
Paula J. Caplan and Lisa Cosgrove

**PART I THE CREATION OF BIAS IN
          PSYCHIATRIC DIAGNOSIS**

1   The Construction of Illness   3
    Meadow Linder

2   The Deep Structure of Bias in Psychiatric Diagnosis   9
    Jeffrey Poland and Paula J. Caplan

3   Creating Post-traumatic Stress Disorder: A Case Study of the
    History, Sociology, and Politics of Psychiatric Classification   25
    Meadow Linder

4   Abnormal Psychology Textbooks Exclude Feminist
    Criticism of the *DSM*   41
    Autumn Wiley

**PART II LEGAL IMPLICATIONS OF BIAS IN
           PSYCHIATRIC DIAGNOSIS**

5   Psychiatric Diagnosis in the Legal System   49
    Emily J. Caplan

6 Bias and Subjectivity in Diagnosing Mental Retardation in
       Death Penalty Cases   55
       Paula J. Caplan

7 What Is It That's Being Called "Parental Alienation Syndrome"?   61
       Paula J. Caplan

PART III SOME FORMS THAT BIAS TAKES

8 The Intersection of Racism and Sexism in Psychiatric Diagnosis 71
       Alisha Ali

9 Clinical Cases and the Intersection of Sexism and Racism   77
       Nayyar Javed

10 Should Racism Be Classified As a Mental Illness?   81
       Wesley E. Profit

11 Ageism in Psychiatric Diagnosis   89
       Rachel Josefowitz Siegel

12 The Psychiatric Policing of Children   99
       Louise Armstrong

13 Confusing Terms and False Dichotomies in Learning Disabilities 109
       Paula J. Caplan

14 Diagnosis of Low-Income Women   115
       Heather E. Bullock

15 Seeking "Normal" Sexuality on a Complex Matrix   121
       William R. Metcalfe and Paula J. Caplan

16 Gender Bias and Sex Distribution of Mental Disorders
       in the *DSM-IV-TR*   127
       Lisa Cosgrove and Bethany Riddle

17 Mislabeling Anxiety and Depression in Rural Women   141
       Nikki Gerrard

PART IV SPECIFIC LABELS

18 Bias and Schizophrenia   149
       Jeffrey Poland

19 The Truth about "False Memory Syndrome"   163
       Karen A. Olio

20 Reclaiming the Meanings of "Self-esteem"   171
Nayyar Javed and Nikki Gerrard

21 Agoraphobia   177
Maureen McHugh and Lisa Cosgrove

22 Depression in Women   183
Sarah McSweeney

23 The "Eating-Disordered" Patient   189
Judith R. Rabinor

24 The Fine Line between Clinical and Subclinical Anorexia   193
Emily Cohen

25 Histrionic Personality   201
Pamela Reed Gibson

26 Post-traumatic Stress Disorder   207
Dana Becker

27 Some Gender Biases in Diagnosing Traumatized Women   213
Vincent Fish

28 Medicalizing Menstrual Distress   221
Lisa Cosgrove and Paula J. Caplan

PART V MOVING AHEAD

29 A New View of Women's Sexual Problems   233
The Working Group on A New View of Women's Sexual Problems

30 Resisting Diagnosis   241
Gloria Anthony

31 The Importance of Critical Inquiry   243
Lisa Cosgrove

32 Some Future Contenders   249
Paula J. Caplan and Wesley E. Profit

Index   255

About the Contributors   263

Foreword

As the Coordinator of the Association for Women in Psychology (AWP), I am delighted to be involved with the development and distribution of this book as a project of AWP. Encouraging psychologists and other mental health workers to develop a critical perspective on diagnosis is an important mission and a form of advocacy for women. This charge has a long tradition within AWP.

The Association for Women in Psychology (AWP) is a scientific and educational feminist organization devoted to reevaluating and reformulating the role of psychology in women's lives. AWP challenges the assumptions of clinical and professional practices that limit the understanding and treatment of women (and men). Its role includes the critique of sexism and other forms of oppression and bias in professional and institutional practices and the education and sensitization of mental health professionals. Since 1969, AWP has provided opportunities for creative feminist contributions and the dissemination of feminist ideas through its conferences, workshops, and newsletter.

AWP was founded in 1969 when disenfranchised members of the American Psychological Association met with local feminist activists to discuss discrimination in the academic and professional worlds of psychology and to examine the contribution of psychology to women's oppression (Tiefer 1991). Since then, AWP members have been active in the both the critique of psychology and the development of feminist approaches to theory, research, teaching, and practice. Sexism in psychotherapy was among the original targets for change. In the 1970s, AWP attempted to define feminist therapy and its principles and to identify feminist therapists. In 1979, AWP endorsed the principles concerning the therapy and counseling of women written by a committee in the counseling division of the American Psychological Association. In the 1980s, AWP protested several new diagnostic categories (i.e., Self-defeating Personality Disorder, Premenstrual Dysphoric

Disorder, Sadistic Personality Disorder, and Paraphilic Coercive Disorder) proposed for the revision of the *Diagnostic and Statistical Manual of Mental Disorders-Third Edition* (American Psychiatric Association 1980). Joined by other women's groups and caucuses, AWP wrote letters and picketed the 1986 convention of the American Psychiatric Association. Following months of opposition, the disputed diagnostic categories were included in the *DSM* in a newly created appendix. Feminists have pointed out that masculine-biased assumptions about healthy behavior are codified within diagnostic labels (Kaplan 1983) and that diagnostic labels applied to both women and men reflect gender role stereotypes (Fodor and Rothblum 1984; Landrine 1989).

AWP supports *Bias in Psychiatric Diagnosis* as part of its action initiative to address contemporary issues in the (mis)diagnosis of women. In her *Brief History of the Association for Women in Psychology, 1969–1991*, Tiefer (1991) concludes that, in the early 1990s, AWP had a diminished activist role because it had not created a structure to find and fight new battles. Recently, AWP has attempted to recreate the activist role of the organization by developing Social Action Initiatives. The Social Action Initiatives are activist projects consistent with AWP's mission. Action Initiatives are adopted at the national level, and members are invited to work at the local level. Misdiagnosis of women has been adopted as one of the first three initiatives of AWP. As part of that initiative, AWP is supporting the efforts to address the problem of sexism in diagnosis already undertaken by longtime AWP member, Paula J. Caplan. In a second Social Action Initiative, AWP has supported the New View Campaign, a movement led by another longtime AWP member, Leonore Tiefer, to expose and critique the medicalization of women's sexuality and sexual problems. The New View Campaign and its efforts to challenge the drug-industry-supported diagnosis of Female Sexual Dysfunction are the subjects of Tiefer's chapter in *Bias in Psychiatric Diagnosis*. This book represents a continuation of AWP's proud history of analyzing sexist practice within psychology, by challenging diagnostic categories and labels that pathologize the gendered experiences of women.

While the primary emphasis in our analysis is gender, the text also addresses the ways that race, social class, age, physical disability, and sexual orientation affect the classification of human beings into categories of psychiatric diagnosis. Other marginalized groups, such as poor and rural women, are also considered. Members of each of these groups suffer when we base our conceptions of normalcy on the behavior and worldview of dominant social groups, and when the consequences of sexism, racism, homophobia, and "the struggle with poverty are misinterpreted as evidence of individual psychopathology" (Bullock, chapter 14 in this volume). As Caplan points out, "these are just a sampling of the huge number of biases" that operate in human interactions, especially in interactions of individuals who differ in their access to power (Caplan and Cosgrove, introduction in this volume).

Feminists have historically examined the politics of gender, that is, the experience of women (and men) as affected by the operation (and abuse) of power in interpersonal and institutional settings. Many of the authors in this book use the classic feminist analytic strategy of asking the basic political questions: Who says so? Who defines the problem? Who profits? Who pays? What is the price? Authors of other essays closely examine the methods and measures used to investigate and validate diagnostic categories. These classic feminist perspectives are offered here alongside contemporary postmodern perspectives on diagnosis as discourse and diagnostic categories as sociopolitical constructs. In addition to applying these analyses to various populations, settings, and diagnostic categories, the text teaches us to expose implicit assumptions in psychological practice and to examine critically the assignment of diagnostic labels. Our goal is to have every therapist and mental health worker who is trained in or employs diagnostic categories to be exposed to the feminist critique of diagnosis. While not satisfied with our impact on psychology and psychological practice to date, members of AWP are proud of our past and our continuing efforts to understand how inequality and oppression impacts women's lives, and how better to advocate for women (and men) in distress. *Bias in Psychiatric Diagnosis* represents a continuation of our efforts.

Maureen McHugh

REFERENCES

American Psychiatric Association. (1980). *The Diagnostic and Statistical Manual of Mental Disorders-III.* Washington, DC.

Fodor, I., and E. D. Rothblum. (1984). Strategies for dealing with sex role stereotypes. Pp. 86–95 in C. Brody, ed. *Women therapists working with women.* New York: Springer.

Kaplan, M. (1983). A woman's view of the *DSM-III. American Psychologist* 38, 786–92.

Tiefer, L. (1991). A brief history of the Association for Women in Psychology, 1969–1991. *Psychology of Women Quarterly* 15, 635–49.

Acknowledgments

This book is a true collaboration, and we would like to express our gratitude to the Association of Women in Psychology (AWP) and especially Joan Chrisler and Maureen McHugh for their vision, enthusiasm, and support for this project (and without whom this book would not exist). It has been a great pleasure to include so many AWP members as contributing authors, as well as all of the authors who generously gave of their time, energy, and wonderful ideas and whose patience with the process of getting this book into print is deeply appreciated. Kate Jagodzinski assisted with numerous editorial and administrative tasks; her efficiency, reliability, and intelligence are unparalleled. We thank Mary Ann Palko for her adminstrative help and good energy. We deeply appreciate, at Rowman and Littlefield, the graciousness, efficiency, and helpfulness of Lissa Jean-Jacques, and we are grateful to our production editor Erin McKindley for all of her help and support, to Alex Masulis for his help and doggedness from under his enormous pile of manuscripts, and to our copyeditor Elizabeth Pohland for her painstaking and excellent work. Paula J. Caplan also wishes to thank Robert Lescher for his wise and compassionate counsel, Catherine Krupnick for her gracious help, and, as always, her parents, Jerome Arnold Caplan and Tac Caplan, and her children, Jeremy Benjamin Caplan and Emily Julia Caplan, for their love and support. Lisa Cosgrove wishes to thank Doreen Hiltz, Jane Matz, Maxine Weinreb, Varda Konstam, and Shams Pai, who always made time to listen and read; I hope you know how much your perspective and friendship mean.

Is This Really Necessary?

Paula J. Caplan and Lisa Cosgrove

The judges of normality are present everywhere.

—Michel Foucault, *Discipline and Punishment*, 304

an official announcement [reads that] . . . nearly half of all Americans experience a psychiatric disorder. . . . does that mean no one is normal . . . ?
Or [do] we live in such a crazy-making, sick, impersonal society that it
does serious psychological damage to half of us? . . . should we be calling
[people the] mentally ill, . . . or . . . society's wounded?

—Paula J. Caplan, *They Say You're Crazy: How the World's
Most Powerful Psychiatrists Decide Who's Normal*, 6

The word "name-calling" provokes negative associations, but the term "diagnostic labeling" has an aura of scientific precision, objectivity, and professionalism that lends it tremendous power. Language confers power (Miller and
Swift 1977), and that power is "not distributed equitably across the social hi-
erarchy" (Hare-Mustin and Marecek 1997, 106), a fact that has had tremendous impact on those who have sought mental health services. Diagnosis of
physical problems has often been extremely useful,[1] and in principle, psychiatric diagnosis can be helpful, too (e.g., Emily J. Caplan, chapter 5 in this volume). Unfortunately, psychiatric labeling has been conceived of and applied in
extremely biased ways and is surprisingly unwarranted by scientific research,
and thus it can result in serious harm (P. Caplan 1995). As Hare-Mustin and
Marecek note, "a diagnostic label . . . has a profound influence on what we
think of people so labeled and how they think about themselves" (1997, 105).
In addition, diagnostic labels often create problems with employers and the
military and can potentially result in the loss of child custody, health insurance,
and the right to make decisions about one's legal affairs and medical care

(Emily J. Caplan, chapter 5). Furthermore, the topics deemed important for a client's therapy sessions can be heavily determined—sometimes for better but often for worse—by the diagnostic system and the label(s) given to that client. These dangers and others, combined with many forms of bias, help to determine *who* gets diagnosed and *with what labels*.

In the United States, distress is intensely psychologized,[2] including the proliferation of diagnoses and therapists, drugs marketed for every psychological state imaginable, cocktail party conversation in which laypeople analyze their own behavior and that of others, increasing use of mental health experts and social scientists as witnesses in court, and even New Age practices that involve psychological concepts. Thus, it is all the more alarming that, as Autumn Wiley shows (2001), authors of abnormal psychiatry textbooks almost or entirely ignore the extensive critiques of bias that have been published for years about the *Diagnostic and Statistical Manual of Mental Disorders* (*DSM* [American Psychiatric Association 2000]). It is not surprising, then, that undergraduate psychology majors "learn" about forms of alleged mental illness that have never been proven to exist and about diagnostic terms, but they do not learn about the biases involved in their creation and use. It is not that assigning a psychiatric diagnostic label is never helpful, but it is widely—and wrongly—believed that diagnostic labels are very helpful to therapists for choosing treatments and predicting treatment outcome. Unfortunately, in the realm of mental disorders, this is rarely true.[3]

The terms "mental illness," "mental disorder," "abnormality," "normality," and even "insanity" are constructs, terms that do not correspond to clearly identifiable, "real" objects. Constructs are defined by whoever does the defining, and the power to make a definition stick resides usually in groups that have the most social, political, and/or economic power. Beginning in the last twenty years of the twentieth century, the small number of primarily white, high-status, male psychiatrists who make the ultimate decisions about what goes into the therapists' diagnostic "Bible," the *Diagnostic and Statistical Manual of Mental Disorders,* have had more power than any group to decide who is and is not psychologically normal. But the *DSM* authors are not the only creators of diagnostic categories, for drug companies and book authors with "M.D." or "Ph.D." after their names have also been granted authority by the media and the wider public.

Biases in diagnosis of "mental disorder" take effect on shifting sands, because no one has ever been able to come up with a definition that they considered satisfactory, as the *DSM* authors have courageously acknowledged (Kirk and Kutchins 1992). The subjectivity is evident in the following italicized terms: mental disorder, the *DSM* authors say, is a *clinically significant syndrome or pattern* that is *associated with distress or disability* or with *significantly increased risk of suffering, death, pain, disability, or an important loss of freedom* and must be considered *a manifestation of a behavioral, psy-chological, or biological dysfunction* in the individual. The further proviso, that it must not be an *expectable and culturally sanctioned* response, presents particularly thorny problems in light of the richly *multi*cultural world in which we live. The problems with this definition remind us poignantly that "mental disorder" is, after all, a construct.

The fact that psychiatric diagnosis is ubiquitous (in the mental health system and in noninstitutional contexts like social gatherings and the media) has tremendous impact on psychiatrists, social workers, pastoral counselors, guidance counselors, psychologists, family therapists, nurse practitioners, psychiatric nurses, and others. As many clinicians realize, demonstrably far more helpful than labeling in mental health settings is an intense focus on any or all of the following: therapists' and others' provision of listening ears, support, respect, familiarity with relevant research and with effective clinicians' experiences, and a questioning approach to the literature and clinical narratives (P. Caplan 1995). Another helpful tool that is far too rarely used is *formulation*, the working out of the most likely explanations, insofar as one can tell, of the causes or perpetuating factors of the person's problems (Block 2002).

When *DSM* began increasing in size because of its skyrocketing number of categories and subcategories, its authors claimed that their labels were "atheoretical," not tied to any theory or treatment, and solidly based in empirical research (American Psychiatric Association 1980). Partly because of this atheoretical approach, the formulation that had been so important in psychoanalysis and many other "talk" therapies has become dwarfed and, in some cases, replaced by an emphasis on diagnosis. This change was impelled by the prominence of the *DSM*, the American Psychiatric Association's aggressive marketing strategy for it, and the ready acceptance of its hundreds of categories and subcategories, by many therapists and researchers. The number of *DSM* labels has skyrocketed over the past fifty years. With each subsequent revision, new diagnostic categories have been added and others sometimes changed or deleted. In the seven years between the 1987 and 1994 editions, for example, the number of categories and subcategories increased from 297 to 374 (P. Caplan 1995). In addition to growing in size, this manual has become increasingly influential, due to the fact that third-party reimbursement now usually requires that patients receive a *DSM* diagnosis. Increased emphasis on diagnosis was impelled by insurance groups and health maintenance organizations (that want therapy to be brief and therefore want particular problems matched with particular drugs and quickly cured), by those media people who are too impressed by the psychiatric establishment to do real investigative journalism, and by laypeople who understandably want to believe that, as with a broken bone, diagnosis can lead to cure.

In addition to these concerns, six other factors inspired this book:

- The burgeoning literature about bias in diagnosis is not reflected in most programs in which psychotherapists of any kind are trained (or in undergraduate psychology courses (Autumn Wiley 2001, chapter 4 in this volume), although students in an increasing number of disciplines are being trained to become licensed therapists. Students in *all* therapy training programs need to think critically about diagnosis, the *DSM,* and the medical model on which much training is based.
- Increasingly, accrediting bodies for therapy training programs require the inclusion of materials about bias, and the literature about bias in diagnosis has been sparse.
- Harmful forms of bias are both morally wrong and therapeutically counterproductive, yet, even now, more than three decades after the publication of Phyllis Chesler's landmark book, *Women and Madness* (1972), trainees and faculty who attempt to point out instances of bias are often subjected to ostracism or mockery.
- The whole enterprise of psychiatric diagnosis is entirely unregulated, a fact to which the attention of students in training programs is rarely, if ever, drawn.
- Diagnosis of "mental illness" is more an art than a science, and many labels, even in the *DSM*, have not been shown by high-quality research to represent real entities (research by Pantony, reported by P. Caplan 1995). This contributes to the low agreement rate between clinician pairs about which *DSM* diagnosis to give a patient (Kirk and Kutchins 1992; P. Caplan 1995), and without this agreement (reliability), there *can be no validity.* As a result, any professional who applies to a patient a label that has not been validated and then bases treatment on that label is, in essence, submitting the patient to experimental treatment without their knowledge and consent. This has serious moral, ethical, and legal consequences.
- The possible negative fallout of diagnosis makes it important for therapists to realize that their patients will be at differential risk for those consequences, depending on their sex, age, racial classification, and so on.

Therapists who, uncritically following the medical model, believe that all emotional problems are caused by factors within the individual make what social psychologists call the fundamental attribution error (Ross 1977; Wiener and Marcus 1994), failing to consider the effects of social factors. Therapists working within the mental health system have developed alternatives to the medical model. For example, in 1987 Janet Stoppard led the Women and Mental Health Committee of the Canadian Mental Health Association (CMHA) in producing a report called *Women and mental health in Canada: Strategies for change* (Women and Mental Health Committee 1987). They dispensed with unvalidated systems of diagnostic labels, instead naming many of the known and proven causes of women's suffering, including poverty, violence, and lack of social and political power and resources. They proposed that money and energy be channeled into eradicating these causes, ending the report with point-by-point recommendations for action in therapists' training programs, various levels of government, and the CMHA itself. Unfortunately, the CMHA allowed the report to go out of print shortly after it was published, and neither the CMHA nor any other group or individual has reported having tracked whether any recommendations were followed. There is little evidence that they were, and there is little evidence in Canada or the United States that attempts to call attention to these major sources of emotional difficulty have permeated the mental health system. Clinicians and researchers could advocate for replacement of current diagnostic labels with descriptors like "the consequences of poverty," "the consequences of violence," "the effects of homelessness," "the damage done by interpersonal discrimination/demeaning treatment," and so on. The *DSM* authors provide one axis on which "psychosocial stressors" are to be listed, but the terms on Axes I and II are the focus of diagnosis and practice, and psychosocial stressors are often left out entirely by clinicians.

Much current research is based on *DSM* categories, even when those categories have not been shown to represent real entities (P. Caplan 1995; Eli Lilly and Company Limited, 2003), and use of *DSM* categories can appear to some grant proposal reviewers to legitimize the proposed research. Futhermore, research reports in which *DSM* categories were used provide further apparent support for the legitimacy of the *DSM*, even when studies have no bearing on the validity or practical usefulness of a *DSM* category. However, as discussed in a number of chapters in this volume (e.g., Olio; Javed and Gerrard; P. Caplan, chapter 7 in this volume; Caplan and Profit, chapter 32 in this volume), even non-*DSM* labels can have tremendous power and be used in biased ways. For instance, labeling people as "stressed" has become so nearly ubiquitous that it threatens to lose its meaning. Often, the word is used when accurate labels would be, for instance, "ashamed" or "terrified." Paula J. Caplan heard a psychologist describe a woman recently diagnosed with late-stage breast cancer as feeling "stressed" by the news. It is troubling enough when the label "stressed" masks the intensity or character of any emotion, and it is even more disturbing when it masks the effects of oppression and violence. A brilliant dramatization of labeling's masking effect is evident in Carolyn Gage's play, *Harriet Tubman Visits a Therapist*, in which runaway slave Tubman tells a therapist about the tragedy and horror of slavery, and the therapist responds with the recommendation that Tubman perform stress-reduction exercises (Gage 1999). Sadly, this mimics what sometimes happens today with labeling of the consequences of oppression.

By and large, research on human behavior tends to be conducted by individuals who interpret their results in ways that are consistent with prevalent forms of bias (Caplan and Caplan 1999). Racism, sexism, classism, ageism, mother-blaming, ableism, and other forms of bias are sustained both within and outside the social sciences and mental health fields (Burman 1998; Fine 1992; Wilkinson and Kitzinger 1995; Caplan, 2000). Further, drug companies fund much research that is used to advocate new diagnostic categories, because finding or creating a diagnostic label for use in connection with a drug maximizes the likelihood of FDA approval and simplifies marketing. In the recent proliferation of television commercials for prescription drugs, many include a description of an ordinary phenomenon (such as shyness), the relabeling of it (shyness becomes "Social Anxiety *Disorder*") in ways that alarm people because the message is that they are mentally ill, and finally the announcement that a brand-name drug is just what the "disordered" person needs. Research on these and other drugs is frequently performed by drug companies' in-house researchers and sometimes by "independent" scientists. Drug companies do not pay the latters' salaries but give them research money and often prohibit them from publishing results that show the drugs to be ineffective or dangerous. Researchers and, indeed, at least one editor of a major medical journal are concerned about the association between funding source and study outcome (e.g., Angell 2000; Bodenheimer 2000; Davidson 1986; Friedberg, Saffran, Stinson, Nelson, and Bennett 1999; Korn 2000). Former *New England Journal of Medicine* editor Dr. Marcia Angell reports that finding a research psychiatrist to write an editorial on treatment of depression was difficult because "we found very few who did not have financial ties to drug companies that make antidepressants" (Angell 2000, 1516).

Therapists who choose or are required to diagnose their patients are likely to read research reports in "scholarly" journals, the media, or both; and research-supported biases tend to affect the diagnoses they select for their patients. One example is the tendency to label abused women as "masochistic" based on poorly designed and misinterpreted research supposedly proving that aggression is biologically impelled and thus nonpathological in men (Caplan and Caplan 1999; Caplan 1993a; Fausto-Sterling 1992). But the existence of even greater bias against women is evident in this example because of the powerful catch-22 situations in which they are placed: Women *victims* of violence are diagnosed as "masochistic," but because aggression is coded as naturally masculine, women *perpetrators* of violence, even in self-defense, are often labeled pathological for being "unwomanly," "castrating," or "psychopathic." Similarly, women who stay with abusive partners are labeled "masochistic," but women who leave are labeled "rejecting and cold" (P. Caplan 1993a; Stahly 2003; Fausto-Sterling 1992).

As human beings, mental health professionals who conduct psychological or psychiatric assessments and apply diagnostic labels can never be totally free from bias (Caplan and Wilson 1990; Fox 1997). However, many lawyers and judges operate as though assessors were infallible professionals whose work is objective science, and in this context therapists' biases can lead to infringement of the legal rights—even constitutional protection—of members of marginalized groups. When making diagnoses and recommendations, a therapist can choose which theoretical or interpretive framework to use. To simplify only a little, there are two kinds of theories, one of which tends not to be supported by good research and (probably not coincidentally) to be racist, sexist, or otherwise negatively biased, and the other tends to be based on good research and not to be negatively biased. Serious legal principles are ignored when an assessor chooses to bring one of the former into play (P. Caplan 1993b).The courtroom is a stage on which some of the tragic consequences of diagnostic labeling are frequently played out through judicial edicts that basically constitute the rubber-stamping of a therapist's diagnostic report. Consider this case: A woman and man divorce soon after their daughter is born. He has physically abused his wife. They agree that the mother will have care and custody of the child. When the daughter is a preschooler, she shows signs of having been sexually abused. The mother is alarmed but fears what her ex-husband will do if she contacts the relevant authorities. She calls her lawyer, who advises her to make a formal report of suspected abuse, which she does. Informed about this report, the judge remarks in a conference with the lawyers that if the Department of Child and Family Services fails to find that the child was abused, he will transfer custody to the father. The mother's lawyer tells her what the judge says, and she is beside herself, feeling terrified and helpless. The next day, the mother has her first appointment with the psychologist whom the judge has ordered to conduct psychological assessments of both parents. The psychologist administers her a Minnesota Multiphasic Personality Inventory, and, although all her scores fall within the "normal" range, he writes in his report that her MMPI profile showed her to be extremely defensive and that her claim that the daughter might have been abused proved her to be an hysteric, a diagnosis almost always applied to women. In the "diagnosis" section of his report, on Axis II, he says that she has "Self-defeating Features." This mother had sufficient resources to pay a good lawyer and two psychologists who could testify that (1) nothing in the court-appointed psychologist's notes or xxviPaula J. Caplan and Lisa Cosgrove

data suggested that she was defensive or hysterical, and (2) the assessor used *DSM* format and terminology to diagnose her, but the term "Self-defeating" is not in the current *DSM*. This example appears here because this scenario is tragically common.

The chapters in this book represent only a sampling of the huge number of kinds of bias in mental health diagnosis, including sexism, racism, ageism, homophobia/heterosexism, and classism. We include papers about some individual labels, as well as about problems that result from various manifestations of bias in diagnosis. We hope that awareness of some of these issues will sensitize both trainees and faculty to the sorts of things to look for in other instances, since critical thinking is developed in part by questioning the assumptions we are most likely to take for granted. Like K. Gergen (1994; 2001), we believe that productive and constructive critique engenders dialogue rather than impeding it. When we transcend dichotomous and other simplistic forms of thinking (e.g., science/politics; normal/abnormal), and when we dare to envision new ways of understanding the world, education becomes "the practice of freedom"(hooks 1994, 12), an aim that informs the spirit and content of this book.

Some of the chapters in this collection are about forms of bias—such as racism, ageism, sexism, heterosexism, classism—that affect large numbers of diagnostic categories. Some are addressed to such general topics as the "deep structure" (different levels) of bias in diagnosis or case studies of the history and politics of particular categories. Still others are about particular diagnostic categories. At the end of this chapter is a list of some of the useful journals and references for general readers or professionals who wish to read further. We hope clinical faculty will interweave their courses and case conferences with discussions of the ways biases interfere with clinical treatment, we hope students will form informal discussion groups about these matters, and we hope that general readers will discuss these matters with family, friends, and clinicians.

PIONEERS

It is important to review some of the classic work by those who have written about bias in "mental illness" diagnosis. Writing in 1923, when Sigmund Freud's theories were becoming well known and in some quarters treated as gospel, psychiatrist and psychoanalyst Karen Horney had the courage to challenge two of the most central psychoanalytic diagnoses (Horney 1973). She questioned Freud's notion of "penis envy" as a label for much of women's and girls' behavior and his claim that all females have not only "penis envy" but also the wish to castrate the "favored male" (Horney 1973, 37). Criticized and ridiculed by Freud and his inner circle, Horney suggested that females' envy of or anger at males came not from wishing to have a penis but from understanding that males had more power and influence in many realms and fewer restrictions than did females. The "penis envy" and castration wish that Freud claimed as universal were examples, she said, of psychoanalysis's own revelation "that much that we have regarded as constitutional merely represents a blockage of growth, a blockage which can be lifted" (Horney 1973, 13).

Another diagnostic term that psychoanalysts claimed to be fundamentally, immutably female was "masochistic." Horney pointed out that what was called masochism was actually women's silent acceptance of the socially imposed conditions that made them unhappy (Horney 1939). In fact, she wrote that what was called masochism was in fact an effort to *avoid* suffering, to find safety by not making demands or being noticeable.

Sociologist August B. Hollingshead and psychiatrist Fredrick C. Redlich had found in their classic work, *Social class and mental illness* (1958), a strong relationship between individuals' socioeconomic class and the psychiatric diagnoses they were likely to receive.[4] Hollingshead and Redlich pointed out the ways that the beliefs of staff members in different clinical settings led to different views of patients,[5] and their findings were striking. They assigned participants to social class, using an index combining the person's area of residence, occupation, and education. (People in the "lowest" class, Class V, had the least education and lowest incomes and lived in the least expensive neighborhoods.) They found:

- The "higher" the social class, the less likely an individual was to become a psychiatric patient of any kind; people in Classes IV and V combined were 2 1/2 times as likely as people in Classes I and II to enter psychiatric treatment, twice as likely to reenter treatment, and 5 times as likely to remain in continuous treatment.
- Diagnoses of "neuroses" were most likely to be given to members of higher than of lower social classes, and the reverse was true for "psychoses."

Hollingshead and Redlich attributed these class differences in diagnosis and treatment to social factors. They note, for instance, that "the external problems of lower class individuals, as well as threats to their economic, social, and physical security, are much stronger than to members of the higher classes" and recommend "that psychiatrists need to understand the social system of the community if they are to diagnose accurately" (365 and 371).

In *The politics of therapy*, Seymour L. Halleck (1971) addresses the social and environmental factors that give rise to problems, the expression of which often leads people to being psychiatrically diagnosed with labels that carry either implicit or explicit attributions of the problems to individual, intrapsychic factors. Halleck expressed concern that people might be simply diagnosed as "mentally ill" rather than listened to and understood to be attempting to influence environments that are causing them harm. Halleck warned against therapists' attempts to remove symptoms (so that people would no longer appear diagnosable) without giving careful thought to the role those "symptoms" played in the patients'" attempts to improve their environments. He suggested that instead of diagnosing old people as depressed and treating the depression as though it were the source of their problems, "the psychiatrist should try to identify those factors . . . that help to make old age a nightmare . . . not only to care for the victims of a brutal process, but to prevent this process from becoming worse" (114). Halleck did not claim that all severe emotional problems were environmentally caused, but he made an impassioned plea with regard to the diagnosis and treatment of people whose primary struggles had such causes.

"Obviously if enough tranquilizing medication were dispensed, black protest could be eliminated" (74). He observes that the people who have been most concerned and militant about oppression tend to be prone to periods of anxiety and depression, even to "intense despair" (75). But, he asks, "what if while they were in jail Henry Thoreau, Eugene Debs, Martin Luther King, and Malcolm X had been given the opportunity to improve their mental outlook by taking a powerful antidepressant?" (75). Furthermore, in words that are powerful in their prescience, Halleck says that therapists ought to urge drug companies to "curb their merchandising fervor [which led to advertisements that would often] depict patients who are overwhelmed with social problems; then they recommend dealing with these patients by simply tranquilizing or stimulating the patient" (77).

*   *   *

Please keep in mind that this book is specifically about *diagnosis*, because much has already been written about the wide variety of problems and biases in *treatment*. Some implications for treatment (or lack of) are mentioned or will be obvious but are not explored here in detail. We hope that you will enjoy the range of voices and viewpoints that are represented in this book (e.g., academic, clinical, and explicitly political perspectives) as well as the broad range of the authors' formal and experiential qualifications. We want to emphasize that no author in this book claims to have easy answers or all the answers for preventing harmful biases.

WHAT TO DO

Clinicians often ask what they can do to try to insulate patients from negative consequences of receiving a diagnosis. Clinical judgments are always involved in the process of diagnosis, whether in psychiatry or other fields. In some cases, the patient clearly meets the requisite number of criteria for one of the official diagnostic categories. However, there are cases in which questions arise about which is the most accurate diagnosis, and in those cases, clinicians might take particular care to consider the effects of their diagnoses on clients' lives outside of treatment, as well as of the treatment implications of giving a patient one diagnosis rather than another.[6] For instance, insurance companies often provide reimbursement for more therapy sessions for patients with certain diagnoses than with others. It is important to select a label that seems to represent accurately as many of the patient's difficulties as possible and does not misrepresent any dangers or increase the potential risk to the patient or others. When there is any question about which diagnosis is most appropriate, the clinician can record which labels beside the chosen one were seriously considered and whether or not they were ruled out. Whatever diagnosis one gives a particular patient, it is important to be aware that diagnoses frequently have negative effects on patients' rights to child custody, employment, health insurance, or the right to make decisions about their lives.

Clinicians who feel in a given case that it is consistent with their clinical assessment and judgment to do so can write on the patient's chart next to the diagnosis such statements as, "The fact that this patient has received this diagnosis does not in and of itself indicate that the patient lacks such capacities as the ability to be a good parent, caretaker of others or employee or to make decisions about their medical and psychological care, their legal affairs, or other important aspects of their lives." Some therapists offer to give their clients letters in which they make statements about the diagnosis that are relevant to the particular person's life situation and needs. For example, a therapist who had diagnosed a woman as having Chronic Adjustment Disorder gave her a letter in which he stated that her disorder was a result of severe, ongoing crises in her life and that it was likely, if the crises abated, that she would be employable and that she would not necessarily always have the disorder and be mentally ill if her life circumstances improved.

It is wise for clinicians to make sure that their words and actions are consistent with the ethical standards of their respective professions and to check with attorneys about how best to choose to protect both the patient and the clinician.

Clinicians should also fully inform patients: (1) that they have to give them a diagnosis, (2) the reason that they have to do this (most often because required by their place of work and/or required for reimbursement by insurance companies and because diagnoses are used in treatment planning), (3) that there are potentially negative consequences of receiving a diagnosis and what these can be, and (4) what the clinician is doing—or will do in the future, if relevant—to try to protect the patient as much as possible from those consequences.

Finally, it is important to initiate and engage in ongoing discussions with colleagues and consultants about the various potential and actual positive and negative consequences of diagnosis, and it is important to educate the public about these matters, to make the realm of diagnosis more transparent to all.

Journals:
APA Division 44—Society for the Psychological Study of Lesbian, Gay, and Bisexual Issues—Newsletter: *SPSLGI Newsletter; Cultural Diversity and Ethnic Minority Psychology; Feminism and Psychology; International Journal of Critical Psychology; Journal of Feminist Family Therapy; Journal of Social Issues; Psychology of Women Quarterly; Radical Psychology; Theory & Psychology; Women and Therapy;* Special issue, *Independent Thinking Review,* on "Critical Thinking about Psychology" (1995). Volume 1, Number 4.

Websites:
Critical Psychology Homepage http://www.uws.edu.au/criticalpsychology/crit-psych-net.htm
Psychologists for Social Responsibility http://www.psysr.org/
Psychology of Women Resource List listserv@uriacc.uri.edu
Radical Psychology Network http://www.radpsynet.org/
Support Coalition International www.mindfreedom.org

NOTES

1. However, the history of medicine includes many examples of serious errors in diagnosis; for instance, tuberculosis was believed to be psychogenic until the tubercle bacillus was discovered.

2. Goode (2002) reported an increase in the number of people who are in psychotherapy and noted that the increase was greatest for older adults and the unemployed, a pattern that appears to reflect, at least in part, the social factors that lead people to seek therapy.

3. See Harris, Hilton, and Rice (1993, 267–85) who found minimal relationships among the way a patient was diagnosed, the patient's problems, and the kinds of drugs that were prescribed. Psychotropic drugs were the primary form of treatment.

4. Dohrenwend and Dohrenwend (1969, 174) also reported this pattern and wrote that "Social environmental pressures in normal civil life, even in the lowest social class, produce symptoms that persist only as long as the situational pressure continues or in the absence of secondary gain," explaining that at least some symptoms were environmentally caused. In a related vein, Berton H. Kaplan, in collaboration with Alexander H. Leighton, Jane M. Murphy, and Nicholas Freydberg (1971, 24) observed that some people were diagnosed as mentally ill because of "interference with striving" caused by conditions among the lower classes.

5. They further noted that their therapists had difficulty in distinguishing among subcategories of "schizophrenia;" their decision to compress them all into one group foreshadowed the ongoing difficulties of the authors of the *DSM*. That is, although justifying the enormous, rapid increase in their manual's subcategories by asserting that they improve the accuracy of diagnosis, they in fact found that the only way to obtain anything close to a positive correlation between the diagnoses assigned a patient by two different professionals was largely to ignore the subcategories and use the overarching categories (Kirk and Kutchins 1992; P. Caplan 1995).

6. This is not a suggestion to distort, cover up, or otherwise misrepresent the patients' symptoms or problems. In fact, for many reasons, only one of which is that harm can come from diagnosis, it would be particularly troubling if negative consequences resulted from a diagnosis that was a misrepresentation.

REFERENCES

American Psychiatric Association. (2000). *Diagnostic and statistical manual of mental disorders-IV*. 4th edition. Washington, DC.

———. (1980). *Diagnostic and statistical manual of mental disorders-III*. 3rd edition. Washington, DC.

Angell, M. (2000). Is academic medicine for sale? *New England Journal of Medicine* 342, 1516–18.

Block, Paul. (2002). Personal communication.

Bodenheimer, T. (2000). Uneasy alliance: Clinical investigators and the pharmaceutical industry. *New England Journal of Medicine* 342, 1539–44.

Burman, E., ed. (1998). *Deconstructing feminist psychology*. Thousand Oaks,CA: Sage.

Caplan, Paula J. (2000). *The NEW Don't blame mother: Mending the mother-daughter relationship*. New York: Routledge.

——— (1995). *They say you're crazy: How the world's most powerful psychiatrists decide who's normal*. Reading, MA: Addison-Wesley.

———. (1993a). *The myth of women's masochism*. Toronto: University of Toronto Press.

———. (1993b). The justice system's endorsement of mental health assessors' sexism and other biases: Charter issues and other forms of injustice. Pp. 78–87 in B. Dickens and M. Ouellette, eds. *Health care, ethics and law/Soins de santé, éthique et droit, 1993*. Montreal: Canadian Institute for the Administration of Justice/Institut canadien d'administration de la justice, Les éditions Themis.

Caplan, Paula J., and Jeremy B. Caplan. (1999). *Thinking critically about research on sex and gender.* 2d ed. New York: Addison Wesley Longman.

Caplan, Paula J., and Jeffery Wilson. (1990). Assessing the child custody assessors. *Reports of Family Law* 3rd ser., 27 (2), 121–34.

Chesler, Phyllis. (1972). *Women and madness.* Garden City, NJ: Doubleday.

Davidson, R. A. (1986). Sources of funding and outcome of clinical trials. *Journal of General Internal Medicine* 1, 155–58.

Dohrenwend, Bruce P., and Barbara Snell Dohrenwend. (1969). *Social status and psychological disorder: A causal inquiry.* New York: Wiley Interscience.

Eli Lilly and Company Limited (2003). Letter to healthcare professionals. December.

Fausto-Sterling, Anne. (1992). *Myths of gender.* New York: Basic Books.

Fine, M. (1992). *Disruptive voices: The possibilities of feminist research.* Ann Arbor: University of Michigan Press.

Foucault, M. (1977). *Discipline and punish: The birth of the prison.* New York: Vintage Books.

Fox, D. (1997). Psychology and the law justice diverted. Pp. 217–32 in I. Prilleltensky and D. Fox, eds. *Critical psychology: An introduction.* Thousand Oaks, CA: Sage.

Friedberg, M., B. Saffran, T. J. Stinson, W. Nelson, and C. L. Bennett. (1999). Evaluation of conflict of interest in economic analyses of new drugs used in oncology. *Journal of the American Medical Association* 282, 1453–57.

Gage, Carolyn. (1999). Harriet Tubman visits a therapist. Pp. 23–34 in *Off-off Broadway festival plays, twenty-third series.* New York: Samuel French.

Gergen, K. (2001). Psychological science in a postmodern world. *American Psychologist* 56, 803–13.

——. (1994). *Realities and relationships: Soundings in social construction.* Cambridge, MA; Harvard University Press.

Goode, Erica. (2002). Psychotherapy shows rise over decade. *New York Times*, November 20.

Halleck, Seymour L. (1971). *The politics of therapy.* New York: Science House

Hare-Mustin, R. T., and J. Marecek. (1997). Abnormal and clinical psychology: The politics of madness. Pp. 104–20 in Dennis Fox and Isaac Prilleltensky, eds. *Critical Psychology: An introduction.* Thousand Oaks, CA: Sage.

Harris, Grant T., N. Zoe Hilton, and Marnie E. Rice. (1993). Patients admitted to psychiatric hospital: Presenting problems and resolution at discharge. *Canadian Journal of Behavioural Science* 25, 267–85.

Hollingshead, August B., and Fredrick C. Redlich. (1958). *Social class and mental illness: A community study.* New York: John Wiley and Sons.

hooks, b. (1994). *Teaching to transgress: Education as the practice of freedom.* New York: Routledge.

Horney, Karen. (1973). *Feminine psychology.* New York: Norton.

——. (1939). *New ways of psychoanalysis.* New York: Norton.

Kaplan, Berton H., in collaboration with Alexander H. Leighton, Jane M. Murphy, and Nicholas Freydberg. (1971). *Psychiatric disorder and the urban environment: Report of the Cornell Science Center.* New York: Behavioral Publications.

Kirk, Stuart, and Herb Kutchins. (1992). *The selling of the DSM.* New York: Aldine De Gruyter.

Korn, D. (2000). Conflict of interest in biomedical research. *Journal of the American Medical Association* 284, 2234–37.

Miller, Casey, and Kate Swift. (1977). *Words and women.* Garden City, NY: Anchor Books.

Ross, L. (1977). The intuitive psychologist and his shortcomings: Distortions in the attribution process. In L. Berkowitz, ed. *Advances in experimental social psychology: Volume 10.* New York: Academic Press.

Stahly, G. B. (2003). Battered women: Why don't they just leave? Pp. 310–30 in J. C. Chrisler, C. Golden, and P. D. Rozee, eds. *Lectures on the psychology of women.* Boston, MA: McGraw-Hill.

Wiener, M., and D. Marcus. (1994). A sociuocultural constrction of "depressions." Pp. 213–31 in T. R. Sarbin and J. I. Kiuse, eds. *Constructing the social.* Thousand Oaks, CA: Sage.

Wiley, Autumn. (2001). The absence of the feminist critique from abnormal psychology. Presented in "Bias in Psychiatric Diagnosis" symposium. Association of Women in Psychology conference. Los Angeles.

Wilkinson, S., and C. Kitzinger, eds. (1995). *Feminism and discourse: Psychological perspectives.* Thousand Oaks, CA: Sage.

Women and Mental Health Committee. (1987). *Women and mental health in Canada: Strategies for change.* Toronto: Canadian Mental Health Association.

Part I

THE CREATION OF BIAS IN PSYCHIATRIC DIAGNOSIS

Chapter 1

The Construction of Illness

Meadow Linder

Health, *illness*, and *medical care* "are socially constructed categories that define and give meaning to a certain class of events. Whether or not members of a society view particular behavior or experience as a sign or symptom of illness depends on cultural values, social norms, and culturally shared rules of interpretation" (Mishler 1981, 141). A person seeking medical assistance for distress is simultaneously subjected to two processes that define and shape the illness experience: the official medical designation of the diagnostic criteria for a disease and individual clinicians' interpretation of their patients' complaints and their translation of those signs into the symptoms of a disorder. Both the clinician's interpretations of the signs and the diagnostic criteria to which the symptoms are fitted are reflections of the broader society. The process of translating personal distress into socially constructed disease categories is one form of what is generally called "medicalization" (Conrad and Schneider 1992).

As societies change, illness categories are created, modified, and abandoned. Psychiatric disorders are no exception. For instance, combat-related neuroses were dropped from the second edition of the *Diagnostic and Statistical Manual of Mental Disorders* (*DSM-II*) only to reappear in the third edition as Posttraumatic Stress Disorder (Linder, chapter 3 in this volume). The large number of appearances, disappearances, reappearances, and reformulations of psychiatric disorders speaks to culture's influence on the field of psychiatry. Psychiatry, like biomedicine, is engaged in a dialogue with society. Society informs the practice of psychiatry and, in turn, psychiatry reinforces the normative structure of society. The relationship is osmotic.

An individual seeking medical care is also seeking legitimacy for their suffering. Legitimacy is attained through diagnosis. However, once diagnosed, individuals are expected to comply with certain socially prescribed kinds of illness behavior (Poland, chapter 18 in this volume). These include taking the necessary steps to regain a state of health. In the words of Talcott Parsons (1951), the individual must fulfill the responsibilities of the *sick role*. In exchange for their cooperation, society absolves the individual of many other social responsibilities. This exchange ensures that the individual behaves normatively. Thus, diagnosis is a mechanism of social control. It could do harm, or it could help, but in either case it is a mechanism of social control (Poland and Caplan, chapter 2 in this volume; E. Caplan, chapter 5 in this volume).

Medical diagnosis can also fulfill a more overtly coercive social control function. For instance, when the behavior or attitudes of one group are considered deviant by a dominant group, they may be classified as the symptoms of an illness (Conrad and Schneider 1992). Members of groups in structurally dependent positions endure this invasive form of medicalization more often than members of groups that possess greater social resources. Women constitute one of these groups (Schur 1983). As a social construct, gender exerts a powerful influence in the sphere of health and illness. Gender's effect can be seen in the domains of illness definition, diagnosis, doctor-patient relations, and treatment (e.g., Lorber 1997; Caplan 1995). The medical profession subjugates women by defining female functions in the stigmatizing language of disease. The recent explosion of drugs to "treat" menopause, a natural and inevitable phase of a woman's life, and the inclusion of a premenstrual-related disorder in recent editions of the *DSM* (Cosgrove and Caplan, chapter 28 in this volume) are noteworthy illustrations. The subjective nature of mental illness makes it highly susceptible to differences in diagnosis as well. In one study in which psychiatrists were asked to assess written case studies, the researchers found that men and women with identical case profiles were given different psychiatric diagnoses (Loring and Powell 1988).

CONSTRUCTION OF THE DSM

Often referred to as the Psychiatric Bible, the *Diagnostic and Statistical Manual of Mental Disorders (DSM)* determines how professionals practice psychiatry and how laypeople are classified. The *DSM* has undergone a series of revisions over the years, reflecting the "evolution of American psychiatry's attempt to define the boundaries of its jurisdiction" (Kutchins and Kirk 1997, 26). *DSM-I* and *DSM-II*, published in 1952 and 1968, respectively, bear little resemblance to *DSM-IV-TR*, published in 2000. The authors of the first edition classified mental disorders on the basis of etiology and framed the manual around the psychodynamic theoretical orientation. The authors of *DSM-II* removed explicit references to a specific theoretical framework and excised the etiologic term "reaction." Both editions suffered from poor diagnostic reliability. However, reliability was not considered a necessity, given the nature of available treatments. This began to change with the development of lithium in the 1950s and its approval in the 1970s by the Food and Drug Administration for the treatment of what was then called manic-depression (Figert 1996).

The availability of lithium and other psychopharmacological drugs increased the demand for accurate diagnoses as well the application of scientific and biomedical principles in the practice of psychiatry. However, the empirical assessment of the diagnostic categories in *DSM-II* and *DSM-III* was limited by the ambiguity of the classification systems. The authors of the *DSM-III* announced that they would address both limitations by defining disorders on the basis of observable signs (Kirk and Kutchins 1992; Figert 1996). In effect, the publication of *DSM-III* and the manual's grounding in symptomatology was generally regarded as affirming psychiatry's commitment to evidence-based medicine and restoring the profession's flagging legitimacy.

In the introduction to the third edition of the *Diagnostic and Statistical Manual of Mental Disorders*, the authors outlined the key objectives behind the development of the revised manual. These include an increased commitment to reliance on data, clinical usefulness, diagnostic reliability, consistency with research on the validity of diagnostic categories, and the creation of a common language for clinicians and researchers (APA 1980, 1–3). Two of these objectives warrant further discussion: the validity and reliability of the diagnostic categories. "Validity" refers to the conceptual reality of the disorder: Does the mental disorder have a reality outside of the *DSM*? Does the condition exist? However, the difficulty of ascertaining the validity of a mental illness is widely recognized and, as the authors state in the introduction, "the most important part of the [field trials] was the evaluation of diagnostic reliability"(APA 1980, 5). The key objective with regard to reliability was that professionals applying the criteria in similar cases would arrive at the same diagnosis.

Diagnostic reliability is a function of consensus about etiology and invariance of symptoms and signs across persons and environments (Mishler 1981, 145). Reliability is also a function of professional interpretation. A medical encounter begins with an examination to uncover the signs of disease. The patient is asked questions, and the answers are reframed in the language of biomedicine. The health professional making the diagnosis emphasizes the importance of some signs while determining that others are extraneous. The clinician's interpretation is the product of their professional socialization and the norms and values of society.

Although the selection of the diagnostic criteria for a disorder is based on professional consensus, the agreement between researchers is often tenuous (see Linder, chapter 3 in this volume; Metcalfe and Caplan, chapter 15 in this volume). So while a diagnostic category's inclusion in *DSM-III* and subsequent editions has implied that it satisfied some of the *DSM* authors' task force members' objectives, the lay public and many mental health practitioners have often been unaware of its empirical limitations. The creators of *DSM-III* regained medical legitimacy by purporting to demonstrate the reliability of the categories, but the extent to which the *DSM-III* was successful in obtaining reliable diagnoses and the methods they employed in the demonstration have been questioned. In addition, the public may not distinguish between the reliability and the validity of a psychiatric diagnosis. This conflation undergirds the assumption about the authenticity of psychiatric diagnoses and the objectivity of the science behind their creation.

Critics claim that the boundaries set out in the *DSM* are arbitrary, not scientific. According to Kutchins and Kirk, "defining a mental disorder involves specifying features of human experiences that demarcate where normality shades into abnormality" (1997, 27). Psychiatrists have decided how many days of sadness are appropriate after the death of a loved one, when anxiety over job security is apropos, and how friendly or reserved a person should be at a dinner party. These determinations are value judgments that one social group makes about another (Scheff 1984). Psychiatry's authority to define the boundaries of normality and deviance was established by the incorporation of biomedical principles into their disease classification (Caplan 1995), but that does not change the fact that the behavior labeled deviant reflects social norms, not science. The labeling process is an agreement between society and the profession of psychiatry. In exchange for the right to benefit, economically, from the "ownership" of the social problem (Gusfield 1996), psychiatry agrees to perform duties of social control by labeling individuals who deviate from socially prescribed behavior.

Although many of these criticisms and concerns are valid, psychiatry and the *DSM* also serve beneficent societal functions. Diagnoses of mental illness can legitimize personal suffering and aid in the acquisition of treatment and benefits. Taking a judicious perspective on psychiatry, the *DSM* and the diagnostic categories in the *DSM* involves recognizing their potential benefits as well as their potential dangers. The balance between the two depends on the specific diagnosis and how it is applied by mental health professionals.

BIBLIOGRAPHY AND REFERENCES

American Psychiatric Association. (1980). *Diagnostic and statistical manual of mental disorders*. 3rd edition. Washington, DC.

Caplan, Paula J. (1995). *They say you're crazy: How the world's most powerful psychiatrists decide who's normal.* Reading, MA: Addison-Wesley.

Conrad, Peter, and Joseph W. Schneider. (1992). *Deviance and medicalization: From badness to sickness.* St. Louis, MO: C. V. Mosby.

Figert, Anne E. (1996). *Women and the ownership of PMS: The structuring of a psychiatric disorder.* New York: Aldine De Gruyter.

Gusfield, Joseph R. (1996). *Contested meanings: The construction of alcohol problems.* Madison: University of Wisconsin Press.

Kirk, Stuart, and Herb Kutchins. (1992). *The selling of the DSM.* New York: Aldine De Gruyter.

Kutchins, Herb, and Stuart Kirk. (1997). *Making us crazy.* New York: The Free Press.

Lorber, Judith. (1997). *Gender and the social construction of illness.* Thousand Oaks, CA: Sage.

Loring, Marti, and Brian Powell. (1988). "Gender, Race, and DSM-III: A Study of the Objectivity of Psychiatric Diagnostic Behavior." *Journal of Health and Social Behavior* 29 (March), 1–22.

Mishler, Elliot G. (1981). The social construction of an illness. Pp. 141–68 in Elliot G. Mishler, ed. *Social contexts of health, illness, and patient care.* Cambridge, UK: Cambridge University Press.

Parsons, Talcott. (1951). *The social system.* Glencoe, IL: The Free Press.

Scheff, Thomas J. (1984). *Being mentally ill: A sociological theory.* New York: Aldine Publishing Company.

Schur, Edwin M. (1983). *Labeling women deviant: Gender, stigma, and social control.* Philadelphia, PA: Temple University Press.

Chapter 2

The Deep Structure of Bias in Psychiatric Diagnosis

Jeffrey Poland and Paula J. Caplan

A bias is any inclination or tendency toward responding or acting in one way rather than another, and it is not necessarily negative. Although many biases result from deep-seated personal, social, economic, or political interests and values, some arise from the practical demands of specific situations or from human cognitive limitations. For mental health professionals, it is particularly important to be aware of our biases because we represent ourselves as, and are seen as, helpers.

We shall provide a framework for thinking about bias in the clinical setting by addressing the following questions:

1. What kinds of actions by the clinician are manifestations of bias?
2. What sources within the clinical setting itself give rise to such biases?
3. What are the deeper cultural and ideological roots of bias?

WHAT KINDS OF ACTIONS ARE MANIFESTATIONS OF BIAS?

Imagine we are interns in an outpatient clinic, observing Dr. Z, a senior staff psychologist performing intake interviews with patients. The clinic is experiencing an overload of walk-in patients, and Dr. Z has little time to spend with each one.[1] Although the following description of Dr. Z's approach to Ms. A and Mr. B may appear extreme, sometimes these kinds of things do happen. We have chosen to use this situation here because it allows us to throw the workings of some biases into high relief and illustrates how contextual factors can promote bias, since stereotypes are even more likely to come into play under time constraints than otherwise.

9

The first patient is Ms. A, a Haitian woman who moved to the United States two years ago. She appears agitated and distraught. She complains that her ex-husband is stalking her and says that she feels desperate and doesn't know how much more of this she can take and that something must be done about him. She reports that she has been attending a job-training program because she wants to get off welfare but has been so frightened by her husband's stalking that she cannot concentrate in the training classes. Dr. Z manages to reach Ms. A's husband by phone and asks him about the stalking, but he denies doing it. Dr. Z diagnoses her with "paranoid personality disorder," writes in her chart that she is a danger to others and possibly to herself, and Dr. Z tells us, "I am calling in a psychiatrist because this woman should be placed on a tranquilizer, and I am considering having her committed to a locked ward. I am having Ms. A wait in the consulting room until the psychiatrist arrives."

The second patient is Mr. B, a white surgeon who is asking the psychologist for advice about how to get his wife, from whom he has recently separated, to stop harassing him. He furiously reports that she constantly telephones his secretary to ask where he is having lunch and with whom, as well as what time he leaves the office each day. He says he is at his wits' end and is having trouble sleeping because he is so humiliated that his secretary is aware of what his wife is doing. Dr. Z assures Mr. B that his reaction is perfectly normal and suggests that his secretary document these telephone calls so that he can make a police report. Dr. Z expresses concern, saying to Mr. B, "It sounds as if your wife is a deeply troubled and possibly dangerous woman," and he asks Mr. B if he would like a prescription for a few sleeping pills.

Obviously, the psychologist has no idea whether either patient has an ex-partner or whether they are accurately describing the behavior of those ex-partners or of themselves. The psychologist is manifesting the following biases:

- Focusing on certain kinds of information rather than others
- Uncritically interpreting information acquired in the artificial context of a clinic
- Making a decision about the normality or pathology of a patient on the basis of little information and little time spent with the patient
- Making a decision about the appropriateness of prescribing medication on the basis of very limited information
- More readily taking at face value what male patients say than what female patients say
- More readily judging a patient mentally ill if the patient is a woman and/or member of a racialized group and/or poor
- More readily judging women than men to be overly emotional, even dangerous

- More readily assuming that men need protection from women than the reverse
- More readily prescribing mood-altering medication for women than for men
- More readily offering men than women the *option* to take medication
- More readily assuming that women more than men need ongoing monitoring and treatment
- Tending to assume a higher-status role in relation to women patients than to men, including making male patients part of the decision-making process

WHAT SOURCES WITHIN THE CLINICAL SETTING GIVE RISE TO BIAS?

The many factors described above that give rise to the manifestations of bias overlap and interact with each other. These cases suggest that bias can arise because of factors concerning the clinician's individual psychology, professional identity, and practices and from contextual factors. The following discussion of these factors may be disconcerting because there is a widespread assumption that therapists overcome their biases. But that assumption is a myth because biases are unavoidable (Caplan and Wilson 1990). The key issue is whether clinicians are critically aware of their biases and of their impact on patients.

PSYCHOLOGY OF THE CLINICIAN

The process of trying to understand the nature of people's anguish, fears, and depression is quite complex; there are usually many unknowns, and settling on a tidy diagnosis can reduce one's anxiety. As a result, the clinician's human need to simplify the picture comes into play. This is intensified under pressures from health maintenance organizations and insurance companies or when the patient is dangerous. Thus, in making clinical diagnoses, the therapist will attend to, emphasize, and use certain information while de-emphasizing or ignoring other information, and biases shape the nature of that selectivity.

First, the clinician's attitudes and beliefs about certain groups of individuals are sources of bias, such as the notion that gay, bisexual, or transgendered individuals are developmentally arrested. Biases also come from more emotional reactions, for example, when the patient reminds the therapist of someone they intensely dislike. In addition, clinicians' personal identities and demographic characteristics are known to influence how they relate to their clients (Rawlings and Carter 1977; Robbins and Siegel 1983). Along these lines, it is important to ask whether therapists consider themselves similar to their patients or qualitatively different from them (Caplan 1984). The latter attitude is reassuring to those who fear that they are like or will be regarded as similar to their patients. These therapists distance themselves from their patients, often thinking of them as broken mechanisms that should be fixed rather than as people encountering problems in their lives and with whom therapists can have more interactive and less hierarchical relationships.[2] Such considerations are important for diagnosis because the collection of information and the development of clinical understanding depend essentially upon the character of clinician-client relationships.

Second, a number of capacities that vary widely among clinicians can be sources of bias, including perspective-taking; critical self-reflection; tolerance for informational complexity, ambiguity, and uncertainty; tolerance for stress and fear; and tolerance for difference. In the case studies described above, Dr. Z was able to identify with the problems of one client but not much with the problems of the other. And with regard to managing informational complexity and uncertainty, those with the most limited capacity in these areas may rely most heavily on stereotypes to simplify information and resolve uncertainty.

Third, the clinician's "cognitive architecture"—perception, attention, information search, memory, and inference—provides a different set of entry points for bias in diagnostic assessment. What sorts of information the clinician does or does not perceive, attend to, search for, and remember, and how the clinician uses available information (e.g., what inferences are drawn) play central roles in the development of clinical understanding leading to diagnosis. A clinician who tightly focuses on clinical pathology and ignores information concerning the broader context in which the client is embedded will tend to develop a pathology-oriented body of information, resulting, for instance, in a failure to grasp the significance *for a given patient* of apparently delusional speech or to develop a more comprehensive and more accurate picture of the person's strengths and functioning.

A variety of well-known cognitive biases are associated with information processing activities such as attention, perception, information search, memory, and inference.[3] For example, highly salient features of a context tend to capture attention, and this is problematic because each piece of information takes on significance only in the context of other information. The information concerning Ms. A's recent immigration, desire to get off welfare, and attendance at a job training program are de-emphasized by Dr. Z in favor of what he feels is more salient information about her distress concerning her husband's behavior. This leads to Dr. Z's view of Ms. A as distraught and potentially dangerous, rather than as hardworking and determined to improve

Table 2.1   Information Processing Biases

confirmation bias	the tendency to seek out and record information that confirms previously held beliefs and expectations and to ignore or minimize information that fails to fit in
availability bias	the tendency to give priority to information that is highly salient or more easily remembered
stereotype-based memory bias	the propensity to recall information that is part of a stereotype being applied to an individual even when the information is false
illusory correlation	the tendency to see as significantly related traits or events that co-occur on a particular occasion but in fact are independent of each other
anchoring effect	the tendency to assign higher priority to initial information received than to subsequently collected information
halo effect	the tendency to assign positive (or negative) traits to a person who exhibits other desirable (or undesirable) traits, even though the traits are not correlated
actor-observer attribution bias	the tendency to see one's own problems, or the problems of someone with whom one identifies, as resulting from situational factors while regarding the problems of others, especially those with whom one does not identify, as resulting from inner causes

her situation. In the latter context, her distress makes a very different kind of sense. Table 2.1 contains other information processing biases can influence diagnosis.

It is especially important to focus on the role of background assumptions in clinicians' inferences. On the one hand, clinicians' background beliefs influence the way they diagnose a person (Kim and Ahn 2002). If Dr. Z believed that racialized women were more likely than white men to suffer from paranoid disorders, this might explain the difference in diagnosis between Ms. A and Mr. B. On the other hand, when one infers that a patient is mentally ill, one is ruling out alternative explanations of their complaints and distress. In diagnosing Ms. A with Paranoid Personality Disorder, Dr. Z ignored or ruled out the possibility that either her fears were warranted by her ex-husband's behavior or they were the natural result of an otherwise upsetting situation.

Further, some therapists make decisions about medication[4] without considering the assumptions underlying what they are doing. After talking with a woman who is depressed because her husband verbally abuses her, some

clinicians will prescribe an antidepressant without stopping to realize that
they are:

(1) assuming she has a brain disease, and that is why she needs a chemical
    that will change her brain; *or*
(2) assuming that it is all right to give her brain-changing drugs even though
    her problem might come from a source other than her brain

To those who would say, "Such assumptions are justified because all mental
processes are obviously based in the brain," we would reply that, although the
brain is a substrate of mental processes, it does not necessarily follow that
nothing *except* the brain is involved in mental processes, and hence that only
the brain should be a target of intervention. Any emotional problem may have
many causes, one of which *may be* a brain dysfunction or disease but others
of which may be environmental, relational, or the manifestation of a normal
psychological process. In addition, although changes that begin in the brain
can lead to changes in emotion and thinking, at other times the cause-effect
sequence is the opposite, with, for instance, traumatic experiences or prolonged isolation leading to changes in the brain. To prescribe drugs routinely
is to act as though (1) the brain is the sole or primary cause of emotional problems; *or* (2) the brain is the most common or most important cause; *or* (3)
brain-altering drugs will probably have beneficial effects on some of the other
causes or on the person's way of dealing with the other causes. However, always prioritizing brain processes is totally unwarranted by current understanding of human functioning, and the assumptions underlying any decision
to employ medications should be critically examined.[5]

PROFESSIONAL IDENTITY AND PRACTICE

Clinicians' training promotes the development of a professional identity (social worker, psychiatric nurse, etc.) and a specific form of clinical practice,
each of which can give rise to bias. Bias can come from terminology, such as
labels for diagnostic categories; accepted beliefs, theories, and models of human functioning and pathology; questions believed to be of primary importance (e.g., what mental disorder does a person have? were they abused?); ob-
servational and assessment practices, such as structured diagnostic interviews
and test batteries; inferential and explanatory practices, including the use of
psychiatric diagnostic manual criteria for differential diagnosis; views about
clients (e.g., as passive victims of disease) and their problems (brain disease,
problems in living); and views about the nature of clinical roles, relationships,

and settings. For example, for historical reasons, social workers (more than other therapists) may take social, economic, and cultural factors into account in trying to understand what is happening to a patient and how to diagnose them, whereas psychiatrists may be more inclined to think in terms of brain-based problems.

Especially important for diagnosis are the clinician's preparation for being a responsible consumer of research and for managing conflicting demands in clinical practice. Instructors in training programs too rarely teach (or encourage) their trainees to be responsible consumers of research about diagnosis and treatment. For instance, trainees should learn to think critically about research that has been influenced by biased researchers and other stakeholders, such as drug companies. After beginning their training programs, students soon realize—perhaps unconsciously—that they are expected to help patients and to know more about them than the patients know about themselves. The daunting nature of these expectations and the propensity of some instructors to misconstrue trainees' questions as hostile, inappropriate challenges (Caplan 1995b) leads many students to avoid ambiguity and feelings of incompetence by accepting researchers' claims at face value (see Caplan and Caplan 1994, who describe skills for critical thinking about research).

An especially important dimension of clinical training concerns clinicians' management of multiple interests, values, and constraints, as presented in table 2.2.

Improper weighting of these interests, values, and constraints can lead to harmful practices. Professional codes of ideals and constraints for clinicians

Table 2.2.   Bias from Information, Values, and Constraints

Personal	career development, financial rewards, personal safety, freedom from lawsuits, family responsibilities and aspirations
Professional	professional status and reputation, guild identity, status of the guild, values promoted by the guild, financial interests of the guild, professional ethics, professional standards of care, relationships to members of other professional communities
Institutional	economics of a clinical setting, administrative rules and policies, organizational structure, specific role within an organization
Social	legal requirements and social responsibilities for protecting the public, advocacy roles with respect to policy and legislation, role as expert in adjudication of competence, responsibility, and other legal proceedings
Consumer-Oriented	interests of the client seeking help, protection of the client from harm, interests of the client's family and friends

constitute a reasonable start but are often inadequate for the clinician who is coping with the demands of day-to-day practice. For instance:

- Clinicians may engage in defensive clinical practices which are designed to avoid lawsuits but which are harmful to the client.
- Psychologists who testify at government hearings or in courts juggle at least three potentially conflicting sets of interests: personal (e.g., prestige), professional (e.g., status of their guild), and social (e.g., concerns about social justice).[6]
- Some therapists avoid damage to their reputations or loss of their jobs through avoiding any deviations from usual practices in diagnosis, however useful such deviations might be for clients.

CONTEXTUAL FACTORS

The final set of sources of bias involves the contexts in which clinical practices are pursued, as shown in table 2.3.

For example, the necessity of quickly assigning a specific diagnosis may lead a clinician to elicit only some of the important information in interviewing the patient, or reimbursement for services may heavily depend upon which diagnosis a patient is given. Alternatively, when under time constraints and pressure from legal mandates concerning dangerousness, a clinician might diagnose a client based on unproven, third-person information, such as a report that the patient has been violent in the past.[7] Finally, the examples just given illustrate how clinicians' personal and professional lives are threatened by the consequences of departing from institutional, legal, and social norms, even if such norms are indefensible.

Table 2.3.   Bias from Contexts of Practice

Systemic Factors	Resource availability (space, money, personnel), sources of funding, funding policies, institutional roles and responsibilities, authority structure, institutional missions/mandates, inpatient or outpatient facility, availability of seclusion and restraint, availability of a licensed physician, chart auditing, standards of care, social organization (e.g., team structures), level, frequency and quality of supervision and in-house training
Specific Conditions	Time pressure, danger/fear, ambiguity/uncertainty, client identity, access to information, character of relationships, ethos of the clinical setting (e.g., morale, pressures from peers and supervisors), research interests and projects, expertise and experience of personnel

WHAT ARE THE DEEPER CULTURAL AND IDEOLOGICAL ROOTS OF BIAS?

All of the sources of bias discussed thus far are created or supported by deeper, interrelated, cultural structures and practices, many of which promote the importance of psychiatric diagnosis. Citizens of Western culture have become so dependent on technology and awestruck by the scientific and medical enterprises that many believe the technology-science-medicine (TSM) complex can provide a solution for every problem, once a diagnosis is made. People want to believe there are cures for everything, and the increasing pace and demands of life in the workplace limit one's time to seek solutions, making the prospect of the quick fix powerfully seductive. Unfortunately, research on mental illness is exceedingly complicated, and little is known about causes and cures of the phenomena called "mental illness" (Poland, chapter 18 in this volume; Caplan 1995a; Poland and Spaulding, forthcoming).[8] In clinical research it is impossible to identify all factors that might contribute to people's emotional problems, and in laboratory research one can only study certain things and control a limited number of variables (Caplan and Caplan 1994). But the public and even some therapists believe that clinicians have substantial expertise, that treatment is solidly based in scientific research, and that therapists know the truth and usually make objective judgments based primarily on science. These beliefs are due partly to mental health systems, mental health professionals' guilds that function largely as lobby groups to increase their members' influence and income, the pharmaceutical companies, and media people who are largely uncritical of pronouncements by researchers and clinicians.[9] These major powers work hand-in-glove in a myriad of ways. For instance, pharmaceutical companies are major funders of symposia and conferences of therapists and researchers and make large campaign contributions to politicians whom they want to vote against legislation that would reduce the companies' profits (Caplan 1995a). The major group associated with diagnosis, the authors of the American Psychiatric Association's psychiatric diagnostic manual, the *Diagnostic and Statistical Manual of Mental Disorders* (known as the *DSM*: American Psychiatric Association 2000), identify or invent one condition after another and include them in the *DSM* (Caplan 1995a). This provides new markets for drug companies, and the advertisements of specific drugs for treating specifically labeled entities lends prescribing physicians the legitimacy of supposedly diagnosing physiologically based problems, each treatable with a pill.

Insurance companies pay for treatment of emotional suffering *only if* the patient's condition is given psychiatric labels. Otherwise, a patient cannot receive reimbursement for seeing a therapist because of loneliness and isolation after moving to a new city, fear as the target of racist speech at work, a major existential crisis, involvement in a child custody dispute, or grief three weeks after a significant loss. Consequently, laypeople and professionals tend to believe that anyone grappling with a problem needs to be diagnosed with a mental disorder and handled in the mental health system. Insurers, of course, want to pay for treatments that seem to hold promise for quick cures, and drug companies' effective marketing techniques are more persuasive than pleas for longer-term or more nuanced treatment.[10] This all fits in with many professionals' narrow focus on medicalized diagnosis of human anguish.[11]

Turning to educational practices, the abnormal psychology textbooks used in undergraduate courses to teach both future therapists and many current or future consumers of mental health services disturbingly lack much of the critique of diagnosis that has been generated in recent decades (Wiley, chapter 4 in this volume; see also Caplan 1995a; Horwitz 2002; Kirk and Kutchins 1992; Poland, Von Eckardt, and Spaulding 1994; Poland and Spaulding, forthcoming; and Whitaker 2002). The same absence characterizes most textbooks and training at the graduate level. And, when students, trainees, and consumers enter the world of psychology or psychiatry, they learn a great deal of jargon, which all too often does not facilitate communication but rather impedes clear thinking about diagnosis (Caplan, chapter 13 in this volume).

Therapists' increasing propensity to attribute emotional problems to brain disease that the TSM complex can allegedly fix leads to patient and public education practices that reinforce a narrow, medicalized approach (that mental problems are "brain diseases") and to the consequent stigmatizing of consumers of mental health services. Many professionals and public figures claim that the problem is not psychiatric labeling itself but rather the *stigma* attached to people who are so labeled, and some have led campaigns to stop stigmatizing the "mentally ill." But in contemporary Western culture it is hard to imagine how being identified as someone with a brain disease that compromises mental faculties could *fail to* lead to being stigmatized. The scapegoating of the lay public for allegedly initiating the stigmatizing takes the focus off the real sources of stigma, and few trainers of therapists, *DSM* authors, drug company CEOs, and media people have tried to alter this state of affairs.

The expansion and publicizing of the *DSM* fuel the belief that diagnosis is based on science and that therapists work with phenomena that they can understand and effectively treat. By aggressively promoting a narrow, medicalized approach centered on *DSM* categories, the *DSM* developers say, in effect, "The only important history is ours;"[12] and, because of their monopolistic power, they confer on HMOs, insurance companies, drug companies, professional guilds, and certain educators, hospitals, and clinics apparent legitimacy, authority, and even cachet (Caplan 1995a). Thoughtful critics, however, suggest that the *DSM* authors' claim to scientific credibility and expertise is dubious and that the *DSM* is a weak link in the chain of institutional relationships underlying diagnostic and treatment practices (Kirk and Kutchins 1992; Caplan 1995a; Kutchins and Kirk 1997; Poland, Von Eckardt, and Spaulding 1994; Poland and Spaulding, forthcoming; Horwitz 2002; Whitaker 2002).

Buttressing the powerful influence that these institutions have on mental health practice is the vulnerability to and dependence on mental health expertise that characterizes the public as well as various social authorities and institutions. When it comes to coping with painful and difficult psychological problems, limited knowledge and experience combined with the steep rise in the average person's work week in recent years (Hochschild 1989; 1997) has intensified many people's need to rely on experts to "Just tell me what to do."

The justice system is similarly dependent upon mental health expertise and has played a significant role in legitimizing psychiatric diagnosis by increasingly deeming mental illness relevant to legal proceedings—including those about competency, insanity, diminished responsibility, and child custody. However, though they frequently recognize the limitations of psychiatric labels for legal purposes (e.g., in insanity cases), lawyers and judges often inadequately look for and recognize bias in diagnosis (Caplan and Cosgrove, chapter 1 in this volume; Emily J. Caplan, chapter 5 in this volume; P. Caplan, chapters 6 and 7 in this volume).

Consumer advocacy groups are also significantly dependent upon mental health experts. For example, parents of people with severe psychological problems have been wounded by the tradition of blaming parents, usually mothers, for whatever happens to their children (Caplan and Hall-McCorquodale 1985a; 1985b; Caplan 2000). They have often found solace in therapists' announcements that their children suffer from brain diseases that are not the parents' fault. Although it is important to avoid parent-blame, it is equally important to be aware that probably the largest group of such parents has come together under the title of National Alliance for the Mentally Ill and that they receive substantial funding from pharmaceutical companies. It is understandable that these parents are relieved when told that they did not cause their child's problem and feel hopeful when informed that "miracle drugs" can help. Some people report that these drugs do help, and the prospect of a magic pill to cure mental suffering remains tantalizing even for parents of patients whom medication has not helped "yet." It is disconcerting to write a paragraph like this one, because it would be nice to be able to say that there is hope for an easy cure and that this will eliminate parent-blaming, but it is troubling that the longings of patients and their parents add momentum to the practice of basing diagnoses on the premise that all serious emotional problems come from brain diseases.[13]

Ironically, fundamental sources of bias are involved in the proposal (before the U.S. Congress as this book goes to press) for "parity," that is, insurance plans to pay as much for care of psychological problems as for physical problems. It is a delicate matter to express reservations about parity, because we want people who need psychological care to have their public or private insurance pay for it. However, the advocates of parity use *DSM* diagnoses conceived of as brain diseases as the standard for deciding that psychological treatment is needed. It is not surprising that they chose the *DSM*, because no other standard is as widely accepted (but see Anthony, chapter 30 in this volume). However, parity in this form will further entrench and strengthen the powers of the *DSM* authors (the American Psychiatric Association), drug companies, and insurance companies, and, although people with serious problems should have access to resources, the price of such access—to be labeled with brain diseases—may be too steep to pay. It is a dilemma with no simple solution.

CONCLUSION

It is currently next to impossible to hold accountable any of the major systems responsible for bias in diagnostic practices, because their power, prestige, and access to immense sums of money render most forms of opposition fruitless.[14] One can imagine that in a different culture, very different institutions or people could become the major players in the diagnostic enterprise.

Nonetheless, although one cannot change many sources of bias on one's own, some are amenable to change by individuals. Simply being aware of the wealth of these sources and the ways they operate can inoculate clinicians against harmfully biased treatment of people who turn to us for help. Health issues are, after all, issues of social justice, and, in matters of social justice, it is important to be relentlessly vigilant about identifying and rooting out biases that can harm those members of our society who have little or no power.

NOTES

1. Virtually every chapter in this volume includes systematic studies of and/or case examples of therapists' biases coming into play in clinical settings. Because the effects of these biases can be devastating, a great deal more research concerning the frequency, forms, and conditions of the operations of these biases should be a high priority.

2. A critical question for all clinicians to ask concerns the extent to which we objectify people who seek help. Do we pathologize and manipulate them, or do we view

them as people living in the world and having features other than those included in the definition of their mental illness? (Although every person should be viewed in the latter way, there is sometimes value in technological manipulation as well.)

3. For a useful survey of cognitive and social sources of bias, see Plous (1993).

4. Drugs are *the* physiologically based treatment prescribed far more often than any other, and they are more likely to be prescribed when formal diagnoses are given. Saying that a person has "Major Depressive Disorder" because she feels helpless, hopeless, and sad two months after being raped is more likely to lead to treatment with psychotropic medication than to a recommendation that she be given a great deal of support by as many loved ones as possible for as long as she needs it.

5. A note on *false dichotomies*: No one should ever deny anyone access to biochemical or other physiologically based treatments if they can be helpful, but it is not helpful and can be harmful to assume that for every problem there is a chemical or other physiological solution. There is no justification for such an assumption. Furthermore, a needlessly adversarial situation has emerged: many therapists and laypeople believe that one has to choose, across-the-board, whether to believe that emotional problems are brain-based and have chemical solutions. Rather, although this may be true of some emotional problems, others have different kinds of individual or social-economic-political causes and solutions.

6. Thanks to Robert Schopp at the University of Nebraska for this point.

7. Note that there is considerable controversy concerning the "prediction of dangerousness." The point we are making in the text is that contextual pressures influence how one responds to potentially dangerous situations, regardless of the difficulty of accurate prediction.

8. This is not to say that nothing is known, but virtually none of the standard diagnostic categories has been empirically validated. What is known concerns more specific phenomena and the kinds of techniques that can be helpful (e.g., for reducing psychotic symptoms, helping regulate mood, or assisting in the development of skills). Even in these areas, knowledge of causes is limited, and techniques are far from perfect.

9. I (Paula J. Caplan) have written about how most media people distorted their reporting of the debates about "Premenstrual Dysphoric Disorder" in the direction of favoring the category's advocates (1995a). I was recently asked for another interview on that subject. After spending more than an hour in the interview, during which I explained my concerns about media distortions, I received a copy of the article that the editor planned to print. Alarmed by the number of factual errors in the piece, I spent ninety minutes writing to the journalist to explain their harmful potential. The journalist responsibly (unusually!) sent a much-amended version that, however, still contained some errors of considerable concern. After more feedback from me, the journalist took the exceptional step of altering the article yet again, and, when it was published, it was almost entirely accurate in its representation of both sides' views and the relevant data and history. Later, the editor notified me that she planned to publish a Letter to the Editor that she had received and wondered if I wished to write a reply. When I sent my reply, the editor said she would have to remove a statement I had made about a pharmaceutical company. She agreed to

leave it in after I pointed out that it was true and had already been reported in the article itself.

10. Longer-term treatment is not always necessary or more effective than other kinds of treatment for emotional suffering.

11. A somewhat different factor that promotes bias in diagnosis is that, although many therapists and laypeople are consciously or unconsciously aware that much of what is called "mental illness" actually results from oppression, violence, anomie, and dramatic imbalances in the distribution of power and wealth, it is daunting to imagine combating those forces. It is easier to operate as though the bias toward medicalizing virtually all psychological problems is the best way to go.

12. It is important for clinicians to learn more about the history of mental health practice and the many past and current clinical traditions in order to appreciate why the *DSM* framework constitutes a harmful, narrow, and distorting approach to clinical practice.

13. See Spaulding, Sullivan, and Poland (2003) for a comprehensive approach to treating severe mental illness that does not depend on either *DSM* diagnostic categories or the assumption that all mental illness involves brain disease.

14. Although the state has an interest in regulation of clinical practice, most states hand over much of that responsibility to professional associations, and some professional regulatory bodies protect their members more than patients or the public (Caplan 1995b.) Furthermore, regulatory bodies do not regulate diagnosis *per se*—indeed, no one does, so in order to succeed in complaint proceedings or court cases against a therapist about diagnosis, a patient would probably have to prove personal harm because the therapist used an unvalidated diagnosis without fully informing the client. Although damaging consequences of receiving a diagnosis itself can be numerous, people who seek therapy are almost never in an emotional *and* economic position to file a complaint or a lawsuit, and the workings of the diagnostic process are so opaque to most laypeople that it would never occur to them to look to diagnosis as a cause of their problems.

REFERENCES

American Psychiatric Association (2000). *Diagnostic and Statistical Manual of Mental Disorders-IV-TR*. Washington, D.C.: American Psychiatric Association.

Caplan, Paula J. (2000). *Don't blame mother: Mending the mother-daughter relationship*. New York: Routledge.

———. (1995a). *They say you're crazy: How the world's most powerful psychiatrists decide who's normal*. Reading, MA: Addison-Wesley.

———. (1995b). "Weak ego boundaries": One developing feminist's story. *Women and Therapy* (special issue on feminist foremothers) 17, 113–23.

———. (1994a). *The myth of women's masochism*. Toronto: University of Toronto Press.

———. (1994b). *You're smarter than they make you feel: How the experts intimidate us and what we can do about it*. New York: The Free Press.

———. (1993). The justice system's endorsement of mental health assessors' sexism and other biases: Charter issues and other forms of injustice. Pp. 79–87 in Bernard Dickens and Monique Ouellette, eds. *Health care, ethics and law/Soins de santé, éthique et droit.* Canadian Institute for the Administration of Justice/Institut canadien d'administration de la justice: Les éditions Themis.

———. (1984). The myth of women's masochism. *American Psychologist* 39 (2), 130–39.

Caplan, Paula J., and Jeremy B. Caplan. (1994). *Thinking critically about research on sex and gender.* New York: HarperCollins.

Caplan, Paula J., and Ian Hall-McCorquodale. (1985a). Mother-blaming in major clinical journals. *American Journal of Orthopsychiatry* 55, 345–53.

———. (1985b). The scapegoating of mothers: A call for change. *American Journal of Orthopsychiatry* 55, 610–13.

Caplan, Paula J., and Jeffery Wilson. (1990). Assessing the child custody assessors. *Reports of Family Law,* third series, 27 (2), October 25.

Coser, Lewis. (1956). *The social functions of conflict.* New York: The Free Press.

Hochschild, Arlie Russell. (1997). *The time bind: When work becomes home and home becomes work.* New York: Metropolitan.

———. (1989). *The second shift.* New York: Avon.

Horwitz, Allan. (2002). *Creating mental illness.* Chicago: University of Chicago Press.

Kim, Nancy, and Woo-kyoung Ahn. (2002). Psychologists' theory-based representations of mental disorders predict their diagnostic reasoning and memory. *Journal of Experimental Psychology: General* 131, 451–76.

Kirk, Stuart, and Herbert Kutchins. (1992). *The selling of DSM: The rhetoric of science in psychiatry.* New York: Aldine De Gruyter.

Kutchins, Herbert, and Stuart Kirk. (1997). *Making us crazy: DSM the psychiatric bible and the creation of mental disorders.* New York: The Free Press.

Plous, Scott. (1993). *The psychology of judgment and decision making.* New York: McGraw-Hill.

Poland, Jeffrey, and William Spaulding. (forthcoming). *Crisis and revolution: Toward a reconceptualization of psychopathology.* Cambridge, MA: MIT Press.

Poland, Jeffrey, Barbara Von Eckardt, and William Spaulding. (1994). Problems with the *DSM* approach to classification of psychopathology. Pp. 235–60 in George Graham and Lyn Stephens, eds. *Philosophical psychopathology.* Cambridge, MA: MIT Press.

Rawlings, Edna I., and Dianne K. Carter, eds. (1977). *Psychotherapy for women: Treatment toward equality.* Springfield, IL: Charles C. Thomas.

Robbins, Joan Hamerman, and Rachel Josefowitz Siegel, eds. (1983). *Women changing therapy: New assessments, values, and strategies in feminist therapy.* New York: Haworth.

Spaulding, William, Mary Sullivan, and Jeffrey Poland. (2003). *Treatment and rehabilitation of severe mental illness.* New York: Guilford Press.

Whitaker, Robert. (2002). *Mad in America: Bad science, bad medicine, and the enduring mistreatment of the mentally ill.* Cambridge, MA: Perseus Books.

Chapter 3

Creating Post-traumatic Stress Disorder: A Case Study of the History, Sociology, and Politics of Psychiatric Classification

Meadow Linder

Post-traumatic Stress Disorder (PTSD) first appeared in the *Diagnostic and Statistical Manual of Mental Disorders* (*DSM*) in 1980 in response to the lobbying efforts of distressed Vietnam veterans and their psychiatric allies. This is important because the foundation of a diagnosis affects the final form and applicability of the criteria. Today, PTSD is the catchall category for victims of trauma, including victims of domestic violence and survivors of sexual assault and natural disasters. However, it is unclear whether PTSD's patently male, wartime origins have been adequately diversified to justify and render useful its current applications.

My research reveals striking differences between the construction and revision of PTSD and the assumptions clinicians make about that process, especially the way the domain of traumas expanded in the absence of supporting research and before the diagnosis was socially and professionally validated. The overall process of social problems claims making, the institutionalized procedures of the bodies creating the *DSM*, and the misguided beliefs of many clinicians contribute to the reification of the diagnosis and circumscribe challenges to the criteria. Many mental health professionals assume that the diagnosis has been depoliticized and sufficiently validated for each trauma to which it is now applied.

Multiple definitions of PTSD emerged in interviews I conducted with clinicians and *DSM* committee members. There is considerable intra-group, as well as inter-group, disagreement, producing a tenuously negotiated order. The definitional incongruity leads to a number of modifications in clinical practice, ranging from relaxing the diagnostic criteria to deliberate misdiagnosis or rejection of the entire diagnostic system. It appears as though elements of the posttraumatic response that are crucial to treatment or capture important variations related to trauma type were lost in the construction of the initial criteria and later expansion of the category to include new victim groups. Consequently, many clinicians modify the diagnostic category to suit their clinical experience.

LITERATURE AND BACKGROUND

A Brief History of War-related Trauma

Before the creation of PTSD, soldiers in the world wars who exhibited "neurotic" symptoms were given a variety of diagnoses, depending on the medical thought of the time. During World War I, "war neuroses" were arrayed on a continuum of legitimacy according to their presumptive cause (Young 1995). "Shell shock" was reportedly the result of neurological damage sustained in combat, but "hysteria" and "neurasthenia" were considered results of psychological stress. The public and the medical community regarded "shell shock" as legitimate because it was supposedly caused by a physical injury, but "hysterics" and "neurasthenics" walked a fine line between being regarded as having legitimate distress and malingering.

W. H. Rivers was one of the first to suggest that "shell shock" was a reaction to the fear of being killed or maimed and suppressing the natural fight-or-flight response to danger (Young 1995, 63). Rivers's rationale was that the soldier, torn between a desire to protect himself and his duty to the group, was psychologically traumatized. Similarly, Sigmund Freud attributed war neuroses to psychological conflict in the face of physical danger. These ideas were further developed by Abram Kardiner in *The Traumatic Neuroses of War* (1941), which is considered a landmark in the history of PTSD and is the source of many items on its symptom list (Young 1995, 89). Kardiner, a Veterans Administration doctor, defined "traumatic neurosis" as "a type of adaptation in which no complete restitution takes place but in which the individual continues with a reduction of resources or a contraction of the ego" (1941, 79). Symptom formation "is an effort to eliminate or control painful and anxiety-inducing changes that have been produced by the trauma in the organism's external and internal environments. The kind of adaptation that occurs in a particular case will depend on the individual's psychological resources and his [sic] relations to his primary social group" (Kardiner 1941, 141). His description combines psychodynamic elements, including Freud's defense mechanisms, with environmental and relational components. Despite the many similarities between the *DSM* criteria and the symptomatology developed by Kardiner, there are some critical differences. Kardiner leaves room for variation, and perhaps even different clinical types, in the expression of the neurosis based on individual, trauma, and contextual factors, but while developing the PTSD category for *DSM-III*, its creators emphasized the commonalities rather than the differences in individuals' posttraumatic responses. The focus on observable phenomena as the foundation for the diagnostic category is also a departure from Kardiner's more process-oriented approach. The former approach is problematic because it may limit the validity of the construct since the most easily discerned elements are not necessarily the heart of the disorder.

DSM-I included the category Gross Stress Reaction (GSR), which is characterized as a psychoneurotic disorder originating in an experience of intolerable stress (American Psychiatric Association 1952). GSR is not included in *DSM-II,* published during peacetime. Consequently, the only *DSM* diagnosis available to professionals to account for psychological disturbances resulting from the Vietnam War was Transient Situational Disturbances. As the name suggests, the symptoms of distress were expected to fade once the source of distress was removed. After the Vietnam War, the media reported an epidemic of "suicides, antisocial acts, and bizarre behaviors" committed by veterans; journalists detailed the personal battles soldiers had waged since returning home; and doctors' offices were filled with troubled young men (Young 1995, 108). Soldiers' accounts of atrocities in Vietnam were initially discredited, and the VA medical community claimed that the soldiers had preexisting psychological problems. Sarah Haley, a psychiatric social worker at Boston's VA Medical Center, was the first to suggest otherwise publicly (Scott 1990). Haley discovered that many clinicians were making diagnoses of "traumatic war neurosis" in the margins of their notes, despite the absence of such a category in *DSM-II*. Her findings were persuasive evidence that a new diagnostic category was needed (Kutchins and Kirk 1997; Scott 1990). The public's awareness of many veterans' instability was an incentive to explain the veterans' emotional problems. As the effort to revise the *DSM* began, the head of the task force, psychiatrist Robert Spitzer, formed the Reactive Disorders Committee to investigate veterans' issues. Despite the publicity and public support for the veterans, *DSM* officials said that a new diagnostic category would not be included without empirical confirmation (Scott 1990, 303).

A small group of mental health practitioners and members of the National Veterans Support Network formed the Vietnam Veterans Working Group (VVWG) to gather evidence about a "post-combat disorder." Their documentation included published reports of the sequelae of natural and human-made catastrophes, case histories of veterans, clinical accounts from clinicians, and endorsements from experts on pathogenic stress (Young 1995, 110). The VVWG presented Catastrophic Stress Disorder (CSD) to the Reactive Disorders Committee in 1978. The VVWG noted similarities between the symptoms of veterans and those of Holocaust survivors. Gradually, the conceptualization of the disorder began to shift from one about war trauma to a more generalized catastrophic trauma (Kutchins and Kirk 1997, 113). The inclusion of more trauma types broadened support for the diagnosis and led to a greater focus on the symptoms shared by the different groups. CSD's reference to etiology, its grounding in Freudian theory, and its empirical limitations violated three of the basic guidelines laid out by the task force for *DSM-III* (Kutchins and Kirk 1997, 114). In spite of this, and perhaps due to the intersection between the politics and science of the diagnosis, the Committee on Reactive Disorders recommended that the diagnosis, now titled Post-traumatic Stress Disorder, be included in the *DSM-III* under "Anxiety Disorders."

For *DSM-III*, veterans' distress was translated into psychiatric symptoms, which were compiled into the diagnostic criteria for PTSD. In order to meet the criteria for a diagnosis of PTSD, an individual had to (1) have experienced an etiologic event outside the realm of usual human experience that was sufficient to evoke stress in most people, and (2) have an observable set of symptoms.

PTSD Today

The impetus for creating the diagnostic category, that is, the psychological problems of primarily male veterans, and making them eligible for government compensation, does not reflect the clinical use of PTSD today. In addition to war veterans, victims of interpersonal violence, natural disasters, and accidents are now treated under the umbrella of PTSD, as revisions to its trauma criterion in *DSM-III-R* and *DSM-IV* broadened the concept of trauma. In *DSM-III-R*, traumatic events were limited to those "outside the range of normal human experience" (APA 1987). The aim of including this criterion was to distinguish catastrophic events from other, more normative occurrences, such as the death of an aged spouse. However, the range of normative experiences varies dramatically across groups and individuals. Recent estimates of the frequency and prevalence of physical and sexual assaults against women during their lifetime indicate that these events are not only not outside the range of normal female experience but actually disturbingly common (Herman 1992). Findings that "persistent low level stress" can lead to PTSD also weaken the distinction between the impact of unusual occurrences and the effect of more mundane events (Kutchins and Kirk 1997, 118). The *DSM-IV* authors address this by removing the phrase "outside the range of normal human experience."

Expansion of the trauma category was based on the assumption of commonality in response to disparate types of stress. It was also based on an assumption of comparability across individuals and social groups. Proposals for new diagnostic categories addressed to issues related to interpersonal violence suggest that some in the psychiatric establishment may be uncomfortable with the widening umbrella of PTSD. Some *DSM-III-R* authors proposed a category they called Self-Defeating Personality Disorder for inclusion in the manual, and Victimization Disorder was considered for *DSM-IV*. Neither was widely successful, although Self-Defeating Personality Disorder was placed in the III-R appendix (but excluded from *DSM-IV*), and both categories were harshly criticized for victim-blaming and stigmatizing women.

Other revisionists have proposed strengthening distinctions among trauma groups. For example, psychiatrist Judith Herman presented evidence that traumas characterized by captivity produce posttraumatic responses different enough to warrant their own diagnostic category. Herman refers to this variation as "Complex PTSD" and states that "the experience of terror and disempowerment during adolescence effectively compromises the three normal adaptive tasks of that stage of life: the formation of identity, the gradual separation from the family of origin, and the exploration of a wider social world," producing a more complex posttraumatic picture than is adequately captured by PTSD as it is written (1992, 61). The complexity includes difficulties that arise from the erosion of personality.

Construction and Clinical Use of PTSD

This investigation is based on archival analysis and semi-structured interviews. The archival records were documents in the American Psychiatric Association (APA) archives that pertained to the construction and revisions of PTSD, including minutes from committee and task force meetings, internal memos, position papers, and documents pertaining to field trials. Most of the boxes containing information about *DSM-III* and some that were relevant for *DSM-III-R* were unavailable. Consequently, the documentation obtained from the APA archives came primarily from *DSM-III-R* and *DSM-IV*. The paucity of archival material from *DSM-III* is counterbalanced by interviews I conducted with members of the *DSM-III* Reactive Disorders Committee. Interviews were conducted with three members of the six-member Reactive Disorders committee that created the diagnosis and one member of the committee responsible for its most recent revision. I also spoke informally with a psychologist who was involved with the *DSM-IV* field trials on PTSD but who did not sit on the committee. In addition, I interviewed fifteen clinicians with trauma expertise. The interviews were semi-structured, and I used predesigned interview instruments. Interviews were later transcribed and analyzed for themes and content. More detailed information about the research methodology is available upon request.

THE CONSTRUCTION AND RECONSTRUCTION
OF A DISORDER

The Reactive Disorders Committee for *DSM-III* included Dr. Nancy Andreasen (chair), Dr. Robert Spitzer (head of the *DSM-III* task force), Dr. Lyman Wynne, Dr. Chaim Shatan, Dr. Robert Lifton, and Jack Smith. There is great variability among the members' expertise on reactive disorders, as well as reasons for being appointed to the committee. As task force head, Spitzer sat on all *DSM* committees. He appointed Andreasen and Wynne to the committee, although their primary interests lay in the psychoses. Only Shatan, Lifton, and Smith had expertise on disorders resulting from extreme stress. Psychiatrists Shatan and Lifton were active protesters against the Vietnam War, and Smith, a doctoral student in psychology and Vietnam veteran, was also involved in the antiwar movement. Shatan, Lifton, and other sympathetic practitioners were collaborating with the Vietnam Veterans Against the War (VVAW) to gather data on the problems facing veterans. Shatan and Lifton presented papers on the issues at professional conferences, and Shatan was invited to write an opinion piece for the *New York Times*. The committee included three relative outsiders to the APA as well as three task force members.

At the 1975 meeting of the American Psychiatric Association, a panel was convened to discuss issues pertaining to Vietnam. Shatan, Lifton, and Sarah Haley, the social worker from the Boston VA hospital, presented their findings, which included a list of symptoms unique to veterans. According to one of my interviewees, researchers from the Washington University (WU) Department of Psychiatry painted a very different picture, saying that the psychological problems of veterans were driven by their predisposition to depression. The WU group argued that there was no need for a new diagnostic category. Spitzer approached Shatan, Lifton, and Haley after the presentation and challenged them to substantiate their claims to the contrary. The Vietnam Veterans Working Group was formed in response to Spitzer's challenge. Shatan chose Jack Smith to head the group of approximately forty-five psychiatrists, psychologists, chaplains, and veterans responsible for various aspects of data collection on a sample of seven hundred veterans. Lifton, Shatan, and Smith presented their findings to Spitzer in 1977. Afterward, Spitzer invited them to join the Reactive Disorders Committee, of which Andreasen, Wynne, and Spitzer were already members.

As noted, the empirical data used in the creation of PTSD came from a single source, the VVWG. Other literature used to support the existence of the disorder was primarily clinical, based on case studies or very small samples, but it appears that these latter sources of information were important in the final decision to include PTSD in *DSM-III*. According to one committee member, Andreasen was initially opposed to the creation of a new category. However, the committee members from VVWG noted many similarities between the reactions Andreasen had reported in burn victims and those of veterans. Literature reviews also demonstrated similarities with World War II and Korean War veterans as well as those with Holocaust survivors that were mentioned earlier. Expanding the applicability of the category was crucial to garnering support from Andreasen, Wynne, and Spitzer for the inclusion of the new category, and convincing Andreasen of the reality and seriousness of veterans' problems was critical to the later inclusion of the new category.

Although data used to support the creation of PTSD came primarily from one source and one type of trauma, after the publication of *DSM-III* the diagnostic criteria were used to diagnose PTSD in victims of many different types of trauma, and, although the VVWG data were almost entirely based on men, PTSD was applied extensively to women. Many clinicians mistakenly believe that the criteria were evaluated for many types of victims, and as a result they overestimate the empirical strength of the criteria. They mistakenly assume that the validity of each disorder in *DSM-III* was tested and subjected to a disinterested professional debate that ended in consensus about the diagnostic criteria. However, although the field trials were far better than the case studies and clinical opinion pieces relied on previously, they were by no means comprehensive, and the data did not cover the broad spectrum of victim populations to which the diagnosis was later applied.

As stated in the introduction to *DSM-III*: "For most of the categories the diagnostic criteria are based on clinical judgment, and have not been fully validated by data about such important correlates as clinical course, outcome, family history, and treatment response" (APA 1980, 8). The authors then say that further study will likely lead to revisions of the criteria. Furthermore, no matter how much one may be concerned about the victims of trauma, from a scientific standpoint, as well as in relation to clinical applicability, it is important to keep in mind that PTSD data were gathered by individuals with a stake in getting PTSD into the *DSM*.

According to one committee member, votes establishing diagnostic criteria are often divided, such as a 7-to-6 vote on Schizoaffective Disorder. This same member noted that the task force, which makes the final decisions about criteria for each disorder, frequently lacks any member with expertise on the disorder in question. My interviews revealed that these facts are not widely known. The Reactive Disorders Committee reached a consensus about the criteria for PTSD, but a few issues were left unresolved. One dispute concerned the distinction between trauma of human design and trauma of natural cause. Some committee members felt that this was a critical distinction because catastrophe caused by humans would arouse a set of issues, including trust and intimacy, that a natural disaster or accident would not. This distinction was not acknowledged in the final criteria but instead was noted in the prefacing text: "The disorder is apparently more severe and longer lasting when the stressor is of human design" (APA 1980, 236). This omission is significant, because symptoms or specific features of a disorder that are not mentioned in the diagnostic criteria are not included in the "mini-D" (the pocket version of the *DSM*, on which many clinicians rely) and may not be mentioned in psychiatric texts used to train medical students during their psychiatric rotations.

Each member of the Reactive Disorders committee with whom I spoke conceives of the criteria, as laid out in *DSM-III*, differently. For one, the criteria were satisfactory merely because they presented a general description of the suffering experienced by veterans, and describing the symptoms legitimized them in psychiatry and society. This committee member continues to conceive of the symptoms in his own nonclinical terms rather than those of the *DSM* and advocates flexibility in the application of the diagnostic criteria.

A second committee member regarded the creation of the category in strictly functional terms; there was a clinical need for the category, and the objective was to come up with diagnostic criteria so that clinicians in different settings could reliably identify the pattern. From this perspective, it is possible to begin with data from various sources and reduce them to core symptoms that can be uniformly applied to anyone who has experienced a life-threatening event, and variability in the clinical picture is simply *an addition* to the central features but not a replacement.

A third member was also surprised at how little had changed in the revisions of the diagnostic criteria. This member described *DSM-III*'s diagnostic criteria as hypotheses to be tested before the publication of later editions and felt that the revisions were published before there had been time for adequate evaluation of the criteria. The publication of *DSM-III-R* reinforced the impression that the diagnostic criteria were scientifically grounded: "[T]oo many people took the criteria as the final definitive gospel word of truth and did not really take them as hypotheses that needed to be not only defined better but also with much better specification of the circumstances and context in which the symptoms occurred." The same respondent stated that he has not seen sufficient evidence that responses to all types of trauma belong in "the same wastebasket."

Committee members also disagree about the political climate in which PTSD was created. When asked whether there was any controversy, two members told me unequivocally that there was no controversy, while the third described controversy and conflict both inside and outside the APA and conjectured that the APA might not have included the disorder had there been no political pressure. The differences in these reports about controversy over the diagnosis raise questions about the efforts undertaken by APA members and other psychiatrists to appear apolitical and objective. Admission that politics played a role in the creation of a disorder could undermine the impression many people have that psychiatric diagnoses are legitimate.

Of the fifteen clinicians I interviewed who had no involvement with the creation or revision of the diagnostic criteria for PTSD, five said they believed that the women's movement had played an important role in adding the category to the *DSM*, but all members of the *DSM-III* committee with whom I spoke insisted that the intent to include sexual and domestic abuse under the rubric of PTSD came much later, in *DSM-III-R*. According to one of the *DSM-IV* members, the women's movement was active in defining things like "rape trauma syndrome" and "battered women's syndrome," but after the inclusion of PTSD in 1980, these advocates determined that those disorders could be included under the PTSD rubric. Consequently, no further efforts at definition were made. I conjecture that clinicians not on the *DSM* committee had this belief about the women's movement because they often give the label to victims of domestic and sexual types of trauma. Some clinicians I interviewed did connect the construction of PTSD solely to Vietnam veterans, and a few of those had a good understanding of the politicized nature of the *DSM* and its creation and revision. However, the large number of practicing clinicians who were not aware of the history demonstrates important gaps in clinicians' education about the history of mental disorders and diagnosis (see Wiley, chapter 4 in this volume, and Caplan 1995). The historical background has practical implications because lack of knowledge contributes greatly to the reification of a socially constructed reality, as described by Berger and Luckmann (1966). In this case, those who are unaware of the role that advocacy efforts played in the creation of PTSD and many other disorders are likely to assume that it was done objectively, thereby contributing to the reification of the disorder.

In *DSM-III-R* several changes were made to the diagnostic criteria for PTSD. Most notable perhaps was the change to Criterion A, which in *DSM-III* specified that a trauma could be considered to cause the "disorder" if it was: "a recognizable stressor that would evoke significant symptoms of distress in almost everyone" (APA 1980, 238). In *DSM-III-R* Criterion A was amended to read: "The person has experienced an event that is *outside the range of usual human experience* and that would be markedly distressing to almost anyone" (APA 1987, 250, emphasis added) and is followed by a list of events that qualify under that definition. The inclusion of the phrase "*outside the range of usual human experience*" was widely criticized, perhaps most vocally by the advocates for victims of sexual assault and domestic violence, who cited epidemiological studies showing the shockingly high prevalence of rape, childhood sexual abuse, and other forms of domestic violence (see Fish and Becker, chapters 26 and 27 in this volume).

Minor changes were made to the language and wording of other criteria, as well as the addition of some examples of symptoms and ways that one of the criteria might be expressed in children. The reference to symptom expression in children is a result of the committee's explicit decision to expand the category to include victims of child abuse, according to one *DSM-III* committee member.

How do we evaluate the revisions that were made to PTSD in *DSM-III-R*? Do they reflect the research performed in the years between the publication of *DSM-III* and *DSM-III-R*? Do the criteria adequately capture the broadened victim population to whom they are now likely to be applied? One *DSM-III* committee member was surprised by how little was changed. It seems reasonable to ask whether the construct of PTSD was so quickly reified, considered to be a real entity whose parameters were already known, that it excluded the possibility for further questioning of the nature of the construct and independent research that would shed light on commonalities and differences among survivors of various traumata at various ages and on the number of optimally useful criteria. It also seems possible that debates about other *DSM-III-R* categories might have obscured legitimate concerns about PTSD and drained resources (e.g., see Cosgrove and Caplan, chapter 28 in this volume; Caplan 1995).

More the Same than Different: PTSD in DSM-IV

To achieve a deeper understanding of the process and events involved in the most recent revision of PTSD, it is critical to examine each organizational layer and to frame the discussion within the larger context of the APA and the field of psychiatry. For *DSM-III-R*, PTSD was considered on its own by a group that was not part of the Anxiety Disorders Committee. In response to criticism about this separation, a subcommittee on PTSD was created for *DSM-IV* as an advisory group that reported to the Anxiety Disorders Work Group (ADWG). Each subcommittee for a specific disorder reported its findings and made recommendations to the work group for that category of disorders in which it was included. Each work group then reported to the overall *DSM* task force, who made the final decision about what disorders and which criteria would appear in *DSM-IV*.

The cochairs of the *DSM-IV* subcommittee on PTSD, Drs. Edna Foa and Jonathan Davidson, also sat on the Anxiety Disorders Work Group. This is important because of the ADWG's role in setting the agenda for the subcommittee on PTSD. PTSD had been removed from the Anxiety Disorders category in the International Classification of Diseases-Tenth Edition (ICD-10), so where PTSD should be placed in the *DSM* became a primary debate within the sub-committee. Letters and documents preceding the finalization of the ADWG's composition suggest that the persons chosen for the ADWG would favor keep-ing PTSD in the Anxiety Disorders category. Since the ADWG would make recommendations to the task force, the exclusion of persons in favor of moving PTSD out of the Anxiety Disorders section would reduce the likelihood that such a change would occur. Letters among members of the ADWG show that they considered the primary symptoms of PTSD to be similar to those of other Anxiety Disorders (AD) and believed that patients often benefited from treat-ment prescribed for other kinds of AD. Minutes from an ADWG meeting reveal that the PTSD subcommittee disagreed, believing that PTSD should be placed in a new category of Stress Disorders in *DSM-IV*. Recommendations made by members of the PTSD subcommittee, who were considered experts on the spe-cific subject, were often rejected or disregarded by the ADWG.

Other discussions about potential changes to Criteria A and C reveal that the *DSM-IV* task force was intrinsically conservative about changing the cri-teria for PTSD. It continually stressed that proposals for change would need to be supported by empirical evidence. However, the same, rigid empiricism was not applied to the *initial* decisions that were made about the form and content of the criteria. If different standards were indeed applied at different times, then use of a stricter standard for *changing* the criteria rather than *es-tablishing* them helps reify the disorder by suppressing challenges to the cri-teria as they were initially written.

An examination of the fate of Disorders of Extreme Stress Not Otherwise Specified (DESNOS) sheds further light on the politics that shaped PTSD specifically and the *DSM* generally. The inclusion of DESNOS, described earlier as "Complex PTSD," in the manual as a new trauma-related diagnosis would have enabled clinicians to address many of the problems resulting from domestic abuse with one diagnosis, rather than simultaneously diagnos-ing a Personality Disorder, a Dissociative Disorder, and PTSD. At the time the subcommittee on PTSD was formed, many of the professionals appointed to it supported the addition of Complex PTSD under the label DESNOS to *DSM-IV*. Documents from the May 1990 meeting of the ADWG suggest that the chair of the *DSM-IV* task force opposed the inclusion of DESNOS as a unique category. An interviewee divulged that the PTSD subcommittee voted 19-to-1 to include DESNOS as a separate disorder. Instead of acting in accord with this vote, however, the members of the ADWG later decided to list what would have been the criteria for DESNOS as "associated features" of PTSD.

A PTSD subcommittee member claimed that she was content to have the features listed in the *DSM*, even as "associated features." In this interviewee's mind, the legitimization that came with being included in the "Bible" was success enough. Interestingly, twelve of the fifteen clinicians I interviewed who were not involved in the work of the *DSM* mentioned that they use the criteria for DESNOS informally, to conceptualize their patients' distress cohesively and formulate an integrated treatment plan. They do this informally because the criteria and diagnosis for DESNOS are not available in the *DSM* for official use. This is an excellent example of the gap between the reality constructed by the authors of the *DSM* and the clinical reality of many mental health practitioners. It also demonstrates the types of accommodations clinicians made in order to bridge this gap. The disparities between research and clinical realities are addressed in the next section.

IN THE THERAPIST'S OFFICE: PTSD IN PRACTICE

Interviews conducted with practitioners[1] reveal a disparate understanding of the posttraumatic response from the one constructed by the authors of the *DSM*. Practitioners' definitions differed both from the *DSM* definition of PTSD and from each other's, illustrating how a multitude of meanings converges in the diagnosis of PTSD. The *DSM* is intended to provide clinicians a common language for communicating about their patients and also to act as a guideline for directing treatment. However, the discrepancies in the meanings various clinicians ascribe to a diagnosis of PTSD restrict the diagnostic category's usefulness as such a guide: Clinicians using the term PTSD may not all be talking about the same thing. Many of the clinicians I interviewed amend their practices to deal with the limitations of the diagnosis, and these therapeutic concessions are not uniformly applied.

I asked clinicians to tell me their understanding of PTSD and to describe how they use the label in practice. The working definitions of PTSD that clinicians provided fall into two categories: broad, thematic definitions and specific, symptomatic definitions. When I asked each clinician to describe three patients whom they were treating for trauma, eight clinicians chose some patients whose primary diagnosis was not PTSD, demonstrating their conviction that PTSD is only one in a spectrum of possible trauma-related disorders. (The issue of traumatic responses existing on a continuum or having varied forms will be discussed in detail later.) The clinicians also described many patients without referring to the *DSM-IV* symptoms, despite the fact that earlier in their interviews we had extensively discussed the symptomatology of PTSD and the applicability of its criteria. Although PTSD is one of two diagnoses in *DSM-IV* for which a direct link to trauma is drawn, clinicians do not universally consider PTSD to be *the* representative trauma disorder.

The utility of a diagnosis is also a function of its helpfulness to therapists in choosing and designing treatment, although treatment recommendations are not made in the *DSM*. Most of the therapists interviewed agree that it is important to find ways to help the patient minimize the symptoms of re-experiencing, hyperarousal, numbing, and avoidance. However, many felt that focusing treatment on the symptoms outlined in the diagnostic criteria would not result in a comprehensive recovery and that the critical role that the meaning of the trauma plays in the clinical presentation is the most glaring omission from the diagnostic criteria. The meaning of the trauma refers to how the event affects the victim's sense of self and how they reconstruct the event in the context of their lives. Fifteen people (twelve clinicians and three *DSM* committee members) mentioned the crucial roles played by thoughts and the stories that survivors tell themselves about the trauma in determining the posttraumatic response and the patient's prognosis.

The therapists I interviewed felt that the PTSD criteria were not very help-ful in capturing differences in posttraumatic response among persons who had undergone different kinds of traumata. However, there is no consensus about whether this is problematic for treatment purposes. The authors of the diagnostic criteria do not agree with one another either. The trauma-specific differences described by clinicians centered on variations thought to result from human-caused trauma versus trauma from other causes, whether the trauma was a single event or a series of occurrences, and characteristics unique to sexual trauma. Many clinicians also noted the importance of the victim's age at first trauma. The therapists believed that whether the trauma is of human design is the most crucial distinction and that each of the other features is a corollary of this central distinction. Interestingly, this is the same distinction over which the Reactive Disorders committee members had dis-agreed. Clinicians said that being the victim of a trauma caused by people would produce a much more complicated posttraumatic picture than would trauma from "natural causes." The variations described by Herman (1992) as "Complex PTSD" (DESNOS) were also mentioned by many of the inter-viewees as deserving special recognition because of the frequency of their oc-currence and their destructive impact on the victim's life. The failure of PTSD to capture these differences is a primary source of discontent with the diag-nosis. Differences in coping mechanisms and in attribution of meaning may seem inconsequential to the symptomatology of PTSD, but, in fact, they are of central importance. As one interviewee observed, the symptoms of PTSD are nothing more than ineffective methods of coping with the trauma, mech-anisms that are causing impairment in other areas of the victim's life and abil-ity to enjoy life. According to many of the clinicians interviewed, however, the catalogue of *DSM-IV* symptoms fails to provide a road map to recovery.

Some of the individuals interviewed said that PTSD captures the form of the posttraumatic response and that is what matters, irrespective of any gender- or trauma-specific differences. However, these clinicians' actions are not consistent with that view. An evaluation of their clinical work reveals that they make a variety of efforts to make up for the inadequacies of the criteria. Many have developed their own ways of thinking about trauma, enabling them to understand the differences in symptom content and in the definitions and meanings people ascribe to it. Furthermore, they adapt their treatment in light of these differences. Once again, the issue of individual bias or error is paramount. The adaptations being made are untested and reflect personal choice. This does not mean, however, that they are less useful, reliable, or valid than the *DSM* criteria.

When asked about weaknesses in PTSD criteria, clinicians named two primary failings: the way that trauma is defined and the presentation of PTSD as though it were the only response to trauma. With regard to the first issue, which relates to Criterion A,[2] clinicians' discomfort is due to the implicit assumption that trauma is a discrete event and to its severe limitation of the scope of what can be considered traumatic conditions. For example, one psychiatrist reasoned, "Why was the sexual abuse more traumatic than having a mother who didn't love you? We are falsely dichotomizing." Fourteen people I interviewed echoed her sentiments about the focus on a specific, horrific act. The issue of variation in posttraumatic response is the second major point of clinicians' disagreement with the criteria and the disorder's location under Anxiety Disorders in the *DSM*. The language of the *DSM-IV* implies that all traumas are equal and will produce the same set of symptoms. According to the clinicians interviewed, however, differences cannot be sufficiently captured by changes to the established criteria. Although some of the differences are minor variations in the symptom structure or the number and severity of PTSD symptoms, the range includes posttraumatic pictures that resemble other *DSM-IV* disorders more than PTSD. Addressing the varied presentations would entail a dramatic restructuring of the *DSM*. Several clinicians suggested that a trauma category be created. The envisioned category would include disorders demonstrated to be traumatic sequelae, including PTSD and Acute Stress Disorder but also diagnoses from other categories. These disorders could be listed in their former categories as well. Others described PTSD as one point on a spectrum, rather than as a discrete entity. As one Reactive Disorders Committee member said: "These things are on a continuum, so trying to have categories that are discontinuous may be a conceptual mistake." A continuum of posttraumatic stress responses might have "partial PTSD" (noted by several of my interviewees, both clinicians and *DSM* committee members, as causing significant impairment but lacking one or a few of the

criterial requirements for a PTSD diagnosis) and DESNOS at the two ends of
the spectrum, with PTSD somewhere in the middle.

CONCLUSION

This analysis of the history and politics of the construction of PTSD and of
the ways in which clinicians actually use the label highlights the gap between
the reality the *DSM* authors claim to represent and the reality of clinicians
treating victims of trauma. It reveals why decisions about what goes into the
DSM are not always based on careful interpretations of well-designed and
well-executed research or on professional consensus. In addition, therapists
who specialize in the treatment of trauma use the label in different ways.
Clinicians' working definitions of PTSD vary, as does their use of the category, representing their own beliefs about traumatic sequelae and their experiences treating patients.

NOTES

This chapter is based on Meadow Linder's thesis (2001).

1. Individuals interviewed about their work on the *DSM* were also given the opportunity to discuss the use of PTSD in their clinical work if they felt comfortable doing so. When these responses are aggregated with those of the clinicians, it is specifically noted or described as "people interviewed," as opposed to "clinicians
interviewed."

2. In *DSM-IV-TR*, Criterion A reads: "The person has been exposed to a traumatic
event in which both of the following were present: (1) the person experienced, witnessed, or was confronted with an event or events that involved actual or threatened
death or serious injury, or a threat to the physical integrity of self or others; (2) the
person's response involved intense fear, helplessness, or horror" (APA 2000, 467).

REFERENCES

American Psychiatric Association. (2000). *Diagnostic and statistical manual of mental disorders-IV-TR*. Washington, DC.
———. (1994). *Diagnostic and statistical manual of mental disorders-IV*. Washington,
DC.
———. (1987). *Diagnostic and statistical manual of mental disorders, III-R*. Washington, DC.

————. (1980). *Diagnostic and statistical manual of mental disorders, III*. Washington, DC.

———— (1952). *Diagnostic and statistical manual of mental disorders-I*. Washington, DC.

Berger, Peter L., and Thomas Luckmann. (1966).*The social construction of reality: A treatise in the sociology of knowledge*. Garden City, NY: Doubleday.

Caplan, Paula J. (1995). *They say you're crazy: How the world's most powerful psychiatrists decide who's normal*. Reading, MA: Addison-Wesley.

Herman, Judith. (1992). *Trauma and recovery*. New York: Basic Books.

Kardiner, Abram. (1941). *The traumatic neuroses of war*. New York: Paul B. Hoeber.

Kirk, Stuart, andand Herb Kutchins. (1992). *The selling of the DSM*. New York: Aldine De Gruyter.

Kutchins, Herb, and Stuart Kirk. (1997). *Making us crazy*. New York: The Free Press.

Linder, Meadow. (2001). The diagnostic divide: The construction and use of Posttraumatic Stress Disorder. Published senior thesis. Brown University: Wayland Press.

Scott, Wilbur J. (1990). PTSD in *DSM-III*: A case in the politics of diagnosis and disease. *Social Problems* 37, 294–310.

Thoits, Peggy A. (1991). Gender differences in coping with emotional distress. Pp. 107–38 in John Eckenrode, ed. *The social context of coping*. New York and London: Plenum Press.

Young, Allan. (1995). *The harmony of illusions*. Princeton, NJ: Princeton University Press.

Chapter 4

Abnormal Psychology Textbooks Exclude Feminist Criticism of the *DSM*

Autumn Wiley

The second wave of the women's movement led to a burgeoning of research about sex and gender bias in psychology textbooks (e.g., Peterson and Kroner 1992; Percival 1984; Birk, Barbanel, Brooks, Herman, Juhasz, Seltzer, and Tangri 1974; Gray 1977; Harris and Lightner 1980). This has led to some textbook modifications by those authors who have recognized the importance of removing bias from their books. What had not been determined was whether abnormal psychology textbooks include the broad and deep feminist critique of sex and gender and other forms of bias that are embedded in the widely used psychiatric manual, *The Diagnostic and Statistical Manual of Mental Disorders* (*DSM*).

In the past three decades, many feminist psychologists (Brown 1991; Walker 1987; 1993; Kaplan 1983a; 1983b; Caplan 1995) have described the *DSM* as inadequately researched, demonstrating that many of its categories lack solid empirical foundation. They charge that many *DSM* categories embody stereotypes that lead to the pathologizing of women and members of other marginalized groups (Brown 1991; Landrine 1985; 1988; 1989; Caplan 1992; 1995); thus, it is all the more important to incorporate this critique into textbooks that are used to introduce undergraduates, some of whom will become mental health professionals and therapy clients, to the subject of mental disorders. The *DSM* is a pivotal ingredient of every abnormal/clinical psychology course, used as a framework for classification and assessment of abnormal behavior.

An investigation was undertaken to answer the question, "Have feminists' criticisms of the *DSM* had any impact on the way classification and diagnosis are presented in undergraduate textbooks?" Ten widely used, undergraduate, abnormal psychology textbooks were selected, and, in each one, the chapter specifically focused on the *DSM* and diagnostic classification in general was

41

identified and photocopied. Based on their knowledge of books that are widely used in undergraduate classes, two abnormal psychology professors, one from Brandeis and one from Brown, recommended the textbooks that comprised the sample.

A coding system (table 4.1) was devised for classifying how the textbooks' authors dealt with published, feminist criticisms of the *DSM*; whether or not they treated these critiques as credible; and whether textbook authors who include criticism of race or culture bias in the *DSM* are more likely than other authors to address sex and gender bias. Three important, frequently used psychology of women textbooks were chosen on the recommendation of an expert in the field who is also an author of a psychology of women textbook and who said they were the most-used texts. The fourteen critics of the *DSM*'s sex and gender bias who were the most frequently cited in those three texts were established; the names of those critics are listed in item 5 of table 4.1.

One Jewish American, lesbian, undergraduate senior and one Caucasian, heterosexual male alumnus of a private New England university served as raters, to whom the chapters from the ten abnormal psychology textbooks were presented in randomized order. The raters were instructed to read each chapter thoroughly, underline relevant information, and fill out the coding sheet for each. Using the coding system, raters were asked, among other things, to count the number of pages devoted to various criticisms of the *DSM* and the number of mentions of the previously identified, prominent feminist critics of the *DSM*.

The number of pages devoted to diagnostic classification in the ten textbooks ranged from nine to twenty-six. The classification section for seven of the ten texts includes no mention of sex or gender bias, and in only one text is the word "feminist" even mentioned. None of the fourteen feminist critics is cited in any of the books, and sex and gender bias identified by anyone at all is only minimally addressed. The word "empirical" or synonyms of that word appear a total of twenty-eight times across all ten books combined, ranging from one to five mentions in each text. This is important because such words are used 80 percent of the time to portray the *DSM* as a scientifically grounded document, but they are used to challenge its empirical basis only 20 percent of the time. A chi-square test indicates that this difference is statistically significant (chi-square$+1-.35$, df$=1$, p $<$ .001). There is almost no relationship between number of pages in a chapter and the amount of sex and gender bias mentioned in each textbook; thus, the length at which these biases were addressed is not explained by chapter length (r$=-.09$, n.s.). In addition, there is almost no relationship between the number of pages devoted to any kind of criticism of the *DSM* and the amount of space devoted to discussion of sex and gender bias (r$=-.03$, n.s.).

Table 4.1.   Coding Framework for Abnormal Psychology Textbook Chapters about Diagnostic Classification Systems

Developed by Autumn Wiley and Paula J. Caplan

Name of Rater _____

Name of Textbook _____

1. How many pages are included in this chapter? _____
(*please round to the nearest ¼, ½, or whole page*)

2. How many of those pages are devoted to criticism of the *DSM*? _____
(*please round to the nearest ¼, ½, or whole page*)

3. Which of the following criticisms of the *DSM* are mentioned in the chapter?

Criticism	Yes	No
Categorical/dimensional		
Comorbidity		
Culture and Ethnicity		
Empirical basis		
Medical Model		
Racism		
Reliability		
Sexism		
Stigma		
Validity		

4. For those textbook authors who give examples of cultural and ethnic criticisms of the *DSM*, how many do they give? _____

       4a. How many of these examples include gender bias? _____

5. Count the number of times each of the following is cited in this chapter:

Name	#	Name	#
Broverman et al.		Hare-Mustin, R. T.	
Brown, L. S.		Landrine, H.	
Caplan, P. J.		Lerman, H.	
Chesler, P.		Marecek, J.	
Comas-Diaz, L.		Nolen-Hoeksema, S.	
Committee on Women and Psychology		Rosewater, L. B.	
Greene, B.		Walker, L.	

In connection with the rare mentions of sex and gender bias (in only three of the books), the textbook authors did not cite any of the fourteen feminist critics listed in item 5 of table 4.1. Rather than cite the major feminist critics who had done original work about problems in the *DSM*, in nearly every case they instead cited journalists and *DSM* committee members who had *challenged* the notion that there is sexism in the *DSM*; the only feminist critic they mentioned was Marcie Kaplan, who wrote a pioneering, critical article about the *DSM* in 1983 but had not been cited as frequently as the fourteen identified for this study.

In four textbooks, bias was attributed to the clinician rather than the diagnostic category, meaning that the raters found that the textbook author described bias as a result of clinicians' subjectivity, not because of problems inherent in the category itself. In the six other books, no mention was made about sources of bias. Thus, no textbook author attributed bias to anything about any category or the *DSM as a whole*. When raters were asked to give a global assessment of whether the chapter presents the *DSM* as clinically based, empirically based, reliable, and/or valid, they found six of ten as presenting the *DSM* as empirically grounded, six presenting it as reliable, seven as valid, and nine as clinically useful. Five of the texts were rated as presenting the *DSM* as empirical, reliable, valid, and clinically based.

These findings suggest that decades of feminist criticism have had little impact on the way the authors of abnormal psychology textbooks present the *DSM*. The absence of that criticism from the textbooks is not because it is not available or of the highest quality. These books are used to teach students about mental health in undergraduate courses, and their authors are not acknowledging the problems with many of the *DSM* constructs. This perpetuates gender and other forms of bias and undermines teachers' ability to prepare therapists-in-training to become culturally competent, ethical practitioners.

If feminist critique is omitted from textbooks, it is at risk for being lost to history altogether. For millennia, women's intellectual work has been erased and discredited (Reinharz 1992). It is difficult to fathom how and why none of the fourteen most prominent feminist critics was cited in any of the textbook chapters examined for this study. In fact, according to standard 2.03 of the American Psychological Association's most recent ethical guidelines, psychologists must base their work "upon established scientific and professional knowledge of their discipline" (American Psychological Association 2002). Indeed, psychologists have an ethical responsibility as teachers to "present psychological information accurately" (American Psychological Association 2002, code 7.03 [b]). To omit feminists' criticisms of the *DSM* from abnormal psychology textbooks is extremely problematic because it sustains the very biases and stereotypes that students must learn to challenge if they are to become responsible therapists who demonstrate the highest regard for the well-being of their clients.

If students of abnormal psychology are not privy to important criticism of the *DSM*, if they are taught that the *DSM* is value-neutral, they will not have the opportunity to challenge either the *DSM* or the medical model upon which it is based. However, if students are exposed to the high-quality critical work that has been published about the *DSM*, not only will they have the opportunity to develop important critical-thinking skills, but they will also be more likely to transform, rather than sustain, an unjust status quo.

REFERENCES

American Psychological Association. (2002). Ethical Principles of Psychologists and Code of Conduct. http://www.apa.org/ethics/code2002.html.

Birk, J. M., L. Barbanel, L. Brooks, M. H. Herman, J. B. Juhasz, R. A. Seltzer, and S. S. Tangri. (1974). A content analysis of sexual bias in commonly used psychology textbooks. [Secondary Publication] *Catalog of Selected Documents in Psychology,* 4, 107.

Brown, L. S. (1991). Diagnosis and dialogue. *Canadian Psychology*, 32 (2), 142–144.

Caplan, P. J. (1992). Gender issues in the diagnosis of mental disorder. *Women and Therapy,* 12 (4); 71–82.

———. (1995). *They say you're crazy: How the world's powerful psychiatrists decide who's normal.* Reading, MA: Addison-Wesley.

Gray, V. A. (1977). The image of women in psychology textbooks. *Canadian Psychological Review* 18, 46–55.

Harris, B., and J. Lightner. (1980). The image of women in abnormal psychology: Professionalism versus psychopathology. *Psychology of Women Quarterly* 4, 396–411.

Kaplan, M. (1983a). A woman's view of *DSM-III. American Psychologist* 38, 786–92.

———. (1983b). The issue of sex bias in *DSM-III*: Comments on the articles by Spitzer, Williams, and Kass. *American Psychologist* 38, 802–3.

Landrine, H. (1989). The politics of personality disorder. *Psychology of Women Quarterly, 13,* 325–339.

———. (1988) Revising the framework of abnormal psychology. Pp. 37–44 in *Teaching a psychology of people: Resources for gender and socio-cultural awareness.* Phyllis Bronstein and Kat Quina, eds. American Psychological Association, Washington, DC.

———. (1985). Race x class stereotypes of women. *Sex Roles* 13, 65–75.

Percival, E. (1984). Sex bias in introductory psychology textbooks: Five years later. *Canadian Psychology* 25 (1), 35–41.

Peterson, S. B., and T. Kroner. (1992). Gender biases for textbooks in introductory psychology and human development. *Psychology of Women Quarterly* 16, 17–36.

Reinharz, S. (1992). *Feminist methods in social research*. New York: Oxford University Press.

Walker, L. (1993). Are personality disorders gender biased? Yes! Pp. 21–32 in S.A. Kirk and S. D. Einbinder, eds., *Controversial issues in mental health*. New York: Allyn and Bacon.

———. (1987). Inadequacies of the Masochistic Personality Disorder diagnosis for women. *Journal of Personality Disorders* 1, 183–89.

Part II

LEGAL IMPLICATIONS OF BIAS IN PSYCHIATRIC DIAGNOSIS

Chapter 5

Psychiatric Diagnosis in the Legal System

Emily J. Caplan

Possessing a psychiatric diagnosis can be helpful or harmful within the context of the legal system, and its impact can vary, depending on the person's particular situation, legal precedent, and biases of the judge or jury. Consider, for instance, the laws against employment discrimination. Two federal laws protect employees and applicants for employment who have been discriminated against because of having a disability. The Americans with Disabilities Act of 1990 prohibits employment discrimination against qualified individuals with disabilities—including mental illness—in the private sector or in state and local governments,[1] and the Rehabilitation Act of 1973 prohibits discrimination against qualified individuals with disabilities in the federal government.[2] The laws also contain provisions for remedies and attorneys' fees for aggrieved individuals. In both laws, an "individual with a disability" is defined as having a physical or mental impairment that substantially limits one or more major life activities; having a record of such impairment; or being regarded as having such impairment.[3] In order to establish entitlement to a remedy, one must initially demonstrate that one is "disabled" according to these laws. Interestingly, in the context of employment law, even testimony from a mental health professional that, for instance, the individual is mentally ill or meets the criteria for a diagnostic label in the *Diagnostic and Statistical Manual of Mental Disorders*[4] may be inadequate to establish that she is disabled. Yet someone who has never been labeled by an expert but offers her own and others' testimony and other evidence about her "disability," and thereby is able to convince a judge that she is legally "disabled," could receive protection from the statutes.

Undoubtedly, a psychiatric label can serve as probative and persuasive evidence that one is disabled. Therefore, the employee who has a psychiatric diagnosis seems to have an edge over the employee who has no label for purposes of an employment discrimination case. In the course of a person's life, however, being diagnosed as mentally ill can have varied consequences. To illustrate this, I have created a fictional person who finds herself involved in numerous legal battles throughout her lifetime. In some of these, a psychiatric label is detrimental, and in others it is beneficial.

FAMILY LAW

Tara was born in a town called Springfield. Tara's mother, Ainslie, was a flight attendant, and her father, Kyle, was a lawyer. For several years her parents' marriage was strong and stable. When Ainslie switched airlines, however, and was required to be away from home four days a week, things started to change. Kyle accused Ainslie of being a bad mother and neglecting Tara in favor of her work. Ainslie feared that Kyle was right about her being unfit, and she often panicked. Over time she found that exercising three hours at a time helped her avoid the panic attacks. Kyle often mocked Ainslie and told her she was "crazy." Ainslie eventually sought help from a psychiatrist, who diagnosed her with "Obsessive-Compulsive Disorder (OCD)." Soon Ainslie and Kyle decided to separate. Ainslie was granted temporary full custody of Tara, who was twelve at the time. Kyle eventually filed for divorce, and both parents sought full custody of Tara. In court, Ainslie's attorney argued that Kyle was often not affectionate toward Tara and was sometimes cruel. Ainslie said that she often heard Kyle telling Tara that no boy would ever be interested in her unless she lost weight. Kyle's attorney retorted that Ainslie was unfit because of her "OCD" diagnosis. The judge found that awarding full custody to Kyle was in the best interest of the child.[4]

EDUCATION LAW

Kyle enrolled Tara in public school, but her grades were poor, and when he confronted Tara, she said that she found the course materials difficult, her teachers went too fast, and the children laughed at her and called her "slow." Kyle and Ainslie decided together to speak with Tara's teacher. Tara's teacher had suspected that Tara might have a learning disability and asked her parents' permission to conduct some tests, which they granted. A committee was convened to assess whether Tara could benefit from special education. The committee, which included the school psychologist, determined that Tara probably had "Attention Deficit Disorder" (ADD). They designed an individualized education program (IEP) for Tara.[5] In her special classes, students did not pick on Tara or call her names.

EMPLOYMENT LAW

When Tara graduated from high school, she applied for several jobs. It was a poor job market, however, and no one was hiring. For more than a year, Tara was unemployed and grew very depressed. One day, she learned that a government agency had a vacancy for an administrative assistant. She applied and was hired. Tara did her work well but frequently came to work late. Her supervisor often reprimanded her for tardiness. After the fourth reprimand, Tara explained that her lateness was due to depression, and she asked for a more flexible schedule. Her supervisor responded by firing her. Tara felt that her termination was disability discrimination, and she filed a formal complaint. The parties agreed to give Alternative Dispute Resolution a try. During a mediation session, the agency officials insisted that Tara could not prove that her "alleged depression" constituted a disability. Tara admitted that she had no formal diagnosis of depression. She felt intimidated by the agency's attorneys and could not afford to hire an attorney herself. Furthermore, she was apprehensive about receiving an official diagnosis of depression, since she had already been given one label from the *DSM* and was concerned about being considered somehow doubly mentally ill. The mediation ended with no resolution, and soon after, Tara withdrew her complaint and tried to find a job elsewhere.

CRIMINAL LAW

Tara applied for many jobs, but again, no one was hiring. Her depression deepened. She told her father about her depression, and Kyle insisted that Tara see a psychiatrist. The psychiatrist diagnosed her with Major Depressive Disorder and prescribed medication. Tara told her father about the diagnosis and sent him a copy of the psychiatrist's report to show that she had done as he had asked. The medication did not help, however, and Tara began to feel more desperate. Then Ainslie died suddenly of a heart attack. Tara felt enormous sadness and guilt because she felt she had not adequately cared for her mother while she was alive. Tara stayed in bed all day, for weeks at a time. Because she had no income, she could not pay her rent, and her landlord evicted her. Tara became homeless and hungry, not knowing where to turn. She was too ashamed to ask her father for help. On one occasion Tara entered a grocery store and, when she thought no one was looking, put a box of crackers and some nuts in her purse. A security guard caught Tara in the act and called the police. Tara was arraigned and charged with petty larceny.[6] She was fortunate that a conscientious public defender was appointed to represent her and took the time to listen to Tara's story and prepare a solid defense for her. A psychologist met with Tara once prior to the trial and testified that Tara had "diminished capacity"[7] due to her Post-traumatic Stress Disorder, resulting from a combination of several things: the shock of her mother's unexpected death, her sudden homelessness, and her well-founded terror that she could starve to death or freeze to death from sleeping outside in the frigid Springfield winter. Although Tara was convicted, she received no jail sentence because of her diminished capacity and was given only six months of probation.

PROBATE LAW

Tara was still on the streets, sometimes staying in homeless shelters, and, although she tried sporadically to find employment in the worsening economy, she could find none. Her depression intensified, and she began to think constantly about dying. Tara worried about dying intestate. Upon her death, she wanted her few remaining possessions to be sold and the money given to her favorite charity, one that helped kids with special education needs. Tara wrote down her wishes on a piece of paper, signed, and dated it. After Tara died, Kyle learned about her will and contested it, claiming that Tara was not in her right mind when she wrote it. As proof, he showed the probate judge the psychologist's report in which Tara was diagnosed with Major Depressive Disorder. The judge nullified the will on the basis that, because of her mental illness, Tara had indeed lacked testamentary capacity when she wrote it.[8] Instead, the judge decided that Kyle, Tara's only living relative, was entitled to all proceeds from the sale of Tara's possessions.

Tara's story illustrates the following: In the context of family law, a major factor in Ainslie's loss of custody of Tara was her psychiatric diagnosis. In the context of Tara's education, her diagnosis with ADD was vital to her educational needs being met. As to her employment, Tara gave up on her attempts to secure reasonable accommodation because of her fear that she could not meet the legal criteria for "disabled" without a psychiatric diagnosis. When she got into trouble with the law, Tara received a light sentence because of her diminished capacity, which was established partially through the testimony of a mental health professional about her psychiatric illness. Finally, Tara's will was not honored because a judge believed, and made a formal finding, that her psychiatric label was persuasive evidence that she lacked capacity to base her wishes on a reasonable judgment.

In each situation, depending on the fact-finders' biases and the arguments made by the parties, the result could have been different. For instance, a family law judge might have found that the kinds of behavior associated with OCD do not render Ainslie an unfit parent and that Kyle's cruelty is more likely to be harmful to Tara than Ainslie's compulsive exercise. For some children in need of special education, it is conceivable that even with a psychiatric diagnosis, a child might not receive the attention and special curriculum that she needs. For instance, in an overpopulated school, with underpaid teachers, the resources simply may not be available for children in need of special education, diagnosis or not; in such a case, the simple fact of having been given a diagnosis can stigmatize the child without leading to any help. In the context of employment, a psychiatric diagnosis can be a tool for establishing entitlement to a reasonable accommodation; however, it can also lead to the employee's stigmatization or mistreatment by coworkers or supervisors who are aware of the diagnosis. Some employees may decide to forego requesting reasonable accommodation in order to avoid the mistreatment they fear they will receive on the job by people who will view them as "sick." In criminal law, judges and juries are influenced by their biases when determining whether a defendant's capacity was impaired at the time they committed a crime. The quality of legal representation can also influence the outcome; for instance, if the psychologist who testified about Tara's diminished capacity was not a persuasive speaker, a jury might have found that, although she was homeless and mourning her mother's death, Tara possessed the specific mental state necessary to be held wholly responsible for the crime. In the context of probate law, the judge could have found that Tara's psychiatric illness did not interfere with her judgment to such an extent that she lacked testamentary capacity. There are many factors at play in a legal battle, including the factual scenarios, the biases of the various individuals, and the arguments that they choose to make. The presence or absence of a psychiatric label is merely another of those factors. And yet, as we have seen, there are circumstances when the outcome truly does hinge on the presence or absence of the psychiatric label.

NOTES

1. The Americans with Disabilities Act (ADA) of 1990 (Pub. L. 101–336), as amended, volume 42 of the United States Code.
2. The Rehabilitation Act (Rehab. Act) of 1973 (Pub. L. 93–112), as amended, volume 29 of the United States Code.
3. See Rehab. Act., §706 (8); ADA, §12102 (2).

4. *Diagnostic and Statistical Manual of Mental Disorders-IV-TR* (Washington, DC: American Psychiatric Association).

5. The "best interest of the child" is the standard applied by most courts in child custody proceedings. See, e.g., *Friederwitzer v. Friederwitzer*, 55 N.Y.2d. 89, 432 N.E.2d 765, 447 N.Y.S.2d 893 (Feb. 16, 1982) (citing *Matter of Nehra v. Uhlar*, 43 N.Y.2d. 242, 401 N.Y.S.2d 168, 372 N.E.2d 4 (Dec. 15, 1997) ("Paramount in child custody cases, of course, is the ultimate best interest of the child.").

6. The IEP means "a written statement for each child with a disability that is developed, reviewed and revised in accordance with Section 1414(d)" of volume 20 of the United States Code.

7. Petty larceny is "larceny of property worth less than a statutory cut-off amount, usu. $100." See Bryan A. Garner et al., *Black's Law Dictionary* (St. Paul: West Publishing Company, 1996), 363.

8. Diminished capacity, as described in Garner et al., is "An impaired mental condition—short of insanity—that is caused by intoxication, trauma, or disease and that prevents the person from having the specific mental state necessary to be held responsible for a crime; the court can consider a defendant's diminished capacity when determining the degree of the offense or the severity of the punishment" (79).

9. Testamentary capacity is defined by Garner et al. as "The mental condition a person must have when preparing a will in order for the will to be considered valid; this capacity is often described as the ability to recognize the natural objects of one's bounty and the nature and extent of one's estate" (79).

Chapter 6

Bias and Subjectivity in Diagnosing Mental Retardation in Death Penalty Cases

Paula J. Caplan

The recent U.S. Supreme Court ruling against executing people who have "mental retardation" has given many people the impression that it is a simple matter to find out who has mental retardation and thus to ensure that they will not receive capital punishment. However, the process of deciding who has "mental retardation" and who does not is far from being a simple, objective, scientific process. The dilemma of deciding whom to execute will arise no less frequently than in the past, but much power has now been transferred from the judge to the psychologist, and psychologists' assessments may be compromised by bias. A primary reason for the principle of not executing people with "mental retardation" is that accused persons must be able to participate in their own defense. For instance, someone with cognitive limitations might not recall a witness or that they were in a location far from the murder scene at the time of the murder. Of course, a good defense attorney would ask as many questions as possible to try to determine whether such exculpatory evidence might be available, but many defense attorneys in capital cases are sorely pressed for time, and others are derelict for additional reasons. There are documented cases of false confessions by people considered to have "mental retardation" (e.g., "The policeman told me he would help me if I told him I did it"). Jerome Bowden denied committing a murder but later signed a confession when it was brought to him in his cell, although he could not read (Bonner 2001).

Mental health professionals' efforts to present their work as scientific and objective have appealed to judges confronted with especially troubling cases, and recent decades have marked an increasing trend for judges to transfer these weighty burdens from their own shoulders onto those of clinicians (Caplan and Wilson 1990). It appears that, because the cutoff point listed in the *Diagnostic and Statistical Manual of Mental Disorders* is an intelligence quotient (or IQ score) of 70, the likely cutoff point for capital cases in many states will be 70, with anyone scoring below that number having a greater chance[1] of being rescued from the ultimate punishment. Unfortunately, the process of determining who has "mental retardation" is not a straightforward one and is riddled with inequities, subjectivity, and even politics.

To begin with, there is no such absolute entity as "intelligence." Intelligence is a construct, a concept whose meaning depends on who is defining it and why. Each creator of an IQ test chooses from among a host of possible definitions of intelligence and then selects test items and subtests based on their definitions. Like intelligence, "retardation" is a construct. This context is crucial to understanding the many causes for alarm in regard to the death penalty and mental retardation, because some prisoners will be excluded from the constitutional right to equal protection under the law. How will this happen? The individual states have the power to decide the cutoff score for mental retardation in their jurisdictions, and, as a result, that magic number varies from state to state. It is alarming to consider that, as long as the death penalty is legal, there will be people executed in some states who would not have been killed if they had lived in other states; in other words, a person whose IQ score is 68 and who is imprisoned in a state whose cutoff point is 65 will be executed, but that person might not have been executed if they had lived in a state whose cutoff score is 70. Other concerns discussed below may also constitute denial of equal protection.

There is the matter of test-retest reliability: All psychologists know that many factors can lead to an individual's scoring 73; however, if that person were to have taken the same test one day later or while hungry, they might have scored 68. Further, any test score must be considered in light of "standard error," because of which an IQ score *indicates a range* of what is defined as intelligence. A person scoring 68 cannot be considered definitely smarter than a person scoring 67. Should a person scoring 71 in a state in which 70 is the cutoff point be executed, or should they be spared the death penalty because the range that includes a score of 71 could well include a score of 69? It will be up to the attorneys to bring this to the attention of judges, and it will then be up to judges to decide what to do about it.

Despite the best intentions, no psychologist testing a person on Death Row can be sure to keep every conscious or unconscious feeling they have about their power and about the death penalty from affecting this work. Instruction booklets include directions for "standardized administration," but those directions primarily prescribe the words the psychologist is to speak, and there is no guaranteed way to control a psychologist's tone of voice, facial expressions, or degree of tension, all of which can enhance or impede the prisoner's performance. Might one solution be to have observers present to monitor such events? Who would they be? The prisoner's attorney? The prosecutor? Neutral parties? All of the above? What effect would it have on the test-taker to have other people watching? This last question is all the more worrying because most people on Death Row being administered an IQ test have had lifelong experiences of failure and may be self-conscious and ashamed about their mental functioning, factors which can certainly change their test scores. Death penalty opponents will probably be less concerned about that point than death penalty advocates, of course, since self-consciousness and shame are likely to lower scores, if anything.

Then there is a host of concerns about standardization. Decisions about how many correct questions should qualify a person for a particular IQ score are based, at best, on the testing of thousands of people throughout the country. But this population does not tend to include Death Row inmates or prisoners in maximum-security prisons. To assign an inmate a number representing their IQ based on the scores of people who were tested in vastly different circumstances makes neither scientific nor moral sense. As a death penalty opponent myself, this does not worry me because it probably *lowers* an inmate's score, but from my standpoint as a psychologist and trainer of psychologists, it concerns me when a test is given to people or under conditions very different from the people and conditions that were part of the process of standardizing that test. This bothers me because it makes it difficult to know how to interpret the test results.

Another matter is likely to worry death penalty opponents more than death penalty advocates. The vast majority of people charged with capital crimes have lifelong histories of receiving little or no warmth, encouragement, or patience and are likely to have been abused, neglected, and/or impoverished. All of these factors can impair an individual's intellectual and life skills functioning, and these are the crucial kinds of functioning used in assessing whether a person has mental retardation. Psychologists who favor the death penalty can conceivably be so warm, supportive, and patient when administering the test and so generous in their scoring that some prisoners' scores will be elevated to the point that they do not accurately indicate the level at which they functioned in their pre-prison days (when they committed the crime, if indeed they did). Ironically, then, psychologists opposed to capital punishment might unintentionally create a testing environment and score IQ tests in ways that increase the likelihood that the accused will be executed.

The examiner's subjectivity, fears, and hopes about a prisoner can come into play in the scoring of tests. The scoring booklet for the most widely used test provides examples of which answers warrant two points, which, only one, and which, zero; but one frequently has to make judgment calls because some

responses fail to fall clearly into any point-category. Psychologists opposed
to the death penalty might be tempted, when in doubt, to assign a lower score,
but they have to uphold ethical standards, and score sheets and reports are
supposed to be audited. Psychologists whose reports always read, "The prisoner's IQ is below 70," wouldn't keep their jobs for long and would probably lose their licenses. Examiners who are so opposed to the death penalty
that they would risk losing their licenses by finding justifications for giving
examinees low scores would have to decide how often and when to make
these choices, in essence choosing whom to sentence to life and whom to
death. In an important way, they would be the judges, though not officially.

According to the *DSM-IV-TR*, a diagnosis of mental retardation must also
include an assessment of the person's level of functioning in life tasks. Here,
too, some subjectivity and arbitrariness enter into decisions about *which* life
tasks to include in that assessment, *how* to assess the prisoner's functioning
in those realms (more difficult because prisoners are not allowed to do some
things one might consider measures of functioning), and *how poor* a prisoner's functioning must be in order to qualify them for the label of "mental
retardation." In relation to this, some people consider it unfair to execute
those who cannot tell right from wrong, but it is not always easy to assess
whether even well-educated people know that difference; indeed, making that
assessment is in some ways a philosophical endeavor and involves attempts
to define the constructs of "know," "right," and "wrong." The imprecision of
language makes this more difficult.

In light of these problems, granting the members of one profession with
deeply flawed methods the power to decide who has mental retardation is not
the proper way to choose our executed if, as a nation, we insist on killing at
least some prisoners some of the time.

NOTES

This chapter was based on a colloquium presented on "Mental Retardation and the
Death Penalty: The Roles of Psychologists in Life-or-Death Decisions," Washington
College of Law, American University, November 7, 2002.

1. As in many kinds of legal proceedings, an IQ score indicating what is usually
called mental retardation can be used as an *argument for* not imposing the death
penalty, but it is not a guarantee that the argument will be accepted. This is the case
because Supreme Court decisions can be challenged and because, as with so many
cases involving expert witnesses, the opposing attorney can always argue that the expert did not do their job properly and/or can bring in another psychologist for a "battle of the experts."

REFERENCES

Bonner, Raymond. (2001). Argument escalates on executing the retarded. *New York Times*, July 23.

Caplan, Paula J., and Jeffery Wilson. (1990). Assessing the child custody assessors. *Reports of Family Law,* third series 27 (2), October 25.

Chapter 7

What Is It That's Being Called "Parental Alienation Syndrome"?

Paula J. Caplan

When hearing about a psychiatric label for the first time, it is important for therapists and laypeople to try to discover the following:

- *who* decided to call it a mental illness?
- *how* it is defined?
- *what* information supports the claims that the entity (a) exists, (b) is consistent with some reasonable definition of "mental illness," and (c) the use of the label is helpful more than harmful?

These questions will be addressed with respect to Parental Alienation Syndrome.

As a result of the Second Wave of the women's movement, many people who were sexually abused as children spoke out about it. One consequence was that therapists and laypeople alike learned that sexual abuse of children (CSA) was by no means rare (see Olio, chapter 19 in this volume; Faller 1990), despite claims to the contrary. In fact, between one-quarter and one-third of women and one in six to ten men were sexually abused as children (Faller 1998a). Around the same time, the divorce rate in North America increased dramatically, and both parents and child custody assessors became more likely than before to notice signs that a child was being abused. The overwhelming majority of CSA perpetrators are men (Finkelhor 1994; Watters, Caplan, White, Bates, and Parry 1986), so more mothers than fathers reported that their ex-spouses might be abusing their children. For a short time, children who said they were sexually abused were likely to be believed, but then came a powerful backlash, and many assessors and laypeople reverted to assuming that angry ex-wives were coaching their children to lie. One of the most popular techniques used by the attorneys who represented fathers in these cases was to claim that the mothers suffered from Munchausen's by Proxy (MBP) (see Caplan 2001; Allison and Roberts 1998). MBP indicated that the mother claimed that terrible things were happening to her child, so that she herself could get attention from medical and mental health professionals. The pervasiveness of this problem was discussed in a British Columbia Continuing Legal Education Society seminar (National Association of Women and the Law 1988). Often the allegation that the mother had MBP was based solely on the fact that she had said that her ex-husband might be abusing their child (Chesler 1986). Judges often responded to mothers' allegations of child abuse by transferring custody of the child to the father (even before the allegations had been fully investigated) on the grounds that the mother was attempting to turn the child against the father (Chesler 1986). Then Richard Gardner (1987) created "Parental Alienation Syndrome" (PAS), which quickly came to be used similarly to MBP, to allege that a parent was turning a child against the other parent (Faller 1998a; 1998b). Gardner claims that PAS is a syndrome because it is a group of symptoms occurring together and constituting a recognizable "condition" (Gardner 1998, 311). But that definition of syndrome is so vague (although it appears in the *Diagnostic and Statistical Manual of Mental Disorders* [American Psychiatric Association 2000]) that vast numbers of clusters of *behavior* would fit the definition of "syndrome." Despite the *DSM* authors' frequently lax standards for what they classify as a mental disorder (Caplan 1995; Kirk and Kutchins 1992), PAS has not made it into the *DSM*. Recently, Gardner urged people to tell the *DSM* authors that PAS should go in the manual so that it can be used in court (Gardner 2002; 2002–2003).

From the beginning, Gardner's characteristics of PAS have been little more than a list of ways in which mothers turn children against their fathers (recently, he said that men can do the equivalent). PAS has been used primarily in custody disputes that include CSA allegations, due in no small part to Gardner's focus, but the label is also used when there is no abuse allegation and one party believes the other is swaying the child. Why call PAS a syndrome and a mental illness when it is just a case of one parent trying to turn a child against the other? It's rather crude for a father to tell a judge, "I never abused my child. My nasty ex-wife made that up," but one takes authoritative high ground when one says, in effect, "It is really too bad that my ex-wife has a mental illness called PAS" and a therapist officially diagnoses her that way. Many judges are insufficiently skeptical when a person who has an M.D. or a Ph.D. and has written many publications testifies.[1] Gardner has added a powerful weapon to the arsenals of therapists and lawyers who advocate for people who are accused of abusing their children.

PAS advocates claim that the child's welfare is their concern, that the turning of a child against a parent is bad for the child. However, when PAS is used, the focus is often moved from the child's needs to the rights of the "alienated" parent to see the child (although use of PAS is not the only cause of this change of focus). It is alarming that Gardner has said that pedophilia "serves procreative purposes . . . the [abused, young] child . . . is likely to become highly sexualized and crave sexual experiences during the prepubertal years . . . and more likely, therefore, to transmit his or her genes to his or her progeny at an early age. The younger the survival machine [*Gardner is referring to the abused child!*] at the time sexual urges appear, . . . the greater the likelihood the individual will create more survival machines in the next generation" (Gardner 1993, 115). Gardner classifies sexual abuse of children with other "paraphilias," which, he says, serve "species survival and are therefore part of the natural repertoire of humanity" (Gardner 1993, 113–14). It seems grotesque that someone who writes in this way about CSA would use a manufactured diagnosis to allege that children are *not* sexually abused. Also bizarre is Gardner's claim that child protection workers want to believe some children are sexually abused because the workers find that sexually arousing (see Faller 1998a).

Despite Gardner's disclaimers, the fact that PAS is nearly always used against mothers suggests powerful bias in its use and possibly its creation. Gardner's description of the causes of PAS includes the stereotype of the "woman scorned": He states that women experience their husbands' leaving them as abandonment and make allegations of sexual abuse in order to punish him (1992a; 1998; 1999). And, as Armstrong (1994) has pointed out, the psychiatric diagnosing of victims of abuse, whether with PAS, Post-traumatic Stress Disorder, or other labels, has focused society's attention on psychologizing and pathologizing the survivor of abuse and on the mothers of survivors rather than on identifying perpetrators and holding them accountable.

What evidence does Gardner offer that PAS represents a real entity? Faller has written, PAS "fails to take into account alternative explanations for the child's and mother's behavior, including the veracity of the allegation or that the mother has made an honest mistake. Even in false cases, it does not take into account the full range of motivations and behaviors of children, mothers, and fathers" (1998a, 112). For instance, a parent who refuses to force the children to visit their father (even when an abuse allegation is still being investigated) or does not "cooperate" with a court-ordered assessment is assumed to be involved in PAS rather than *possibly* perceiving accurately or even reasonably believing that the father or assessor may be biased against her child. Gardner claims that false allegations of CSA are frequent features of PAS and that PAS is found in 90 percent of child custody disputes (Gardner 1992a). However, out of 9,000 U.S. custody or visitation disputes in twelve different jurisdictions, only 1.9 percent involved CSA allegations (Thoennes and

Tjaden 1990; Thoennes, Pearson, and Tjaden 1988). Further, research shows that the vast majority of such allegations are very likely to be true (Thoennes and Tjaden 1990; Faller and DeVoe 1995). In fact, disturbingly often, child custody assessors do not take minimal steps to ensure that a CSA allegation is checked out: 13 percent of assessors surveyed reported that they do not refer to a child protective service when a CSA allegation arises in a custody dispute, and 28 percent complete the assessment when there has been such an allegation *even before a determination about the allegation has been made* (Caplan and Wilson 1990). Relevant to Gardner's claim that mothers make nearly all of the false CSA allegations in divorces, Thoennes and Tjaden (1990) found that 28 percent of false CSA allegations were made by fathers and fewer than half by mothers. Furthermore, Armstrong notes, "Those women who were still married when the disclosure [of child sexual abuse] occurred, were advised *by protective services* to take the child, leave the abuser, and file for divorce" (1994, 191); in other words, often the disclosure of abuse led to the divorce, not the reverse.

In Gardner's "manifestations" of PAS, it is not clear whether he intends for the mother, the child, or both to be given the label; he lists "campaign of denigration," which seems to apply to an adult, and also "reflexive support of the alienating parent in the parental conflict," which clearly refers to the child (Gardner 1999, 98). Bone and Walsh have noted that the "diagnostic hallmarks [of PAS] usually are couched in clinical terms that remain vague and open to interpretation" (1999, 44). Some professionals have said that PAS involves a parent's attempt to force the child to choose between the parents (Bone and Walsh 1999, 47), but this is exactly what CSA perpetrators do to ensure that the child will not tell the other parent about the abuse. Professionals often claim that one parent makes the child believe the parent will abandon them if they say anything positive about the other parent (Bone and Walsh 1999), but perpetrators often play on the child's fear of abandonment by *both* parents when they say such things as, "Don't tell Mommy about this. She would get mad at you. You won't get to see me any more if you tell. And I will be mad at you." Whereas *DSM* categories for the most part are listed with a requirement that a patient have a certain number of the symptoms listed in order to receive the diagnosis, Gardner says, "Typically, children who suffer from PAS will exhibit most (if not all) of these symptoms. However, in the mild cases one might not see all eight symptoms initially" (2002–2003, 4). In other words, according to Gardner, there is not even a lower limit to the number of criteria a person must meet in order to qualify for PAS.

Other problems with PAS are evident in Gardner's "Sexual Abuse Legitimacy Scale": The "falsely accusing parent" uses what Gardner calls "the code-term 'the truth'" (Gardner 1992b, 195, 208–09, and 274–75) to refer to the sex-abuse scenario, a claim that reflects his fundamental belief that most parental accusers are distorting the truth. He includes in his scale the item that the accuser often was sexually abused as a child, and Gardner is not the only one to use that claim to suggest that mothers make abuse allegations not because they are warranted but because they imagine that their children were abused because they themselves had been. But that very item of parental history has been used very differently with respect to fathers to justify or diminish the culpability of the father who was abusive. In Armstrong's words, "Thus has childhood sexual abuse been invoked for convenience—as cause for vengeful gratification in women and as cause for a plea of mitigating circumstance in men" (1994, 205). Gardner also says that the "falsely accusing parent" is reluctant to take a lie detector test (Gardner 1992b, 260–62), *but such tests have questionable reliability and are sensitive to anxiety, which one might well feel in such a situation.*

Despite Gardner's denials that his work is biased against mothers, it is clear that this is not the case. Armstrong (1994) has written that mothers who believe their children are being abused are frightened, and they are often caught in catch-22 situations (Caplan 1995). When women tell their lawyers they suspect their child is being abused, attorneys instruct them to keep careful records of everything that happens, even though they are then labeled as obsessive. When mothers try to get protection for the child, they are labeled hysterical and vindictive (Armstrong 1994, 177). The use of PAS to construct negative portrayals of mothers who are involved in child custody disputes cannot be said to redress an anti-father bias in the courts, because *when custody is contested* (mothers usually end up with custody in *un*contested cases, and advocates for fathers use this to claim that the courts are unfair to fathers), fathers are awarded *sole* custody in 79 percent of cases in which a sole-custody award is made (e.g., *Contested Custody Cases* 1991; Chesler 1986).

The created category of PAS is extremely problematic with respect to all three criteria mentioned at the beginning of this chapter, that is, with who decided to call it a mental illness, with how it is defined, and with the nature of the information available in regard to whether the entity exists, whether it is consistent with some reasonable definition of "mental illness," and whether the use of the label is helpful and not harmful.

NOTE

1. I was an expert witness in a case involving sexual abuse allegations in which a psychiatrist had written a letter claiming that, although his patient had over many years

sexually abused both a toddler and a teenager, he was absolutely certain the man would never abuse anyone again. I told opposing counsel that I knew this psychiatrist had written about prediction of dangerous behavior and believed that, in any individual case, it is virtually impossible to predict whether a person will commit a further violent act. But the attorney did not call him as a witness because she had seen him on the witness stand and he appeared utterly self-confident and certain of the truth, so she doubted that what he had written would be enough to overcome the way he presented himself.

REFERENCES

Allison, David B., and Mark S. Roberts. (1998). *Disordered mother or disordered diagnosis? Munchausen by Proxy Syndrome.* Hillsdale, NJ: Analytic Press.

American Psychiatric Association. (2000). *Diagnostic and statistical manual of mental disorders-IV-TR.* Washington, DC.

Armstrong, Louise. (1994). *Rocking the cradle of sexual politics: What happened when women said incest.* Reading, MA: Addison Wesley.

Bone, J. Michael, and Michael R. Walsh. (1999). Parental alienation syndrome: How to detect it and what to do about it. *The Florida Bar Journal* 73 (3), 44–48.

Caplan, Paula J. (2001). *Don't blame mother: Mending the mother-daughter relationship.* New York: Routledge.

———. (1995). *They say you're crazy: How the world's most powerful psychiatrists decide who's normal.* Reading, MA: Addison Wesley.

Caplan, Paula J., and Jeffery Wilson. (1990). Assessing the child custody assessors. *Reports of Family Law*, third series. 27 (2), October 25.

Chesler, Phyllis. (1986). *Mothers on trial: The battle for children and custody.* New York: McGraw-Hill.

Child maltreatment. (1996). Reports from the states to the national child abuse and neglect data system available from national clearinghouse on child abuse and neglect information. Washington, DC.

Contested custody cases in Orange County, North Carolina Trial Courts, 1983–1987: Gender bias, the family and the law. (1991). The Committee for Justice for Women and the Orange County, North Carolina, Women's Coalition. Cited by Joan Pennington. *The hardest case: Custody and incest.* National Center for Protective Parents, February 1993.

Faller, Kathleen Coulbourn. (1990). *Understanding child sexual maltreatment.* Newbury Park, CA: Sage.

———. (1998a). The parental alienation syndrome: What is it and what data support it? *Child Maltreatment* 3, 100–111.

———. (1998b). Response to Gardner. *Child Maltreatment* 3, 312–13.

Faller, Kathleen Coulbourn, and E. DeVoe. (1995). Allegations of sexual abuse in divorce. *Journal of Child Sexual Abuse* 4, 1–25.

Finkelhor, David. (1994). Current information on the nature and scope of child sexual abuse. *Sexual Abuse of Children* 4, 31–53.

Gardner, Richard. (2002–2003). Does *DSM-IV* have equivalents for the parental alienation syndrome? *American Journal of Family Therapy* 31, 1–21.

Gardner, Richard. (2002) PAS and the *DSM-V*: A call for action. www.mensnewsdaily.com/stories/gardner100602.htm.

——. (1999). Differentiating between parental alienation syndrome and bona fide abuse-neglect. *American Journal of Family Therapy* 27, 97–107.

——. (1998). Letter to the editor. *Child Maltreatment* 3, 309–12.

——. (1993). A theory about the variety of human sexual behavior. *Issues in Child Abuse Accusations* 5, 105–24.

——. (1992a). *The parental alienation syndrome: A guide for mental health and legal professionals.* Cresskill, NJ: Creative Therapeutics.

——. (1992b). *True and false allegations of child sex abuse.* Cresskill, NJ: Creative Therapeutics.

——. (1987). *The parental alienation syndrome and the differentiation between fabricated and genuine child sexual abuse.* Cresskill, NJ: Creative Therapeutics.

Kirk, Stuart, and Herb Kutchins. (1992). *The selling of DSM: The rhetoric of science in psychiatry.* New York: Aldine De Gruyter.

National Association of Women and the Law. (1988). Custody litigation and the child sexual abuse backfire syndrome. *Jurisfemme* 8 (3), 21.

Thoennes, N., and P. Tjaden. (1990). The extent, nature, and validity of sexual abuse allegations in custody/visitation disputes. *Child Abuse and Neglect* 14, 151–63.

Thoennes, N., J. Pearson, and P. Tjaden. (1988). *Allegations of sexual abuse in custody and visitation disputes.* Denver, CO: Association of Family and Conciliation Courts.

Watters, Jessie, Paula Caplan, Georgina White, Robert Bates, and Ruth Parry. (1986). *Toronto multi-agency child abuse research project report.* Toronto: The Hospital for Sick Children Foundation.

Part III

SOME FORMS THAT BIAS TAKES

Chapter 8

The Intersection of Racism and Sexism in Psychiatric Diagnosis

Alisha Ali

Conventional beliefs about current-day approaches to psychiatric diagnosis portray a process wherein a highly trained expert employs state-of-the art techniques to arrive at an "untainted" and value-free assessment of an individual's mental state. This portrayal rests on the assumption that diagnosis occurs in a decontextualized space free from prejudice and discrimination. It is increasingly evident, however, that numerous sources of bias can influence the process of psychiatric diagnosis and thereby result in compromised care for certain at-risk individuals. Racialized women and immigrant/refugee women are vulnerable to misdiagnosis due to particular risks associated with the intersecting biases of racism and sexism with which they must contend in the mental health system. Some of these risks will be described as they pertain to women of color and immigrant/refugee women as clients within psychiatric settings employing *DSM-IV-TR* diagnostic criteria (American Psychiatric Association 2000).

THE SEXUALIZATION OF WOMEN OF COLOR

Ideas of normalcy are constructed differently for white and racialized clients within the context of psychiatric diagnosis (Cermele, Daniels, and Anderson 2001; Greene 1995; Root 1996), one consequence being the existence of certain denigrating and stereotypical representations of the latter. An example of this denigration is the reduction of the racialized woman to an exoticized and sexualized entity. Such damaging representations have been identified in the *DSM-IV Casebook* (Spitzer et al. 2002), in which depictions of clients show a marked difference between descriptions of white and racialized women, with the latter represented more often in sexualized terms (Cermele, Daniels, and Anderson 2001). The authors of this study conclude that "sexualizing and objectifying women of color in comparison with white women contributes to the myth that these are inherent characteristics of women of color, rather than products of racist and sexist constructions" (Cermele, Daniels, and Anderson 2001, 244). Sexualization of women of color can also function as a distraction from the seriousness of a mental health problem. For example, with a client experiencing an eating disorder, conceptualizing her drive for thinness solely as a means to attain a sexually attractive body can lead one to discount other more complex aspects of her suffering. Such a conceptualization may also exacerbate a client's symptoms by violating her personal sense of body ownership, focusing on her as a primarily sexual being (Piran 2001).

THE BLAMING OF VICTIMS:
RACISM AS TRAUMATIC STRESS

Another source of potential bias in psychiatric diagnosis is the risk of using the decontextualized nature of the *DSM* nomenclature to blame oppressed individuals for their identified pathologies. Racialized women are vulnerable to this risk because the trauma of racism and related forms of oppression are sometimes dismissed by the diagnosing clinician as irrelevant or even nonexistent (Pauling and Beaver 1997; Root 1996). Consequently, a psychological or emotional reaction to racism is categorized as an illness originating from and existing within the individual, as opposed to an understandable response to a traumatic experience. The trauma of racism can therefore be perpetuated by the racist ideologies that often pervade psychiatric settings. Such ideologies may be particularly pervasive in the content of mental health professionals' interactions with immigrant and refugee women when the traumata associated with acculturative and migratory stress are belittled or ignored (Lee 1988). One further consequence of the dismissal of the reality of racism is that clients may come to adopt the diagnosing clinician's belief that they are responsible for their psychiatric pathology; such "internalized oppression" can contribute to a client's increased suffering (Yamoto 1992).

THE DEROGATION OF THE "OTHER"

Many of the biases in psychiatric diagnosis reflect "Western" ideologies which include the conferring of superior status on "white" culture and the representing of "other" cultures as less advanced and less enlightened. The derogatory category of "other" connotes an inferior subset of individuals who are non-white, non-Western, and non-mainstream. As members of this subset, women of color and immigrant women are often seen as representatives of inferior groups of individuals who do not conform to conventional notions of normalcy. In such instances the pathologizing of the individual can be conflated with pathologizing of their culture. For example, immigrant, racialized, and refugee women are portrayed as the products of cultures that endorse violence, inequality, and woman-beating (Austin, Gallop, McNay, Peternelj-Taylor, and Bayer 1999; Hekmat 1997). Consequently, there is the risk that women from these subsets can be subjected to the overt denigration of their cultural backgrounds on the part of practitioners. Moreover, violence or trauma that immigrant or refugee women might have experienced in their countries of origin may be dismissed as simply part of daily life within those cultures. This invalidates the clients' suffering, and the sequelae of their trauma may be underdiagnosed as a result of such dismissal.

THE SEPARATION OF "SOMA" AND "PSYCHE"

For the most part, mainstream psychiatry has adopted a decidedly nonholistic and nonintegrative approach to conceptualizing mental illness. This approach is embedded in the assumption that the body (soma) must be separated from the mind (psyche) in order to obtain an accurate diagnosis (Hinton and Kleinman 1993). One problem with this approach is that many racialized women may present their mental suffering by using the language of the body (Krause and Liang 1992; Roberts and Cawthorpe 1995). Such idiomatic expression of symptoms is evidenced by clients' descriptions of emotional distress through reference to ailments concerning the blood (Obeyesekere 1977), sensations of heat (Guinness 1992; Mumford, 1989), and the body's nerves (Koss 1990). The artificial separation of body and mind stands in many instances in direct opposition to other cultures' conceptualizations of health and illness. Furthermore, due to the stigma associated with a psychiatric label, a client may choose to describe to a practitioner only the physical aspects of her illness. The separation of mind and body can therefore lead to underdiagnosis of mental health problems among racialized and immigrant women through failure to acknowledge that suffering of the body may be intrinsically connected to suffering of the mind.

CONCLUSION

Although it is challenging to consider the numerous intersecting facets of a client's identity, taking on this challenge is crucial to the provision of care that facilitates clients' recovery and growth. The potential biases outlined here are examples of risks that can hinder the therapeutic process through detrimental diagnostic approaches. It is necessary to consider such risks alongside other forms of diagnostic bias that clients encounter in psychiatric settings. It is also important to note that sexism and racism intersect with other forms of oppression in people's lives. The notion of a fully objective and context-free model for evaluating individuals and their capacities therefore emerges as a fallacy, the adoption of which impedes the effort to provide caring and supportive environments for all clients.

REFERENCES

American Psychiatric Association. (2000). *Diagnostic and statistical manual of mental disorders-IV-TR*. Washington, DC.

Austin, W., R. Gallop, E. McNay, C. Peternelj-Taylor, and M. Bayer. (1999). Culturally competent care for psychiatric clients who have a history of abuse. *Clinical Nursing Research* 8 (1), 5–23.

Cermele, J., S. Daniels, and K. L. Anderson. (2001). Defining normal: Constructions of race and gender in the *DSM-IV* casebook. *Feminism and Psychology* 11 (2), 229–47.

Greene, B. (1995). Institutional racism in the mental health professions. Pp. 113–25 in J. Adleman and G. Enguidanos, eds. *Racism in the lives of women*. New York: Haworth Press.

Guinness, E. A. (1992). Brief reactive psychosis and major functional psychosis: Descriptive case studies in Africa. *British Journal of Psychiatry* (Supplement), 24–41.

Hekmat, A. (1997). *Women and the Koran: The status of women in Islam*. New York: Prometheus Books.

Hinton, L., and A. Kleinman. (1993). Cultural issues and international psychiatric diagnosis. Pp. 111–29 in J. C. Costa-Silva and C. C. Nadelson, eds. *International review of psychiatry*. Washington, DC: American Psychiatric Association.

Koss, J. M. (1990). Somatization and somatic complaint syndromes among Hispanics: Overview and ethnopsychological perspectives. *Transcultural Psychiatric Review* 27 (1), 5–30.

Krause, N., and J. Liang. (1992). Cross-cultural variations in depressive symptoms in later life. *International Psychogeriatrics* (Supplement 2), 185–202.

Lee, E. (1988). Cultural factors in working with Southeast Asian refugees adolescents. *Journal of Adolesence* 11, 167–79.

Mumford, D. B. (1989). Somatic sensations and psychological distress among students in Britain and Pakistan. *Social Psychiatry and Psychiatric Epidemiology* 24, 321–26.

Obeyesekere, G. (1977). The theory and practice of psychological medicine in the Ayurvedic tradition. *Culture, Medicine and Psychiatry* 5, 379–408.

Pauling M. L., and A. S. Beaver. (1997). Treating racism as traumatic stress. Paper presented at the 8th annual meeting of the International Society for Traumatic Stress Studies, Montreal, PQ, November 6–10.

Piran, N. (2001). Reinhabiting the body. *Feminism and Psychology* 11 (2), 172–76.

Roberts, N., and D. Cawthorpe. (1995). Immigrant child and adolescent referrals: A five-year retrospective study of Asian and Caucasian families. *Canadian Journal of Psychiatry* 40, 252–56.

Root, M. P. (1996). Women of color and traumatic stress in "domestic captivity": Gender and race as disempowering statuses. In A. J. Marsella, M. J. Friedman, E. T. Gerrity, and R. M. Scurfield, eds. *Ethnocultural aspects of posttraumatic stress disorder*. Washington, DC: American Psychological Association.

Spitzer, R. L., M. Gibbon, A. E. Skodol, J. B. Williams, and M. B. First, eds. (2002). *DSM-IV-TR casebook*. Washington, DC: American Psychiatric Press.

Yamoto, G. (1992). Something about the subject makes it hard to name. In M. L. Anderson and P. H. Collins, eds. *Race, class, and gender: An anthology*. Belmont, CA: Wadsworth.

Chapter 9

Clinical Cases and the Intersection of Sexism and Racism[1]

Nayyar Javed

Psychiatry books of the eighteenth, nineteenth, and twentieth centuries are filled with fictions about racialized people in the United States because psychiatry emerged in this part of the world during U.S. colonization and slavery. Today, racialized people are misdiagnosed, pathologized for symptoms that are, in fact, reactions to oppression or abuse, even if they are very resilient people who have survived horrific traumas and continue functioning.

The story of a woman from India illustrates the intersection of race and gender in the way she was treated. She was very damaged psychologically because she had been diagnosed as psychotic, heavily medicated, and repeatedly committed to psychiatric wards for more than a decade. When she saw me in the clinic, she said she had married in India, and then her husband left her with her mother-in-law, who was extremely controlling and abusive. She gave birth to a son and was restricted to her home. Then she moved to Canada with her husband, and he was very abusive. As the son grew up, like many sons of racialized, immigrant women, he abused her as her husband had. She was struggling with learning to speak English and was isolated because of language, the abuse, and the racism and sexism directed at her in Canada.

A succession of psychiatrists from her home country had labeled and medicated her. She had tried to make meaning of her painful existence by turning to religious interpretation, according to which she was paying for her sin of disobeying her mother-in-law. Drawing on the mythology of her religion, she said, "Snakes are crawling all over me, biting me," the image of the snake being very powerful and dangerous in her religion and that part of the world. I realized that these were the terms in which people of her religion are taught to think about themselves if they believe they have been bad, and she had been treated as though she were horrible. I explained that I understood about the snakes, validating her reactions, and said I thought she had been misdiagnosed

77

and, as a result, mistreated. Although she remained deeply damaged, she became much better able to function, because, once she was no longer pathologized, she could cry and grieve about the abuse she had suffered and know that she was understood. The wrongheaded labeling of her came from therapists' ignoring her reality because of her race and her gender.

A young woman of Asian origin who was living with a white man came to see me. The man was extremely bright and had been in many postgraduate degree programs but had never finished one. When she tried to talk to him about this and expressed concern, he went on the attack, labeling her "obsessive-compulsive," and demeaning and controlling her in many other ways. After carefully assessing her, I said I did not consider her "obsessive-compulsive," but I said she seemed to be living in an oppressive environment. I suspected that she was suicidal and took her to see a psychiatrist. After seeing her alone, the psychiatrist said, "The partner needs to come." At the next session, which the client, her partner, and I attended, the psychiatrist told her soberly, "You must stop worrying so much. You are obsessive-compulsive." Her partner looked at her triumphantly. This woman, too, had been pathologized in ways that would have been far less likely were it not for her race and sex.

These are two examples of therapists' inability to understand the reality of their clients' lives when the intersection between clients' sex and cultural factors makes the clients different from their therapists. We are told that the *Diagnostic and Statistical Manual of Mental Disorders-IV-TR* (American Psychiatric Association 2000) goes beyond symptoms and helps therapists deal with patients' reality—that all this can be done in a few, short minutes. This is not true because in psychiatry, as in mainstream psychology, little or nothing has been done to raise therapists' consciousness of racism, sexism, or other forms of oppression and the ways they affect diagnosis (see Finkler 1993 for an excellent description of the role of oppression in labeling Native Canadians as mentally ill). Imagine a day when the balance of power shifts, and those of us who are racialized, women, people of other sexual orientations, and the poor have the opportunity to produce their own *DSM*. I don't think we would ever do that. I hope we wouldn't. But, just for a minute, consider this: If it were our turn to assess people who have a great deal of power and have lost total touch with the realities of racism, sexism, ageism, homophobia, and classism, how would we diagnose them?

NOTE

1. This chapter is based on a symposium address delivered at the 2001 Association for Women in Psychology conference.

REFERENCES

American Psychiatric Association. (2000). *Diagnostic and statistical manual of mental disorders-IV-TR.* Washington, DC: American Psychiatric Association.

Finkler, Lilith. (1993). Notes for feminist therapists on the lives of psychiatrized women. *Canadian Woman Studies* 13, 72–74.

Chapter 10

Should Racism Be Classified As a Mental Illness?

Wesley E. Profit

Recently, the American Psychiatric Association began an effort to decide whether racism should be included in the next edition of the *Diagnostic and Statistical Manual of Mental Disorders*. Would it make sense to call racism a mental illness? In order to consider this question, it is helpful to think first about some of the history of the concept of race, especially in the United States, where the *DSM* is written and published. The concept of race is an intellectual beast of burden. It is a construct that has been used in the scientific literature to cover many different things. Its early history shows that the discourse about race has been more about ideology than about science. In the early literature of psychology and psychiatry, it is quite striking to see how the concept of race so clearly reflects the political biases of the day and how, nevertheless, these ideas were published in reputable scholarly journals as though they were true and scientific.

Historically, psychiatrists' efforts to understand matters of race have not always been salutary, to say the least. Two labels for mental disorders that were said to affect slaves were "Drapetomania," also called "running-away sickness," and "Disaesthesia Ethiopica," or "rascality" (Cartwright 1851). Later, psychiatrists proposed to use African Americans to explore Freudian ideas, because, unlike children, they could talk sensibly about dream experiences. However, because African Americans were seen as "childlike," it was thought that the various Freudian ideational processes would be "writ large" in them. Hence, as one doctor put it, "the dream as a simple wish fulfillment in the mind of the Negro" could readily be investigated (Lind 1914). In the 1950s, Kardiner and Ovesey (1951) saw skin color as a "mark of oppression," allowing for no healthy psychological development and resulting in florid self-hatred. When we look at some of the earlier literature today, we think, "What rubbish!" We laugh at the phrenologists of the nineteenth century who claimed to be able to describe a person's personality based on the number and shape of bumps on the head, but what proponents of the concept of race were doing did not differ much because they pushed the notion that one's race was a reliable predictor of one's intelligence, degree of civility, inscrutability, laziness, emotional volatility, honesty, and so forth.

Long before the tools became available for the actual study of genes, it was believed that the human population was divided genetically into categories called "races." Genes were thought to be responsible for determining who was intelligent and civilized and who was inferior and savage. In the encounters between European explorers and Africa and, later, the Americas, the idea of one group distinguished by its physical features as superior to another group was used to explain what the explorers thought they saw. To this, Dr. Fred Hickling (2002), professor of psychiatry in the Department of Community Health and Psychiatry at the University of the West Indies, counters that the colonizers suffered from the "European delusion": "All that I see is mine." Arguably, this view of the dominated as racially inferior receives its most vigorous workout in the United States in connection with slavery and the belief that slavery was justified because the people being enslaved were simple-minded (but not retarded), unable to take care of themselves without assistance and guidance, and lacking in "true" intelligence though sometimes "clever." Slavery was sanctioned in part because it brought "civilizing influences," most notably Christianity, to otherwise "lost souls."

The notion of a "white" race is in some ways peculiar to the United States. In Europe, people might variously consider themselves first to be Italian, German, or French, but after emigrating to the United States, they find that Americans label them first of all as "white." In the United States, being "white" has historically anchored a certain kind of politics in which all "whites," and, some would say, especially poor "whites," were encouraged to consider themselves superior to all "blacks" (Bennett 1975).

Race, at least as it appears in the minds of most people, is a social construct with a culturally specific descriptive meaning (Profit, Mino, and Pierce 2000). Despite the fact that who is "black" and who is "white" depends largely upon when and where and by whom these questions are asked, most Americans believe that the construct "race" has scientific and biologic meaning. In the United States, discussions of race, especially who is "white" and who is "black," are always complicated by beliefs about the purity of blood. Historically, this involved an elaborate classification system, remnants of which still survive in the popular culture, according to which individuals who have one "black" great-grandparent are classified as black ("octoroons") despite having seven-eighths "white" blood. "Blacks" who pass as "whites," therefore, are regarded as betraying their biological roots. Light-

skinned "blacks," in this scheme, are considered by "whites" to be more intelligent than dark-skinned "blacks" because they possess more "white"
blood. From that same viewpoint, intellectual performance is thought to be
closely linked to the degree of one's skin color. "Pure negroes [*sic*]" were reported to have achieved 60 percent of white intellectual efficiency but
quadroons to have reached 90 percent (Ferguson 1916). Ideas about blood
purity also had practical implications: During World War II, the U.S. Army
and the American Red Cross segregated blood by race (MacGregor 1985).
These ideas are still alive today. Recently, a young law school student com-
plained bitterly to me that her excellent performance in a classroom exercise
had prompted one of her classmates to remark with opaque insensitivity,
"You aren't full black, are you?"

So historically, many white mental health professionals and social scientists have actively promoted profoundly racist beliefs. Now that the American
Psychiatric Association is considering inclusion of racism in some form in the
DSM-V, what is the case for or against calling racism a mental illness? I shall
describe three different models or approaches to considering this question.

Racism as mental health and public health illness. Dr. Chester Pierce, professor emeritus of psychiatry and education at Harvard University, defines
racism as a "false belief, born of morbidity, refractory to change when contrary evidence is presented concerning the innate inferiority of any person
with dark skin color" (1970, 266). He points out that racism is a mental health
and public health illness characterized by "perceptual distortion, contagion,
and fatality " which, "besides affecting masses of population, also defies therapy on a one-to-one basis, produces chronic, sustained disability, and will
cost large sums of money to eradicate" (Pierce 1970, 268 and 266). Thus,
racism as a false belief exists both at the level of individual beliefs and actions and as a public health problem because of its widespread and pervasive
presence in the community. For this latter reason, an organized community effort is needed to prevent, control, and eradicate it. But to describe a person
who holds racist beliefs as having a "chronic, sustained disability" appears
counterintuitive in light of the fact that holding racist beliefs in the United
States does not necessarily result in the disabling consequences usually attendant on delusional thinking or mental illness.

Racism as personality disorder. Racism could also be seen as a character
or personality disorder, reflecting habitually maladaptive responses to recur-
ring situations arising during formative stages in the life cycle. According to
this view, certain individuals, influenced by parents, other respected adults,
and significant peers, find reason during childhood and adolescence to sub-
stitute false ideas about race for a more complex and accurate understanding
of the world. As they grow up, these beliefs, when persistent and unchanged,

impair their ability to interact freely and fairly with those about whom they harbor negative and irrational ideas. These individuals, reflexively and without further consideration, act out their belief that a person's worth is determined by membership in a particular racial group. This is an accurate description of probably the vast majority of people who are racist, and, in some ways, it fits the description of a personality disorder as a maladaptive organization of the personality, yet it must be said that in *some* settings racist individuals have nevertheless achieved enormous social, economic, and political power. In this respect, their behavior does not appear maladaptive to them. As with other phenomena that mental health professionals have chosen to classify as personality disorders, whether or not having a particular personality structure will result in negative social consequences for the individual depends, in part, on whether, and how, the larger society chooses to treat such individuals. Consequently, we still come back to the problem of whether *racism* can be classified as a disabling mental disorder when significant elements of the larger society ridicule efforts to suppress its verbal manifestations as mere attempts to be "politically correct."

Racism as one symptom of mental illness. A third approach would be to consider racism not as a mental illness in and of itself but rather as a symptom in the way that we consider violence a symptom. Dr. Carl Bell, a member of both the *DSM* Work Group on Gaps in the Current *DSM* Classification System and the Cross Cultural Work Group, points out: "*DSM-IV* does not specifically highlight racism as a symptom. [But] clinical experience informs us that racism may be a manifestation of a delusional process, a consequence of anxiety, or a feature of an individual's personality dynamics" (Bell 2003).

No doubt, Dr. Bell is correct. Many clinicians have seen patients whose racist beliefs were but one symptom of a larger pathological process or condition, which substantially interfered with their ability to meet the ordinary demands of life. These patients were not sick *because* of their racist beliefs; instead, their racist beliefs were manifestations of their sickness. In principle, listing racism as a symptom of some diagnostic disorders would encourage all clinicians, when seeing racist beliefs in their patients, to take notice of and consider this material when determining a diagnosis or assessing the patient's treatment needs. Presently, with regard to this material, there is no uniform or standard practice within the profession and a clinician who notes racist beliefs of whatever degree need not even include this material in an assessment or diagnostic work-up. Of course, the same is true for a great many deleterious beliefs, and there is nothing to prevent clinicians currently from making a record of racism or anything else in a patient's chart and addressing their meaning in the context of choosing a diagnosis and formulating a treatment plan. Certainly, by no means is every possible or even common delusion listed under Delusional Disorders in the *DSM*.

One problem with treating racism as a mental disorder or even as a symptom of a mental disorder would arise when defendants, who have engaged in racist behavior, would argue that they should be psychiatrically treated, not punished. One can imagine use of this argument to mitigate punishment for conviction of criminal behavior, especially hate crimes. This raises the question: "To what extent do persons with racist beliefs, when they act in racist ways, 'choose' to do so?" If racism is included in the *Diagnostic and Statistical Manual of Mental Disorders*, there can be no doubt that it will speedily make its way into an argument to diminish responsibility for some criminal acts that are racist. Mental health professionals have not been sufficiently diligent about preserving their professional findings from misuse, most notably in the legal system.

Presently, people who could be classified as racist are, in important ways, legally no different from people with Antisocial Personality Disorder. At this point, most courts have not allowed a diagnosis of Antisocial Personality Disorder to be used as an argument for diminished responsibility for criminal behavior, because people who are given this diagnosis are regarded as capable of choosing to behave nonviolently. Thus, at this point in history, in the courts, people are not held less responsible for electing to commit a violent act because they could be classified as having a diagnosable personality disorder. However, as history has shown, these practices can change, and even now there are therapists who would argue that an essential feature of a personality disorder is that one cannot choose how to behave, because behavior is dictated by the rigidity that makes for a personality disorder.

As a forensic psychologist for more than twenty-five years, when I have testified about criminal responsibility, I have adhered to the standard that you may not be held responsible for your behavior if it can be shown that as a result of a mental disease or defect you lacked the substantial capacity to appreciate the wrongfulness of your conduct or to conform your conduct to the requirements of the law. This standard permits a distinction between a personality disorder, on the one hand, and a major mental illness and/or retardation (mental disease or defect) on the other. (Generally, drug- or alcohol-induced behavior is explicitly excluded from consideration.) It is important to restrict the legal definition of insanity. Distortions in mentation and perception brought about by a mental disease or defect cannot be interrupted, evaded, or avoided by an act of will. But criminal behavior by a person with a personality disorder is conduct for which the person can be held legally responsible. The law has made, for the most part, a distinction. Where a mental defect or a major mental illness is implicated in behavior that is criminal, the person suffering from such an illness is not necessarily legally responsible. Such an individual may be legally insane. Everyone else bears some responsibility for the harm that they do. A diagnosable *DSM-IV-TR* (APA 2000) mental illness of whatever kind is not currently recognized as a standard in defense of criminal conduct; legal insanity is. Nevertheless, this has not prevented lawyers from arguing that anything listed in the *DSM* is grounds for claiming, if not insanity, then at least diminished responsibility.

Calling racism a mental illness or a symptom of a mental disorder would probably not lead people to seek and obtain treatment. Both individuals suffering from delusions and those suffering from personality disorders rarely seek treatment voluntarily. While including racism in some form in the *DSM* might eventually lead to greater recognition and understanding of the debilitating effects of racist beliefs on those who hold them, it is more likely that such inclusion would lead to increased frustration for victims in their efforts to hold perpetrators of hate crimes responsible for their conduct. Regarding racism as a mental illness could ultimately diminish efforts to treat racism as what it usually is—a venomous set of attitudes, often followed by hurtful and even dangerous acts, that constitute a serious political, social, and public health problem—and not simply a matter of individual psychopathology.

Racism is certainly a public health problem in that its elimination will require a very public practice of applying psychological principles to social and institutional "carriers," as opposed to the kind of work that occurs in individual and group therapy. It is a fiction that mental health treatment will end racism. From the victim's point of view, racism is first a set of practices, then a set of attitudes, and finally a system of beliefs. Inclusion of racism in the *DSM-V* as a symptom or disorder might speak to the beliefs, and sometimes to the attitudes, but it would hardly illuminate the practices. It is not sufficient to seek out and attend to those individuals whose racist behavior may come to the attention of mental health professionals; it is more important for us as a society to discover and address the arrangements that make the development of this particular social pathology possible and, still worse, permissible. I suspect that two strategies are needed: one for those we might deem sick and another for those who should be damned.

The editors of the current edition of the *Diagnostic and Statistical Manual of Mental Disorders* claimed that identifying and including certain entities in the manual facilitates research and improves communication among clinicians and researchers (APA 2000). This argument would also support the inclusion of ageism, sexism, childism, and a number of other unsuitable and inappropriate belief systems as symptoms, but these have not been proposed for inclusion in the *DSM*, and one has to wonder why this might be. That racism exists is well-documented, but to ask whether racism should be included as a symptom of mental illness is not a question that has a scientific answer; rather, it is arguably better to ask whether evil should be included as a symptom as well. Racism is far too important a social problem to be left solely to mental health clinicians and thereby marginalized and minimalized.

One final point is in order. Effort must be made to distinguish between racism and its effects. In my view, African Americans and others, growing up under a system of racial apartheid, may develop a hatred for those they feel are responsible for their oppression, and they may express this hatred in truly ugly ways, perhaps every bit as violent and dehumanizing as anything that has happened to them. But this countering behavior is not racist (nor, as some would say, "reverse racism") any more than self-defense is the moral or psychological equivalent of initiating violence. If racism is included as a symptom or mental disorder in the *DSM*, it will be distinguished from all other disorders in the manual in that its appearance and prevalence will vary across "racial" groups.

REFERENCES

American Psychiatric Association. (2000). *Diagnostic and statistical manual of mental disorders-IV-TR*. Washington, DC

Bell, C. C. (2003). Personal communication by email.

Bennett, L. Jr. (1975). *The shaping of black America*. Chicago: Johnson Publishing Company.

Cartwright, S. A. (1851). Diseases and peculiarities of the Negro race. *DeBow's* 11, 332.

Ferguson, G. O. (1916). The psychology of the Negro: An experimental study. *Archives of Psychology* 36, 1–138.

Hickling, F. (2002). Lecture, International Division of the Massachusetts General Hospital Department of Psychiatry, The African Diaspora: Psychiatric Issues.

Kardiner, A., and L. Ovesey. (1951). *The mark of oppression*. New York: Norton.

Lind, J. E. (1914). The dream as a simple wish-fulfillment in the Negro. *The Psychoanalytical Review* 1, 295–300.

MacGregor, M. J., Jr. (1985). Integration of the Armed Forces 1940–1965, Center of Military History, United States Army, Washington, DC.

Pierce, C. M. (1970). Offensive mechanisms: The vehicle for micro-aggression. Pp. 265–82 in F. Barbour, *The Black 70's*. Boston: Porter Sargent.

Profit, W., I. Mino, and C. Pierce. (2000). Stress in Blacks. Pp. 771–76 in George Fink, ed. *Encyclopedia of Stress*. San Diego: Academic Press.

Chapter 11

Ageism in Psychiatric Diagnosis

Rachel Josefowitz Siegel

Age bias, which is based on a deficiency model of late life, is one of the least recognized prejudices in our society, and it includes ignorance and avoidance of old age. Like any other bias, it is bound to affect psychiatric diagnosis,

It is no easier to figure out what should be labeled a mental disorder in old people than in the not-old. In important ways, the realities of old people's lives, feelings, and functioning have often been invisible in the process of psychiatric diagnosis, just as old people are often made to feel invisible in Western cultures. Old age is an important developmental stage in the life cycle. It is not an illness or a mental illness, nor is it shameful; yet, it tends to be seen as all of these. However, a number of illnesses and challenges to emotional stability do occur primarily or only in late life and must be made visible by providing more information about the situations, feelings, and needs of old people and by naming ways to help them feel better. Old people, like younger people, feel sad as a result of loss, isolated as a result of being alone or shut out, and frightened by abuse and by the presence or prospect of physical illness, disability, and approaching death.

A significant shift toward a positive view of aging and old people is taking place, especially in industries that provide services to people over sixty-five, although the word "old" is still shunned. However, this shift has not yet tended to trickle down to those clinicians who have no training in geriatrics and are unaware of their own ageism. Being uninformed about normal or predictable psychosocial, medical, and economic conditions of old age is like treating children without knowing anything about child development. Crawford and Unger (2000, 438) report research showing that "Both younger and older respondents evaluated identical behavior differently, depending on the age of the actor," such as viewing an episode of forgetfulness more negatively in a seventy-five-year-old than in a thirty-five-year-old (Rodin and Langer

1980) and that "clinical psychologists evaluated a case study more negatively and were more likely to diagnose psychosis when the client was older" (Crawford and Unger 2000, 438; Settin 1982). Indeed, ageism is frequently cited as a problem in mental health delivery (James and Holey, 1995). Failure to recognize ageism is so widespread that people feel free to laugh when comedians impute stupidity to the old; similar "jokes" about some minority groups would never be tolerated.

The tendency to pathologize everything about old people leads directly to diagnosing many as mentally ill when they are not. In this connection, Seymour Halleck has written, "The psychiatrist who interprets the misery of the elderly as an illness helps to perpetuate a vicious form of oppression" (1971, 113). The previously mentioned factors that have an emotional impact on the well-being of old people are further exacerbated by living in a society in which the old are regularly ignored, demeaned, scapegoated, and treated as distasteful and ridiculous. Such ageist treatment hurts targeted people, making them feel depressed, outcast, angry, and ashamed. The perception of these uncomfortable feelings as evidence that old people are mentally ill is a way of classifying the utterly normal, human responses to rejection as psychopathology.

Age bias includes a troubling combination of invisibility and hypervisibility in the mental health field and in society generally. This combination (which Caplan 1993 describes in connection with race) also manifests itself in the intense phobia affecting people of all ages about calling old people "old." The word is commonly avoided, replaced by " elderly," "senior citizens," or people in "late life," their "retirement years," or "golden years."

Invisibility may lead to underdiagnosing the symptoms that bring old people into mental health offices, and this can result in the withholding of necessary services, while hypervisibility can lead to overdiagnosing, overmedicating, and even institutionalizing people who may not need it, resulting in further deterioration (Ginter 1995). The aged poor are subject to class prejudice as well as age bias and are even more likely to be ignored or overdiagnosed. When institutionalized due to overdiagnosis, they are often subjected to the worst possible treatment in poorly funded, understaffed institutions. Even experienced and well-meaning clinicians may find themselves caught between the two mistakes of either ignoring or overdiagnosing old people, especially if the clinicians do not consistently examine their own ageist assumptions (e.g., Myers 1990).

This is not to say that medication and diagnostic labels are to be completely avoided in treating old people but rather that special care is required to make sure that the old person's complaints are neither dismissed as simply part of aging nor overdiagnosed and overmedicated. When physicians prescribe medication, they may neglect to adjust the dosage for age or to evaluate all of the patient's other medications and medical conditions. Since many medications used by old people affect mood and mental functioning, these need to be considered in diagnostic decisions.

In America's majority culture, people of all ages, including the old, tend to discount or shy away from the realities of old age that are sad or frightening, such as loss of beloved relatives and friends, fear of death, deterioration of health, and the partial or complete loss of capabilities that were previously taken for granted. The too common view is that the old person's mood or feelings in response to these difficult changes do not warrant attention or that old people can no longer benefit from psychotherapy. When depression in old people does not go beyond what most people would feel in similar circumstances, it is important not to pathologize it, but neither should serious depression and anxiety be regarded as "just part of getting old." Invisibility of the emotional needs, especially of old women, reflects the common view that it is normal for an old woman to continue in her role of willing listener to younger people's troubles, but it is selfish, whiny, and needy of her to want to talk about her own life and its joys and sorrows. Thus, the diagnosis of depression in old people is not always necessary or appropriate, but old people's complaints and symptoms need to be taken seriously and validated. Like people of any age, old people can benefit from and are entitled to supportive services, counseling, understanding, and problem solving when they are grieving, isolated, and afraid. Failing strength, illness, isolation, and the fear of death, all of which are associated with aging, though formidable, do not inevitably cause depression. Many an old person can live with grace and dignity. It may be a myth to assume that aging in and of itself causes depression (Halleck 1971).

Because the vast majority of mental health professionals work in systems that require them to assign psychiatric labels to the people they treat, old people may not get the help they need if their miseries are coded as "normal." This is even worse because so many old people, especially women, have very limited financial resources and have to rely on insurance, *which requires a diagnosis.* The impossible choice is between two unsatisfactory solutions: (1) overdiagnose a healthy person in order to get insurance to pay for services or (2) withhold services from a person who needs help because of reluctance to overdiagnose.

One prevalent myth is that old people want to withdraw in preparation for death. The fact is that a number of old people withdraw to some extent for a variety of reasons, such as that they may have less energy than when they were younger, they are ignored in social situations, their friends and agemates have died or moved away, and/or younger people have not responded to their overtures of friendship. When some of these hurdles are removed, when opportunities for engagement and activity are provided, as in some retirement communities, senior centers, and health clubs, old people can be fully engaged in activities and relationships.

What Parker, Georgaca, Harper, McLaughlin, and Stowell-Smith wrote about diagnosis and class applies as well to diagnosis and aging: "it is class that both causes misdiagnosis by professionals (who are likely to be middle class) and causes psychological distress" (1995, 45). Many therapists are young adults or middle-aged but not "old," and few have sufficiently examined or overcome their own age biases, their fear of becoming old, or the conflicts they have with parents who are old. These attitudes and blind spots can seriously interfere with the practitioner's attempts to determine whether an old person's feelings and behavior warrant diagnosis as psychopathology.

"Ageism differs from biases about other marginalized populations, whose 'otherness' can be kept in a distinctly separate category," because all of us will eventually join the old age category if we live long enough (Siegel and Sonderegger 1990, 177). And yet, in white American culture, the young and the "not yet old" seem to need to make the old invisible, assigning their behavior to a personality disorder or perceiving them as ill or even demented. The problem for those who have not yet achieved or acknowledged old age is that they are so uncomfortable when an old person's sorrow, fear, anger, or longing comes to their attention that they attempt to distance themselves from the messenger of such feelings by pathologizing the person and the feelings.

This also takes attention away from the external, social, biased forces that trouble old people and instead treats their pain as though it were proof of individual, intrapsychic illness. This process allows ageist practitioners to evade responsibility for examining their own reactions to such patients. Their biased attitudes and behavior remain unacknowledged, and they remain guilty, without being aware of it, of treating old people in ways that would be devastating to people of any age.

Although unexamined biases are very common, they are not shared by all mental health professionals. A growing number of practitioners are providing excellent, empathic, and unbiased services to old people and teaching others to do the same. Experts in hospice care for the terminally ill have been at the forefront of providing compassionate, non-ageist services and developing support and educational programs that enhance staff awareness and empathy. The same is true in geriatric training programs and the better retirement communities.

Let us look at some specific situations that are prone to lead to the misdiagnosis of old people. When a difficult differential diagnosis is discussed, as when dementia is being considered, the possibility should be raised that the person could instead be diagnosed as grieving or depressed. Such symptoms as apathy, loneliness, and difficulty concentrating might be repercussions of ageism or self-protective responses to the emotional or physical abandonment of old people and the disturbingly common phenomenon of elder abuse (Goldstein 1987; Picard 1989). Serious symptoms of confusion and apparent dementia in old people could be due to a variety of factors that need to be assessed. Change, especially when rapid, may cause confused states which are reversible once the situation is stabilized (Wolanin 1985). Malnutrition, over-medication, or recent trauma, as well as combinations of over-the-counter and therapeutic drugs may produce confusion (Poe and Holloway 1980). For example, as Ginter (1995) has pointed out, depressive symptoms can also be caused by prolonged use of anti-hypertensives and anti-Parkinsonian medications. In addition, "Increasing difficulties in vision or audition, together with decreased opportunities to interact with other people, can increase paranoid-like ideation" (Siegel and Sonderegger 1990, 181). Since cerebral vascular damage increases with age, assessments may be needed to differentiate depression from physical illness (Sherwin and Seltzer 1970).

An important point made by Hare-Mustin and Maracek about psychiatric diagnosis in general is directly relevant to psychiatric diagnosis of the old: "Both overdiagnosing and underdiagnosing have negative consequences. Overdiagnosing may occur because experiences and behavior that are normative for a particular social group are regarded as signs of psychological disorder by the mental health professions. . . . Underdiagnosing refers to overlooking or minimizing a psychological condition. For example, distress and unhappiness may be . . . written off as hypochondriacal complaining for an elderly person, when in fact the individual is experiencing serious depression" (1997, 110–11). Related to this is Halleck's (1971) observation that some pharmaceutical companies advertise drugs for retirement, thus pathologizing another common and by no means inevitably problematic aspect of old age.

Old people who also belong to other marginalized and demeaned groups are at risk of being pathologized as a consequence of multiple biases. For instance, in the case of old women, sex bias as well as ageism comes into play. In the widely used *DSM Casebook* (Spitzer, Gibbon, Skodol, Williams, and First 2002), one finds "The Case of the Wealthy Widow." This seventy-two-year-old woman is described as having no prior psychiatric history and diagnosed with Bipolar Disorder, which is usually described as one of the most severe forms of mental illness. Among the information presented about her are the facts that she is sexually active and that her partner is a considerably younger man. The subtlety with which ageist and sexist bias operate, and their invisibility because they are coded as normal, provide an effective cover-up for the perniciousness of their consequences. When the details of "The Case of the Wealthy Widow" are given to students but with the widow described instead as a widower (Cosgrove 2002), the students find nothing pathological about the man's enjoyment of sexual activity or about his dating a much younger woman. Sexual behavior in old age is often viewed as ludicrous or disgusting, and this bias can affect the mental health worker's judgment.

Another instance of gender-specific age bias is the prevalence of mother-blaming (Caplan 2000). Old women are often perceived as mother figures and treated with unexamined, negative assumptions about mothers (Siegel 1990; Caplan 2001). The stereotype of the "Jewish Mother" adds anti-Semitic prejudice to such mother-blaming (Siegel 1987). Although not found in formal diagnostic manuals, one of the most common labels used to pathologize old women is that of "Jewish mother." Professionals and laypeople who use it show no awareness of the virulent combination of ageism, sexism, and racism the term embodies, nor of the rarity of father-blaming. Mother-blaming attitudes among professionals may cause the practitioner to identify with the old mother's children instead of trying to understand the mother's pain, and this can lead to misdiagnosis. It is akin to accepting parents' descriptions of their child without observing and talking directly with the child.

Fundamental to the process of diagnosing people is the question, "Who is the patient?" Whom are we supposed to treat or diagnose when a relative or caregiver brings an old person to a therapist? Is it the old person, the relative, or the family? There is no simple answer, but the old person's needs must be primary, even when one addresses the relationships of family members. Relatives and caregivers often need help in coming to understand their own feelings, their ambivalence and fears, as well as those of the person they brought for treatment. Whose needs are being met when the old person is given a psychiatric label or is medicated or institutionalized? The practitioner must be careful to recommend what is best for the old person, without colluding with family members in prescribing a solution that is detrimental or distasteful to the old person; the solution that gives relief to relatives who want the old person classified as "the problem" may or may not be what's best for the old person. The available alternatives for old people who need special care are never perfect or easy to choose, but skillful, caring mental health experts can help the family sort it out.

Widowhood in old age is another stressful event that may fail to elicit empathy in the younger professional. The painful and complex transition to widowhood involves learning a new way of life and coping with a host of unfamiliar tasks while feeling depleted and full of grief (Siegel 1994b). Middle-aged children and professionals may grow impatient with the slow pace of the mourning process, reinforcing the grieving person's feelings of deficiency or pathology about what are, in fact, natural reactions. According to the *DSM* authors, a person still grieving two months after the loss of a loved one can be diagnosed with Major Depressive Disorder (American Psychiatric Association 2000). In contrast, my experience in conducting groups for widows shows that normal grieving has no predictable timetable. While diminishing in intensity, it often continues throughout the first two years, or even more.

For assessing whether patients have any signs of psychopathology, it would be helpful to develop criteria that guide practitioners in differentiating between normal or predictable responses and maladaptive or unusual responses among old people, as well as to look for strengths and positive growth. Exactly how much loss of function or damage is "normal" for an old person and at what stage of "old"? In the absence of debilitating physical illness, what is unsurprising at ninety-five is not at sixty-five. Gerontologists recognize late life as an important developmental stage and differentiate among early, intermediate, and late periods of the aging process; starting with age sixty-five, each of these periods can last ten years or more, a possible total of thirty to forty years

The label "old" is associated with a deficit model of advanced age, a model that is grounded in a deep fear of death, an overemphasis on youth and physical perfection, and a multitude of ageist biases and misinformation (Nelson 2002). In white, North American culture, old age is considered undesirable, perhaps because it is regarded as rife with problems and deficiencies and/or because it is perceived as a stage of life in which tremendous effort is required to appear eternally young. Although aging is a natural process experienced by every living organism, ageism is a social phenomenon that is culture-specific, composed of usually negative societal attitudes, assumptions, and behavior regarding aging, old age, and the aged population (Siegel 1993). The deficiency model of aging and the power and pervasiveness of ageism, as well as its invisibility as a form of bias and oppression, increase the frequency with which people are pathologized simply because they are old.

I have proposed a personal growth model of late life, in which old age is considered an important developmental stage in the life cycle, with a focus on the strengths, courage, and creativity that old people exhibit in coping with the numerous and never-ending challenges of old age (Siegel 1994a). This model validates the contributions to society that people make in old age as they continue to touch many lives. The model provides a way to avoid pathologizing our aging population, recognizing instead that late life presents mental health concerns and situations that differ from those of earlier years, including many losses and the oppression of a youth-oriented culture that is

negatively biased against the old. The model allows us to celebrate the
amount of late-life learning and the deep personal growth that take place in
this final stage of life. If generally accepted, this model would reduce the
amount of old age misdiagnosis due to ageism, and the word "old" would take
on a positive meaning, as in "old is beautiful."

NOTE

Thanks to Rebecca Downs Anderson, MSW, and Lisa Cosgrove, Ph.D., for their early
input on this project, and Paula Caplan, Ph.D., for her help and encouragement.

REFERENCES

American Psychiatric Association. (2000). *Diagnostic and statistical manual of mental disorders-IV-TR*. Washington, DC.
Caplan, Paula J. (2000). *Don't blame mother: Mending the mother-daughter relationship*. New York: Routledge.
———. (1993). *Lifting a ton of feathers: A woman's guide to surviving in the academic world*. Toronto: University of Toronto Press.
Cosgrove, Lisa. (2002). Personal communication.
Crawford, Mary, and Rhoda Unger. (2000). *Women and gender: A feminist psychology*. Boston: McGraw-Hill.
Ginter, G.G. (1995). Differential diagnosis in older adults: Dementia, depression and
delirium *Journal of Counseling & Development, 73*, 346–51.
Goldstein, Naomi. (1987). An overview of the elderly in the criminal justice system:
Mental health perspectives. Pp. 289–304 in Richard Rosner and Harold I. Schwartz,
eds. *Geriatric psychiatry and the law*. New York: Plenum Publishing Corporation.
Halleck, Seymour. (1971). *The politics of therapy*. New York: Science House.
Hare-Mustin, R. T., and J. Maracek. (1997). Abnormal and clinical psychology: The
politics of madness. Pp. 104–20 in Dennis Fox and Isaac Prilleltensky, eds. *Criti-
cal psychology: An introduction*. Thousand Oaks, CA: Sage.
James, J. W., and W. E. Haley. (1995). Age and health bias in practicing clinical psy-
chologists. *Psychology and Aging* 10, 610–16.
Myers, J. E. (1990). Aging: An overview for mental health counselors. *Journal of
Mental Health Counseling* 12, 245–59.
Nelson, T. D, ed. (2002). *Ageism: Stereotyping and prejudice against older persons*.
Medford, MA: MIT Press.
Parker, Ian, Eugenie Georgaca, David Harper, Terence McLaughlin, and Mark Stow-
ell-Smith. (1995). *Deconstructing psychopathology*. London, UK: Sage.
Picard, Andre. (1989). Elderly abused by family, study finds. *The Globe and Mail.*
May 26, p. A5.

Poe, William D., and Donald A. Holloway. (1980). *Drugs and the aged.* New York: McGraw-Hill.

Rodin, J., and E. Langer. (1980). Aging labels: The decline of control and the fall of self-esteem. *Journal of Social Issues* 36, 12–19.

Settin, J. M. (1982). Clinical judgment in geropsychology practice. *Psychotherapy: Theory, Research, and Practice* 19, 397–404.

Siegel, Rachel Josefowitz. (1994a). Personal growth model of aging. Unpublished paper presented at the Eastern Psychological Association Meeting in Providence, RI.

——. (1994b). An immigrant again: This time in a country called widowhood. *LILITH: The Independent Jewish Women's Magazine* 19 (1) 25–27.

——. (1993). Old age and ageism are not identical: Uncovering our own reality. *Interchange, Journal of the Advanced Feminist Therapy Institute*, 15–18.

——. (1990). Old women as mother figures. Pp. 89–97 in Ellen Cole and Jane Knowles, eds. *Woman defined motherhood*. New York: Haworth Press.

——. (1987). Anti-Semitism and sexism in stereotypes of Jewish women. Pp. 249–57 in Doris Howard, ed. *Dynamics of feminist therapy*. New York: Haworth Press.

Siegel, Rachel Josefowitz, and Theo Sonderegger. (1990). Pp. 176–84 in Hannah Lerman and Natalie Porter, eds. *Ethical considerations in therapy with older women*. New York: Springer.

Spitzer, R. L, M. Gibbon, A. E. Skodol, J. B. Williams, and M. B. First, eds. (2002). *DSM-IV-TR casebook: A learning companion to the diagnostic and statistical manual of mental disorders, fourth edition, text revision.* Washington, DC: American Psychiatric Press.

Wolanin, Mary Opal. (1985). The aging woman and confusion. Pp. 129–34 in Marie R. Haug, Amasa B. Ford, and Marian Sehafor, eds. *The physical and mental health of aged women*. New York: Springer.

Chapter 12

The Psychiatric Policing of Children

Louise Armstrong

"No term is wholly adequate to convey the range of psychopathology," declared a committee appointed by the Institute of Medicine at the request of the director of the National Institute of Mental Health (NIMH). They wrote:

> The term "disorders" has achieved acceptance, as a broad rubric without theoretical implications about etiology. The term "illness" may convey an implication that the troubles being discussed are like medical diseases or have a clearly established biological basis. "Diseases" conveys a specificity and pathological implication which is inappropriate for most childhood mental disorders. Terms such as "conditions" or "problems" appear frequently in the report and are usually synonymous with disorder or syndrome.
>
> The term "mental" is not quite right either, since it seems to split the child into "mind" and "body." In some circles "mental" is derogatory, and there are advocacy groups, such as the parents of autistic children or those with Tourette's disorder, who feel that having these disorders classified as "mental disorders" has an etiological implication which slights their biological foundations. A triad "mental, behavioral, and developmental disorders" conveys the spectrum, but it may also mistakenly imply that there are conceptually clear distinctions among these categories. There are also semantic concerns about whether the field of inquiry should be called "mental health" (as in this National Institute of Mental Health) or "mental illness/disorder" (for which individuals come to treatment). (National Institute of Mental Health 1990, 19)

So now—what are the particulars of that which we cannot name? The diagnostic criteria for Adjustment Disorder [in *DSM-IV-TR* (American Psychiatric Association, 2000)] are:

A. The development of emotional or behavioral symptoms in response to an identifiable stressor(s) occurring within 3 months of the onset of the stressor(s).

99

B. These symptoms or behaviors are clinically significant as evidenced by either of the following:
   (1) marked distress that is in excess of what would be expected from exposure to the stressor.
   (2) significant impairment in social or occupational (academic) functioning.
C. The stress-related disturbance does not meet the criteria for another specific Axis I disorder and is not merely an exacerbation of a preexisting Axis I or Axis II disorder.
D. The symptoms do not represent Bereavement.
E. Once the stressor (or its consequence) has terminated, the symptoms do not persist for more than an additional 6 months.

Specify if:
Acute: if the disturbance lasts less than 6 months.
Chronic: if the disturbance lasts for 6 months or longer.
(APA 2000, p. 683)

Well, then, what is the practice? What happens when a real psychiatric professional confronts a real child with troubles and has to snuggle that child up under a category in The Book?

Consider Jimmy, who, at nine, is in a foster care kinship home (living with his uncle but a ward of an agency designated by the New York City Child Welfare Administration). The evaluation was prepared by a licensed psychologist, based on a referral from his school. The "Reason for Referral and Background":

Jimmy was referred for a psychological evaluation in order to assess his cognitive and emotional functioning. Jimmy has been disruptive in school. His foster father, who is his uncle, stated that Jimmy may have some learning disabilities. Jimmy's parents were drug addicts and died of AIDS. He then went to live with his paternal grandparents, who died of natural causes soon after his placement with them. Jimmy attends a special education program. He is reported to be attending the third grade. Jimmy is seen for psychotherapy twice a week. He was suspended for two days last year, after banging two of his classmates' heads together. He is reported to flee from class when the door is opened. Foster father reports that Jimmy is worried about his uncle, foster father, dying. Jimmy has told his uncle, "I won't cry! My father taught me not to." He needs to be watched constantly.

It would be hard to argue that Jimmy, as described, is not troubled. But how is it possible to argue that his "symptoms" are "in excess of what would be expected from exposure to the stressor" (APA 2000, 683)? And, though bereavement is here denied prominence, what is a normal and expectable reaction when you are eight and both your parents have died and your grandparents have died; when the school you attend doesn't have time for you; when the norm around you is (more than likely) addiction and violence; and when you are in the custody of a large and impersonal bureaucracy? "Jimmy experienced the most difficulty on a task where knowledge of factual information was tapped. . . . His knowledge of information was extremely limited. He did not know what a baby cow is called. . . . This deficit is probably caused, in part, by previous deprivation." That certainly seems likely. It also seems likely that Jimmy has lots of factual information about things more related to his life and environment than baby cows, if anyone had asked. "Jimmy was most successful when dealing with a non-verbal task where planning and the ability to anticipate were important. On this task he was able to perform within the high average range."

It is certainly plausible that Jimmy is just as bright as he needs to be, given the chance, and that he has been pretty busy dealing with the stuff that has happened to him. Nor is the problem that the evaluator is not sympathetic to Jimmy's reality:

> The most striking aspect of Jimmy's emotional functioning is the extent to which concerns with death pervade his thoughts. He worries about his uncle's dying. He still has not worked through his parents' and grandparents' deaths. This is a youngster who feels that he could be abandoned, yet again, at any time. . . . Jimmy worries about illness causing his world to be turned upside down. . . . Jimmy relies upon the defenses of denial, avoidance and repression. His defenses tend to be quite rigid and limited. Although his reality testing is relatively accurate, his limited defenses are not capable of handling the stress with which he must deal.

Jimmy's diagnosis from the *DSM*: Adjustment Disorder with Mixed Disturbance of Emotions and Conduct. He is also diagnosed with Reading Disorder, Expressive Language Disorder, and Schizoid Personality Disorder. Anyone even marginally familiar with the haphazard nature of New York City's foster care system will agree that Jimmy's appraisal of the potential for disruption in his life is entirely realistic. With all the diagnosing on his record, should any of the disruptions occur, Jimmy is brought one step closer to being a candidate for a residential treatment center. The upshot of the interview is that Jimmy may be referred for a psychiatric evaluation in order to assess the need for medication. Should he be put on medication, the "need" for that will become part of his record as well, further validating the "illness."

The problem is not that either the *DSM* or the interviewing psychologist is deliberately setting Jimmy up. Indeed, it is fairly clear that the interviewing psychologist does not believe that Jimmy's symptoms are in excess of the normal, given the circumstances. What is wrong here is identifying Jimmy as having a *mental disorder*. Joel Kovel, psychiatrist and professor at Bard College, writes:

> Paradoxically, it is when [the *DSM*] tries to become most rational and humane
> that it succeeds in becoming most irrational and dehumanizing. This contradic-
> tion inheres in its most fundamental concept, cushioned in its very title, that of
> the "mental disorder." The mental disorder is the object wrought by the objecti-
> fying gaze. It is not so much what the gaze sees as what it constructs. And with-
> out a coherent notion of mental disorder, [the *DSM*] collapses like a rope of
> sand. Unless mental disorders exist and more to the point, exist discretely, so
> that they can be bounded and clearly differentiated from each other, there is no
> point in measuring them complete to the second decimal place [as is done in the
> *DSM*]. (Kovel 1988, 135)

To pin on Jimmy a label that does not validate and dignify his real-life experience is cruel. It does not require a theory to ascribe Jimmy's misery to actual circumstance. It requires only that you are not committed to colonizing
all human beings under your psy-think system. The kind of system you use
will dictate the kind of information that is considered weighty: When the system is one of grouping mental disorders, weight is given to Jimmy's deficits
as though they existed independent of his reality.

As the public became alarmed in the 1960s and 1970s by young people
challenging authority, the psychiatric policing of children—especially in the
schools—began to gain the legitimacy it now has. As the authors of *The Psychiatric Society* write, "Today . . . it is the school system, backed up by the
family, that has become the center of an impressive and growing system for
detecting behavioral anomalies and treating them medically" (Castel, Castel,
and Lovell 1982, 205). This, if anything, is even truer today than it was two
decades ago.

The political conservatism and economic hedonism of the 1980s coincided
with the upsurge of psychiatric hospitalization of juveniles. While this does
not necessarily imply causality, it does suggest that the climate was compati-
ble with public acceptance of free-market forces in the arena of child
control—so long as it was painted with the pastel colors of "treatment." Ad-
ditionally, faced with an increasingly repressive atmosphere, exhausted by the
apparent futility of efforts at social change, the public was more susceptible
to the psy-sector's salesmanship of personal "mental health" solutions for socially related distress. The greater the sense of helplessness in the face of
oppression—in the face of real events—the greater the appeal of the distrac-
tions offered by psy-think. Greedy entrepreneurs, offering to diagnose children, to intimidate by incarceration (in the name of treatment), were no more
than agents of a more widespread snookery: a snookery entirely dependent on

the medical, the scientific, authority granted to *DSM*. Repeatedly, I returned to this volume, nagged by the feeling there must be something here, something I must be missing. (Else how could so many smart people, some of them caring, take it so seriously?)

By chance, on August 27, 1991, I happened to notice that Sally Jessy Raphael was airing a show on "Borderline Personalities." Borderline! Another favored diagnosis for juveniles! And one I had thus far been unable to decode. Indeed, I had even gone so far as to read a book by the leading authority on Borderline, James E. Masterson (1985). Dr. Masterson's subject inspires in him an oratorical ebullience that is certainly a change from the rather flat tone of *DSM* and its related volumes:

> These patients' stories reveal . . . human beings condemned by birth and subsequent accidents of fate to be victims rather than masters of their own fortune, they are emotionally attacked and impaled before they have developed the resources and weapons with which to do battle. . . . Unable to face their fate, they make of it a virtue. Their chains become a halo; their way of life in all its human misery is defended as their path to salvation. . . . Let the reader now share the adolescent's lonely and painful struggle up through the levels of Dante's Inferno toward a new day that will witness not only survival but also even the mastering of life's blows. (Masterson 1985, ix)

Condemned by birth. Emotionally impaled. By what? Or rather—by whom?

Mother. The Borderline syndrome: a failure of individuation-separation: a distraught-doting, worried-angry-depressed-frightened mother. Mother-blame has of course always been a favorite psy sport: From the refrigerator mother, who was said to cause autism, to the schizophrenogenic mother to the mother who was said to inspire juvenile delinquency in her young. Paula Caplan and Ian Hall-McCorquodale (1985) read 125 articles from nine psy journals and found 72 different kinds of psychopathology attributed to mothers, including avoidance of peers, chronic vomiting, anxiety, arson, delusions, depression, dependency, failure to mourn, fetishism, frigidity, hyperactivity, inability to separate from mother, incontinence, incest, isolation, loneliness, marijuana use, moodiness, narcissism, poor concentration, scapegoating, school dropout, self-induced television epilepsy, tantrums, truancy. So mother-blame is not what takes one by surprise here. It is the opportunity to view the hospitalization of an adolescent from the overseeing psychiatrist's viewpoint; it is what one finds when one witnesses, in action, the (not objective, but as Joel Kovel put it) *objectifying gaze.*

Capsulized from Masterson's book: When Anne was ten, the maid who had taken care of her died, and her mother became ill with porphyria. Anne began acting rebellious, stayed up late, slept in the daytime. She dressed "inappropriately." At fourteen she began to smoke marijuana, was taken to a psychiatrist who said she was hopeless and belonged in a state mental hospital. (Honest. It's right there on page 51.) She was sent to boarding school, became sexually active, was suspended, and was taken to another psychiatrist. Eventually, the doctor insisted she be hospitalized.

"Let us now follow what happens to Anne as she enters the hospital," Masterson writes, and goes on to describe her appearance ("striking"): "shoulder-length black hair, partially covering her eyes, pale white skin, her only makeup blue and white eyeliner, giving her an almost ghostlike appearance. She dressed either in blue jeans with a black turtleneck top and black boots or in very short miniskirts. She wore one blouse open on the sides to the waist without a brassiere" (Masterson 1985, 116). Ah. The objectifying gaze. What Anne said was that she didn't want to be in the hospital. What she *did* ("acting out") was wear miniskirts and adopt a negativistic, sarcastic, flip attitude toward the therapist and *write provocative letters to her friends about hospitalization,* and phone friends, also to make *provocative statements*. Oh—and fail to keep her room clean.

"We," Masterson says, "began . . . by forbidding miniskirts, monitoring her letters, limiting the telephone calls, and expecting her to be at school on time and keep her room clean" (121). War was declared: a war between a rebellious teenager and an authoritarian father, a war in which Masterson et al. seem just as frustrated and helpless as any other parent similarly situated. The difference is that the hospital staff had the power to keep her locked up until she knuckled under. They would tell her no miniskirts. She would say, "How mini is a miniskirt?" They put her on room restriction. They threatened to send her clothes home. She installed a red light in her room and burned incense. They said those things had to go. Finally, she smoked marijuana smuggled in by another patient, and she was put on the restricted floor. The angrier Anne gets, the more gleeful the therapists are because she is releasing her anger. When she tells them the truth—she doesn't want to be there—they tell her she is masking her real feelings. When she tries telling them what she thinks they want to hear, it doesn't help. What is most interesting in this situation is the use of a label meant to connote a medical condition in juxtaposition with the treatment response which clearly presumes acts of will. One feature that sociologists ascribe to those designated "ill"—as opposed to those labeled "deviant" or "bad"—is the exemption from normal responsibilities (Conrad and Schneider 1992). While there is certainly nothing normal about Anne's obligations while in the hospital, she was, in fact, given a whole plateload of responsibilities (tasks that will prove her conformity to the roles of this intensively restrictive social order). These responsibilities could be called extra-normal or supernormal.

The second feature allocated to those cast as sick is that "the individual is not held responsible for his or her condition and cannot be expected to recover by an act of will" (Conrad and Schneider 1992, 32). Yet, Anne is being held responsible for the kinds of behavior that are the only "indicators" of her "disorder," which is precisely what gives the entire scenario the character of a particularly acrimonious household dispute.

However, it is the third feature ascribed to the "sick role" that is the most telling. "[T]he person must recognize that being ill is an inherently undesirable state and must want to recover" (Conrad and Schneider 1980, 32). This is exactly what seems most problematic here. The mission of the treatment is to convince Anne that she is ill (when she quite believes otherwise), to convince her to recognize that the way she is is inherently undesirable, and that changing the way she is (or appearing to do so) is the only way to recover (in a purely nonmedical sense)—to recover what she most wants: her freedom to be who she is.

But back to Sally Jessy Raphael. Let her ask for us: What is Borderline? Addressing us, Sally Jessy asks whether we divide the world into good or bad, black or white, or if we're too hard on ourselves or can't handle rejection? Her guests, she tells us, felt just that way and were given multiple diagnoses over the years, only to realize at last that they suffered from "Borderline Personality Disorder" (BPD). Sally says that when you're not sure what your diagnosis is, it might be Borderline.

We meet Lisa, whose identifying subtitle reads "Borderline Personality Disorder Led to Self-Mutilation." Indeed, Lisa describes being three or four years old, pulling her hair out in wads, and, in first grade, stabbing pencils into her stomach. By grade eight, she was putting safety pins in her legs and fastening them. When she cut herself, she was not, she assures us, just doing it to get attention. "I learned to sew them up, so that I wasn't asking for attention." She delineates her compulsion for sex (a couple of times a day), her continued cutting of herself, her bulimia, and her cocaine use. She rattles off some of the diagnoses she received: schizoaffective, atypical bipolar, manic depressive, cyclothymic, split personality.

Sally introduces our expert, Dr. Jerold Kreisman, who is on the psychiatric staff of St. John's Mercy Medical Center in St. Louis and is medical director of the Borderline Personality Treatment Unit. Dr. Kreisman has written a book: *I Hate You. Don't Leave Me.* Sally invites the audience to ask questions. The first to rise asks Lisa how she finds comfort in cutting herself and tearing out her hair. Lisa tells us it diverts her attention from the pain. The second audience member to speak, however, feels like my stand-in, asking Lisa what makes her certain that *this* diagnosis is the right one. It quickly becomes apparent that the prevailing audience response so far is befuddlement. Lisa replies that at the hospital she was given a book, the *DSM-III*, and told to go through it to see what she thought. She picked Borderline for herself because it seemed to describe what she was going through. Another audience member expresses her frustration: Are we talking about a chemical imbalance? Something mental? Family problems? So, comfortingly, I am not the only person who still does not know what it is we are talking about, or, rather, why we are talking about these various things as being the embodiment of a single thing, a diagnosis called Borderline.

Dr. Kreisman reiterates that a Borderline is someone who divides the universe into good and bad, black and white (which suggests to me a twelve-year-old in full cry, or a president declaiming the "axis of evil"). Kreisman says, "They love beyond measure on Monday those who they may come to hate without reason on Tuesday." (It still sounds like twelve-year-olds and presidential foreign policy to me.) Kreisman explains that the disorder is most often seen in adolescents, but he allows that some people suggest that the term "Borderline Adolescent" may be redundant. In fact, he tells us, Borderline can be identified by extremes: the adolescent who cuts his wrists, who runs away from home, who gets into heavy drug use.

So, once again, it is the behavior that speaks of disease (as surely as the stars and the tea leaves speak of the future?). The problem is that the same behavior may speak of many things. It is common psy currency as well that girls who have been sexually abused by fathers and stepfathers frequently turn to cutting themselves. And sexually abused and battered kids run away from home. And get into drug use. If the behavior is the leading determinant and plays the dominant role in the diagnosis, then diagnoses have virtually no reliable relevance to experiential truth—even if enough psy practitioners have been similarly indoctrinated so that you can show they agree. Faced with this, any reasonable child may stand ready to shout that the emperor has no clothes. But if, given psy power, a kid does shout this out, it is less apt to result in a professional or public epiphany than in a prescription for psychotropic medication.

What all Borderlines have in common, Kreisman says, is self-damaging "impulsivity" and identity problems. "They're Democrats with Democrats and Republicans with Republicans. But at 2:00 in the morning, they're unregistered." Sally acknowledges that the audience does not seem to understand "Borderline" and that perhaps we at home may not understand it either. She asks the doctor for guidelines.

Kreisman attempts again to explain: "The name Borderline Personality has been around for 50 years. And, up until 1980, before it was rigorously defined in the *DSM* . . . it was this wastebasket diagnosis, where you put people you didn't know what to do with. Frequently, it was also a diagnosis if one of the therapists was just ticked off and aggravated at the patient. If they called me in the middle of the night and manipulated me and kept going to the hospital and aggravated me to death, they're a dirty, no-good Borderline, too."

Then Kreisman says, "Well, all psychiatric diagnoses, these days, are defined very clearly in the *Diagnostic and Statistical Manual*. And, every few years, wise psychaitrists go up to Mount Sinai, talk to God, and define all psychiatric illnesses. If you're a manic-depressive, you have three out of these five or four out of these seven. Borderline Personality Disorder is defined by having five out of the eight criteria."

There was, once upon a time, another book from which this kind of scientific certainty was derived. It was the *Malleus Maleficarum*. The certainty then was about who was a witch.[1]

NOTE

1. The witchcraft/Inquisition allusion derives originally from the pioneering work of Thomas Szasz, *The manufacture of madness* (New York: Delta, 1970).

REFERENCES

American Psychiatric Association. (2000). *Diagnostic and statistical manual of mental disorders-IV-TR.* Washington, DC.
———. (1987). *Diagnostic and statistical manual of mental disorders-III-R.* Washington, DC.
Borderline personalities. (1991). *Sally Jessy Raphael Show*, transcript 776, August 27.
Caplan, Paula J., and Ian Hall-McCorquodale. (1985). Mother-blaming in major clinical journals. *American Journal of Orthopsychiatry* 55, 345–53.
Castel, Robert, Francoise Castel, and Anne Lovell. (1982). *The psychiatric society.* New York: Columbia University Press.
Conrad, Peter, and Joseph W. Schneider. (1992). *Deviance and medicalization: From badness to sickness.* St. Louis: C.V. Mosby.
Kovel, Joel. (1988). A critique of *DSM-III. Research in law, deviance, and social control* 9, 127–46.
Masterson, James F. (1985). *Treatment of the borderline adolescent: A developmental approach.* New York: Brunner-Mazel.
National Institute of Mental Health, U.S. Department of Health and Human Services. (1990). *Research on children and adolescents with mental, behavioral, and developmental disorders*, DHHS Pub. (ADM) 90–1650, p. 19.

Chapter 13

Confusing Terms and False Dichotomies in Learning Disabilities

Paula J. Caplan

Editors' note: This paper is about learning disabilities, which, to the surprise of many people, are listed in the Diagnostic and Statistical Manual of Mental Disorders. *This chapter is slightly adapted from Caplan (1988).*[1]

In order to ensure that learning-disabled children's difficulties are properly identified and usefully remediated, it is essential for parents and professionals to understand what they say to each other. Yet no other field is as burdened with incomprehensible, minimally meaningful jargon and variously defined terms. Much of this is a consequence of the paucity of solid information about the causes and varieties of learning disability as well as the lack of successful remedial methods and materials. Thus, labels that sound as though they might be useful are often eagerly grasped by psychologists, pediatricians, psychiatrists, audiologists, special educators, speech pathologists, neuropsychologists, and other professionals who work with learning-disabled children, particularly when they are in training.

One type of problem in thinking about learning disability is the use of a single term, such as "auditory processing deficit," in various vague or contradictory ways. For instance, when I ask three different professionals what they mean when they say a child has an "auditory processing deficit" or is "hyperactive," I get three different answers. This happens whether the professionals come from different disciplines or from the same one. The second type of problem is the setting up of false dichotomies. For example, I have heard both parents and professionals describe a child as "having trouble with verbal tasks but not with concrete ones." But nonverbal tasks are not all concrete, and verbal is not the opposite of concrete. Each of these problems is discussed below in some detail.

VAGUELY DEFINED TERMS

It is dismaying when some professionals are unable, when pressed, to explain how they are using their terms. Some of the most commonly confusing terms are "auditory processing or auditory perceptual deficit," "visual perceptual disorder," and "hyperactivity." Let me focus on "auditory perceptual deficit" as an example. Some professionals say it means "something is wrong with the way that auditory material passes through the ear into the brain." Others say the problem is with what happens *in* the brain to material that begins as sound. And some professionals who use this term have even said vaguely, when I have asked for clarification, that it means "something wrong with the ears."

Recently an old friend told me that her twelve-year-old daughter had been labeled six years ago as having an "auditory perceptual problem," and it was attributed to her early, numerous ear infections, during which time she had presumably failed to learn what she needed to learn. However, most children who are given this label have *not* had multiple ear infections. This illustrates one of the reasons for conflicting definitions: Rarely is the research literature carefully considered at the time of diagnosis and discussion of etiology. The situation is even worse for terms like "crossed dominance" or "mixed dominance," since a great deal of time is wasted in deciding whether a learning disabled child has that kind of dominance, even though no thorough research has ever established that by changing one's dominance one can improve one's school performance. Even so, time is spent not only in determining a child's hand, foot, and eye preference, but also in subjecting her or him to "remedial" exercises aimed at changing this, the unfounded underlying assumption being that this will improve the child's reading or math performance.

In my own experience, children described as having "auditory perceptual deficits" usually appear to have none of the above problems. What *does* tend to be their difficulty? It is usually poor attention span, distractibility. How, then, do they get mislabeled? In virtually all intellectual and psycho-educational tests, orally presented items are presented extremely briefly. By contrast, visually presented items are less likely to disappear instantly. Distractible children, therefore, have a better chance of doing well on visual tests than on auditory ones. If they are distracted when visual items are presented, they find that the item is still there when their attention does return to the task. However, the reason that such children do better on visual than auditory tasks has to do with presentation time, not with the nature of the presented materials or with the presentation modality. Once such a label is in use, tests are identified which, as noted, are claimed to assess whether that label should be applied. This leads to the mistaken belief that the label accurately describes what has been tested. And this, in turn, tends to increase the frequency with which this label is used.

Similar patterns characterize the use of other terms. A very common one is "visual-perceptual problem," which is often used to mean "fine motor problem."[2] For instance, psychologists and other professionals often interpret a child's difficulty on tests that involve drawing as a sign of a "visual-perceptual problem," which they then explain has something to do with the eyes or the processing of information in the brain, or both. In fact, a child's trouble in copying those shapes frequently results from the difficulty in holding and manipulating the pencil.

As with "auditory perceptual deficit" and so many other terms, clear and accurate definitions are essential because sloppiness and inaccuracy in describing the problem will lead to, at the very least, a waste of the child's and the teacher's time in misdirected remediation. At worst, of course, it leads to further, profound frustration—in the children, who think "I'm even more stupid than I thought"; in the teachers, who feel like failures for being unable to teach the children; and in the parents, who misguidedly wonder why their children aren't trying harder and why what the "experts" recommended is not, in fact, helping.

FALSE DICHOTOMIES

When I supervise students who are writing reports of learning disability assessments, I find that I spend a considerable amount of time in pointing out to them their use of false dichotomies. This is especially true for students who have had previous experiences in working with learning-disabled children. Here are some of the common types of false dichotomies:

- *This child has trouble with visual but not with concrete tasks.*
- *This child can do auditory but not abstract tasks.*
- *This child has trouble with verbal but not with concrete tasks.*

In an attempt to bring some clarity to this area, it is important to understand that the poles of a genuine dichotomy must be on the same *dimension*, in the same realm. Many false dichotomies result from the mistaken contrasting of a part of one realm with a part of another realm. Consider the following simple schema for classifying test responses. Any test item can be described according to:

1. *the nature of the stimulus* (verbal vs. nonverbal *or* verbal vs. performance *or* verbal vs. mathematical vs. musical) *and*

2. *the level of abstraction of the stimulus* (concrete vs. abstract) *and*
3. *the time of exposure of the stimulus* (brief vs. long) *and*
4. *the channel of input of the question* (auditory vs. visual vs. tactile, etc.) *and*
5. *the channel of output of the answer* (spoken vs. written vs. pointing, etc.).

The features of every test item or set of items must be carefully classified according to all of these five categories—and perhaps more. Some learning-disabled children have trouble remembering letter shapes but not number shapes over the long term. It does such children no service if, instead of describing their strengths and weaknesses in a straightforward way, we (1) use jargon and (2) describe them sloppily as, for example, having trouble with abstract but not concrete tasks or with verbal but not nonverbal tasks (since "verbal" includes tasks besides learning letter shapes, and "nonverbal" goes way beyond number shapes or even mathematics).

I do not wish to give the impression that it is always easy to decide where on each of these five dimensions a particular item or subtest belongs. (And, indeed, many subtests begin, for example, with more concrete items and move toward more abstract ones.) With regard particularly to dimension number 2, the level of abstraction, after many years of practice with learning disabled children, many years of teaching assessment courses, and many consultations of both dictionaries and philosophers, I find that it is extremely difficult to find an adequate operational definition of "abstract." There seems to be some consensus that items requiring abstract thinking are often lacking in specific, recognizable, everyday details (thus, the WISC's Object Assembly items are less abstract than the WISC-R's Block Design ones), that they are difficult to solve by trial-and-error techniques, and that some type of cognitive leap (which requires careful definition) is required. It is not, then, easy to classify all test items according to each of these dimensions.

However, attempting such a classification serves two important practical purposes. First, it helps to clarify professionals' and parents' thinking about what the child needs, what the child's strengths and weaknesses are, how the difficulty is experienced from the child's point of view. Second, by helping us all to be very specific about the areas of strength and of weakness, it allows both adults and children to make optimal use of time spent in remediation attempts. When one wants to teach to strength, one then has a clear idea of what and how to teach, and the same goes for the times that one wants to teach to weakness.

At a more theoretical level, such specificity is important because ultimately it will help us, through research, to identify the real nature of the various learning disabilities. It will be useful in determining how many of what seem to be learning disabilities involve discrete, highly specific processes and how many involve global underlying difficulties.

ACKNOWLEDGING GAPS

In a study that is now being conducted, Patricia Tobin, Gael MacPherson, and I have been asking parents of learning-disabled children to fill out questionnaires in which they describe their experiences with various professionals. Although the data have not yet all been collected, it is clear that the results confirm what we have found in our clinical work—that many parents either frankly do not understand what the professionals have told them is wrong with their child or they think they understand but realize, as they think about the jargon, that in fact they still do not know what their child can and cannot do.

There is simply no excuse for this. As professionals, our first responsibility is to try to find out how we can help, what we can recommend. A second responsibility, which no one in my graduate training ever mentioned to me, is to let our clients know the limits of our understanding. Fortunately, this is not true of some, hopefully many, graduate programs. This serves the dual purposes of telling them the truth and of destroying destructive aspects of the professional/parent power imbalance. In my own practice I have found that parents are deeply grateful for professionals who can say "I don't know" in response to questions like "Will my child be able to go to college? or "*But why* can't my child pay attention or do math problems?" For those times when we do not have the answers, it is unethical and inhumane to use jargon to mask our ignorance and our helplessness. With regard to our interactions with other professionals and our influence on the development of work in the learning-disability field, it is essential that we use straightforward language and acknowledge our limitations because that is how the real gaps in knowledge are identified, and that is where research—aimed at helping children and their parents—truly begins.

NOTES

1. This article first appeared in *Orbit*, December 1988, pp. 14–15, as "Confusing terms and false dichotomies: A plea for logical thinking about learning disabilities" and is reprinted by kind permission from *Orbit* at the Ontario Institute for Studies in Education, University of Toronto.

2. Since the time that this paper was originally published in 1988, a little more clarity has been brought to the field. For instance, thanks to the efforts of occupational therapists, one less often finds that "visual perceptual problem" and "fine motor problem" are used interchangeably.

Chapter 14

Diagnosis of Low-Income Women

Heather E. Bullock

Although psychotherapists increasingly recognize the importance of gender and racial diversity, they may overlook poverty and social class as significant factors affecting diagnosis. Poverty, homelessness, and other social and economic burdens have profound impact on emotional functioning (American Psychological Association 2000; Task Force on Women, Poverty, and Public Assistance 1998), and the *DSM* authors paid lip-service to these effects when adding Axis IV, for psychosocial and environmental problems, to the list of diagnostic axes (see American Psychiatric Association 1980). In fact, however, Axis IV often either is not mentioned in patients' charts and reports or is ignored in any formulation and recommendation sections of reports. Many clinicians merely assign Axis I (e.g., mood disorders, substance-related disorders, anxiety disorders) and Axis II (e.g., personality disorders, mental retardation) labels without consideration of or reference to Axis IV factors, such as giving an Axis II diagnosis of Hysterical Personality Disorder to a woman who is distraught solely because she has lost her job and fears that she will not be able to provide food and shelter for her children.

Although responsible clinicians are aware of the *DSM* authors' caveat that an Axis II diagnosis is supposed to reflect a longstanding, even lifelong pattern of behavior, living in poverty for an extended period of time can result in fear and anxiety. In this way, results of struggling with poverty are misinterpreted as evidence of individual psychopathology rather than as consequences of a social problem. Diagnostic and therapeutic models are still based on assumptions that privilege the experiences of white, college-educated, middle-class professionals who have the time and resources to pursue therapy (Hill and Rothblum 1996). As a result of these biases, when poor women come to or are brought to therapists, their emotional problems are far too often considered to be individual, intrapsychic problems rather than social and economic problems. These biases render class privilege and economic inequality invisible. They also tend to steer therapy in unproductive, useless, even harmful directions.

The assumption that "everyone is middle class" stands in sharp contrast to the reality of many women's lives (Baker, 1996). Women are overrepresented among the 32.9 million people who are poor in the United States (U.S. Census Bureau 2002). Single-parent households, particularly those headed by women of color, are particularly vulnerable. In 2001, 22.4 percent of white female-headed households, 35.2 percent of Black female-headed households, and 37 percent of Hispanic female-headed households were poor (U.S. Census Bureau 2002). These figures, which are derived from formulas developed over three decades ago, are widely criticized for underestimating the prevalence of American poverty (see Lott and Bullock 2001). Since 1965, poverty thresholds have been calculated by multiplying the cost of a minimally adequate diet by three. If official calculations were updated to include the cost of housing, childcare, and health care, government estimates of U.S. poverty would increase dramatically. These figures, as well as the high rates of depression, anxiety, and domestic violence found among women receiving welfare underscore the need to develop class-sensitive diagnosis and treatment models (Danziger et. al. 2000; Danziger, Kalil, and Anderson 2000; Jayakody and Stauffer 2000; Tolman and Raphael 2000). A vast body of research about the health risks associated with poverty and economic inequality amply document the dangers poor women confront (Adler et al. 1994; American Psychological Association 2000; Kahn, Wise, Kennedy, and Kawachi 2000; Mazure, Keita, and Blehar 2002).

Because middle-class status is considered normative, class bias can affect therapists' attitudes toward low-income clients and the diagnoses that they assign. Deeply held cultural stereotypes characterize low-income women as neglectful mothers, lazy, sexually promiscuous, intellectually incompetent, and uninterested in self-improvement (Azar 1996; Bullock 1995; Lott 2002; Seccombe 1999; Seccombe, James, and Walters 1998; Sidel 1996). Endorsement of these stereotypes may lead therapists to overlook what low-income and working-class women really need (e.g., safe housing, financial security), to overpathologize them, and to problematize women's behavior rather than the structural factors that cause poverty (e.g., wage inequity, unequal access to education, discrimination). When therapists diagnose low-income clients, they may incorrectly attribute the clients' missed appointments and muted affect to irresponsibility and apathy, rather than transportation problems and cumulative trauma, respectively (Schnitzer 1996). As a result, poor women are at heightened risk of receiving more severe diagnoses, labeled resistant, or considered "untreatable."

Research indicates that being poor increases the likelihood of being diagnosed as psychotic and given drugs, while being middle class increases the likelihood of being diagnosed as neurotic and treated with psychotherapy (Judd 1986). Drug therapy is prescribed more frequently to low-income clients, particularly those who are less educated or members of ethnic minorities, and these clients are less likely to receive information about the medications they are given than are clients from higher up the socioeconomic ladder (Killian and Killian 1990). Hollingshead and Redlich's (1958) landmark study provided some of the strongest evidence of class-differential diagnosis and treatment. At the time of their study, lower-income clients not only received more severe diagnoses but were also more likely to receive shock therapy, drugs, lobotomies, or custodial care than wealthier clients (Hollingshead and Redlich 1958). Similar patterns were found across clinics, underscoring the pervasiveness of class bias.

Other forms of diagnostic bias have also been noted. Zellman (1992) asked 1,196 school principals, pediatricians, psychologists, social workers, childcare providers, family practitioners, and child psychiatrists to read family case histories that varied by social class. Child abuse was more often identified as a problem when the family was described as "lower class" than "middle class," suggesting that poor mothers are at greater risk than middle-class mothers of being labeled "abusive." Prognostic evaluations also vary as a function of clients' social class. Sutton and Kessler (1986) found that prognostic evaluations were significantly worse for a client who was described as an unemployed welfare recipient than for one described as a commercial artist or a bulldozer operator. Low expectations may result in diminished interest in and commitment to low-income clients. Related to this is the finding that intake interviewers have been found to perceive poor clients as less intelligent than higher-income clients and to assume that they are less interested in, and will benefit less from, psychotherapy than higher-income clients (Brill and Storrow 1964). These assumptions may lead therapists to neglect the full range of available, and potentially effective, treatment options.

Feminist psychologists have written extensively about the use of diagnostic labels to control "deviant" groups and the tendency to equate "normalcy" with dominant social groups (Blackman 1996; Landrine 1992). Landrine's (1992) analysis of the "politics of madness" documents how closely classist, racist, and sexist stereotypes correspond with diagnostic criteria. She argues that the stereotypic characteristics associated with the "culture of poverty" (e.g., inability to defer gratification, immorality, promiscuity, and an antiwork ethic), a term typically used to denigrate poor, urban African Americans, mimic the diagnostic criteria for schizophrenia so closely that being poor and racialized increases the risk of receiving a psychiatric label. Poor and racialized women, who are cultural "outsiders" by virtue of their gender, class, and ethnicity, are particularly vulnerable to diagnostic bias and mistreatment, as reflected, for instance, in the long history of the sexualizing and criminalizing of their behavior (see Ali, chapter 8 in this volume; Gans 1995).

Pathologizing poor and working-class women as the morally inferior "other" reinforces middle-class status as normative and deepens class divisions that stigmatize the poor (Blackman 1996). Paralleling broader societal beliefs, therapists risk blaming women for being poor and for the psychological stress caused by financial insecurity, rather than problematic social structures. When therapists overlook these structures, they participate in the covering up of the real problems of poverty, racism, sexism, and other forms of bias. Therefore, it is important to raise serious questions about the overdiagnosis and overpathologizing of poor women and working-class women who seek assistance for problems related to economic hardship. In such cases, psychiatric labels do more harm than good.

Many psychologists are from middle-class backgrounds and may be unaware of the difficulties associated with poverty (Lott 2002). Middle-class therapists cannot assume that they will connect with poor and working-class clients simply because they share the same gender or ethnicity (Ferguson and King 1997). Even therapists who are sensitive to class issues in principle may have difficulty fathoming the number and severity of the hardships poor and working-class clients face (e.g., unsafe neighborhoods, the threat of homelessness, difficulties caused by the lack of transportation to get from the workplace to a child's school when the child is ill). It is important, therefore, for practitioners to examine how their own class privilege and biases affect their perceptions and treatment of poor and working-class women (Leeder 1996).

Although therapy may be used by many members of the middle class as a means of achieving personal growth, poor and working-class women are more likely to seek help from therapists for dealing with an immediate crisis or a financial difficulty (Chalifoux 1996). Therapists should not make diagnoses without fully considering the impact of these economic circumstances on clients' behavior. Moreover, the economic constraints of poverty not only make affording therapy difficult, but also financial instability limits clients' ability to adhere to plans, "start over," or "take control." For example, leaving an abusive partner is never easy, but decisions like this are complicated when economic resources are scarce. Ultimately, keeping issues such as these in mind may help reduce classist bias in diagnosis and improve clinical outcomes for poor and working-class women.

REFERENCES

Adler, N. E., T. Boyce, M. A. Chesney, S. Cohen, S. Folkman, R. L. Kahn, et al. (1994). Socioeconomic status and health: The challenge of the gradient. *American Psychologist*, 49, 15–24.

American Psychiatric Association. (1980). *Diagnostic and statistical manual of mental disorders: DSM-III*. Washington, DC.

American Psychological Association. (2000, August 6). *Resolution on poverty and socioeconomic status*. www.apa.org/pi/urban/povres.html (accessed July 29, 2002).

Azar, S. T. (1996). Cognitive restructuring of professionals' schema regarding women parenting in poverty. *Women and Therapy* 18, 149–63.

Baker, N.L. (1996). Class as a construct in a "classless" society. *Women and Therapy* 18, 13–23.

Blackman, L. (1996). The dangerous classes: Retelling the psychiatric story. *Feminism and Psychology* 6, 361–79.

Brill, N. Q., and H. A. Storrow. (1964). Social class and psychiatric treatment. Pp. 241–47 in F. Riessman, J. Cohen, and A. Pearl, eds. *Mental health of the poor: New treatment approaches for low-income people*. New York: Free Press.

Bullock, H. E. (1995). Class acts: Middle-class responses to the poor. Pp. 118–59 in B. Lott and D. Maluso, eds. *The social psychology of interpersonal discrimination*. New York: Guilford Press.

Chalifoux, B. (1996). Speaking up: White, working-class women in therapy. *Women and Therapy* 18, 25–34.

Danziger, S., M. Corcoran, S. Danziger, C. Heflin, A. Kalil, J. Levine, et al. (2000). Barriers to the employment of welfare recipients. Pp. 245–78 in R. Cherry and W. M. Rodgers III, eds. *Prosperity for all? The economic boom and African Americans?* New York: Russell Sage.

Danziger, S. K., A. Kalil, and N. J. Anderson. (2000). Human capital, physical health, and mental health of welfare recipients: Co-occurrence and correlates. *Journal of Social Issues* 56, 635–54.

Ferguson, S. A., and T. C. King. (1997). There but for the grace of God: Two black women therapists explore privilege. *Women and Therapy* 20, 5–14.

Gans, H. J. (1995). *The war against the poor: The underclass and antipoverty policy*. New York: Basic Books.

Hill, M., and E. D. Rothblum, eds. (1996). *Classism and feminist therapy: Counting costs*. New York: Harrington Park Press.

Hollingshead, A. B., and F. C. Redlich. (1958). *Social class and mental illness: A community study*. New York: John Wiley & Sons.

Jayakody, R., and D. Stauffer. (2000). Mental health problems among single mothers: Implications for work and welfare reform. *Journal of Social Issues* 56, 617–34.

Judd, P. (1986). The mentally ill poor in America: The anatomy of abuse. *Journal of Applied Social Science* 10, 40–50.

Kahn, R. S., P. H. Wise, B. P. Kennedy, and I. Kawachi. (2000). State income inequality, household income, and maternal mental and physical health: Cross-sectional national survey. *British Medical Journal* 321, 1311–15.

Heather E. Bullock

Killian, T. M., and L. T. Killian. (1990). Sociological investigations of mental illness: A review. *Hospital and Community Psychiatry* 41, 902–11.

Landrine, H. (1992). *The politics of madness*. New York: Peter Lang Publishing.

Leeder, E. (1996). Speaking rich people's words: Implications of a feminist class analysis and psychotherapy. *Women and Therapy* 18, 45–57.

Lott, B. (2002). Cognitive and behavioral distancing from the poor. *American Psychologist* 57, 100–10.

Lott, B., and H. E. Bullock. (2001). Who are the poor? *Journal of Social Issues* 57, 189–206.

Mazure, C. M., G. P. Keita, and M. C. Blehar. (2002). *Summit on women and depression: Proceedings and recommendations.* American Psychological Association. www.apa.org/pi/wpo/women&depression.pdf (accessed July 29, 2002).

Schnitzer, P. K. (1996). "They don't come in!" Stories told, lessons taught about poor families in therapy. *American Journal of Orthopsychiatry* 66, 572–82.

Seccombe, K. (1999). So you think I drive a Cadillac? Welfare recipients' perspectives on the system and its reform. Needham Heights, MA: Allyn & Bacon.

Seccombe, K., D. James, and K. B. Walters. (1998). "They think you ain't much of nothing:" The social construction of the welfare mother. *Journal of Marriage and Family* 60, 849–65.

Sidel, R. (1996). The enemy within: A commentary on the demonization of difference. *American Journal of Orthopsychiatry* 66, 490–95.

Sutton, R. G., & Kessler, M. (1986). National study of the effects of clients' socioeconomic status on clinical psychologists' professional judgments. *Journal of Consulting & Clinical Psychology* 54, 275–76.

Task Force on Women, Poverty, and Public Assistance. (1998). *Making "Welfare to Work" Really Work*. Washington, DC: American Psychological Association.

Tolman, R. M., and J. Raphael. (2000). A review of research on domestic violence. *Journal of Social Issues* 56, 655–82.

U.S. Census Bureau. (2002). *Poverty in the United States: 2001* (P60–219). Washington, DC: U.S. Government Printing Office.

Zellman, G.L. (1992). The impact of case characteristics on child abuse reporting decisions. *Child Abuse & Neglect*, 16, 57–74.

Chapter 15

Seeking "Normal" Sexuality
on a Complex Matrix

William R. Metcalfe and Paula J. Caplan

In the realm of sexuality and sexual activity, some of the most personal aspects of one's being, groups in powerful positions have declared which feelings, wishes, preferences, and activities are good and which are bad. Often, decisions are made about what is "ideal," and then that is equated with "normal." In most other realms, what is ideal is considered to describe only a few people; think of saints or Olympic athletes. Classification of sexuality by the powers-that-be in the Western mental health system reflects a radical over-simplification. "Sexual orientation," for instance, has been divided into a very small number of categories, as have other aspects of sexuality, and erroneous conclusions have often been drawn about some aspects of a person's sexuality based on what was known about one or more other aspects. First, we shall look at a few examples of kinds of sexuality that have been classified as mental illnesses by the world's most powerful arbiters of psychiatric diagnosis, the authors of the *Diagnostic and Statistical Manual of Mental Disorders* (*DSM*) to see what they reveal about the pathologizing of sexuality. Then we shall propose a radically different framework for thinking about sexuality.

Hypoactive Sexual Desire Disorder (HSDD) is described in the *DSM-IV-TR* as characterized by a low level or absence of sexual fantasies and desire for sexual activity (American Psychiatric Association 2000). How is the therapist to decide? Should a therapist diagnose HSDD in any patient whose desire for sexual activity is less frequent than that of the therapist? Although the description of the "disorder" includes the comment that a person's life circumstances are to be taken into account, the scope for subjectivity is obvious. An extreme example of this is a psychiatrist (encountered by Paula J. Caplan) who labeled as mental illness a woman's wish to avoid having sex with her husband because he had raped her; he said that she should have understood that this was just her husband's way of showing that he loved her.

Despite the great scope for subjectivity in applying this label, the aura of scientific precision of the *DSM* is furthered by the requirement that in diagnosing this "disorder," one should specify whether it is lifelong or acquired, generalized or situational, and due to psychological or "combined" factors. Some people may have a low level of sexual desire and find that this disturbs their lives, but the *DSM* criteria leave a great deal to the judgment of the therapist. Decisions about what warrants diagnosis "are influenced by (and in turn have implications for) medicine, religion, law, science, society, and culture" (Moser 2001, 94).

Gender Identity Disorder (GID), according to the *DSM*, is a strong and persistent "cross-gender identification" manifested by a strong preference for playmates of "the other sex," the wish to engage in games and pastimes that are typical of "the other sex," the wish to engage in make-believe in which one is a member of or wears clothes usually seen on members of "the other sex," or the repeated desire to be a member of "the other sex." In adolescents and adults, the patient has a desire to live or be treated as "the other sex" or the conviction of having feelings and reactions typical of "the other sex." We place "the other sex" in quotation marks to indicate the *DSM* authors' failure to note the many "intersexuals" who are not chromosomally or hormonally members of one of the two most commonly recognized sexes (Fausto-Sterling 2000). This is a particularly curious failure, in light of the fact that the *DSM* authors note that GID should not diagnosed in someone "with a physical intersex condition." In addition to crosscultural differences in clothing, play, toys, and extent to which one plays with members of a particular sex, the increasing trend for people to describe themselves as "transgender," meaning that they do not wish to be classified indisputably and immutably as members of one sex or the other, would qualify many for GID. In many Western and other cultures, the extreme rigidity of prescribed gender roles results in a squelching of many interests and inclinations that is not generally considered to cause mental disorder, but the failure to keep within the rigid boundaries is considered pathological. Inappropriate pathologizing is further reflected by the inclusion in GID of boys' aversion to rough-and-tumble play or their assertion that their penis is disgusting (a common attitude in a culture that treats much about sexuality as shameful) and girls' wish not to grow breasts (many prepubertal girls are self-conscious about their growing breasts) and "aversion toward *normative feminine* clothing" (emphasis added (APA 2000).

Frotteurism: In the *DSM-IV-TR*, "frotteurism" is defined as "touching and rubbing against a nonconsenting person," followed by the highly specific description that a "frotteur" "rubs his [*sic*] genitals against the victims thighs or buttocks" and "usually fantasizes an exclusive, caring relationship with them," and that this occurs "mostly when the person is 15–25 years, after which there is a gradual decline in frequency" (APA 2000, 570). One could create a diagnosis for every act, but it is particularly disturbing that this one involves victims, because this alleged mental illness is used by attorneys to argue that people who engage in these kinds of acts have diminished responsibility for having victimized others (see Caplan 1995). A dentist who "pleaded guilty to having fondled between one hundred and two hundred young girls and women patients . . . that . . . he thought 'were susceptible to being touched,'" sued his insurance company, claiming that his "sexual disorder" made it impossible for him to work as a dentist, so the insurance company should pay him $5,000 a month in disability payments (Caplan 1995, based on Martinez 1994). Psychiatrist Harold Lief supported the dentist's claim and told the court that the dentist suffered from "frotteurism" (Caplan 1995).

Sexual Disorder Not Otherwise Specified is described in the *DSM-IV-TR* as a sexual disturbance not already listed in the *DSM* (APA 2000, 582). Any therapist can decide what to call a sexual disorder.

Homosexuality is no longer listed by name in the *DSM*, but some therapists would consider it a Sexual Disorder Not Otherwise Specified. Homosexuality was listed as a mental disorder in the *DSM* until 1974, when the American Psychiatric Association made headlines by announcing that it had decided homosexuality was no longer a mental illness. The APA's 1974 vote showing 5,854 members supporting and 3,810 opposing the disorder's removal from the manual demonstrates that this "mental disorder" is a construct, that whether or not it is considered a disorder depends on who is classifying or voting on it. The claim that it would be deleted was false: The next *DSM* included homosexuality with which the patient was not fully comfortable (APA 1980). Mental illnesses in general are regarded as intrapsychic problems, so it is troubling that, in a homophobic society, the effects of oppression and marginalizing would be labeled a mental illness. Voting on what is a mental illness is bizarre, as is the fact that that one day the APA called homosexuality a mental illness, and the next day, it did not. The index for *DSM-III-R* (1987) included the listing "ego dystonic homosexuality" with the instruction "see Sexual Disorders Not Otherwise Specified," a clear statement that homosexuality was still officially a mental illness, and, as noted, the *DSM-IV* (2000) includes "Sexual Dysfunction Not Otherwise Specified" and, similarly, "Paraphilias Not Otherwise Specified," allowing ample room for therapists who wish to "diagnose" someone as homosexual.

People who seek help for problems in relationships with partners or others or for problems at work, rather than for help in trying to change their sexual orientation, may nevertheless be pathologized for being homosexual. In important ways, in some cases labeling patients as mentally disordered because of their sexual orientation constitutes unprofessional and possibly unethical conduct by the therapist because of the misleading of the patient about what the therapist may be aiming to do in treatment. This is not to say that no lesbian, gay, or bisexual—or heterosexual—patient has problems in their lives on account of their sexual orientation, but rather that a therapist's attitude and approach to dealing with those problems would likely be shaped by their classification of the discomfort with homosexuality as a mental illness or as an understandable, nonpathological response to rejection and contempt.

The view that homosexuality needs to be changed supports the institution and power of heterosexuality as the norm. It seems possible that underlying the pathologizing of homosexuality is the assumption that heterosexuality is a fragile condition, such that if any of many things goes wrong, the person becomes homosexual.

A MODEST PROPOSAL: SEXUALITY AS A MATRIX

Talk about sexuality tends to include only a few labels, as well as using what used to be adjectives (e.g., "lesbian woman") as nouns (e.g., "lesbian"), as though this were their whole identity as a person. We use even fewer labels— actually, just one: "heterosexual"—as the "normal one." When asked to define the term "homosexual," most people say something like "a person who has sex with members of the same sex." This implies that all homosexuals always and only have sex with people of the same sex as themselves. But many people fall in between the extremes of "exclusive homosexuality" and "exclusive heterosexuality." Females and males are said to be members of "opposite" sexes, and one who is "feminine" in behavior is assumed not to be "masculine" (in any way). Thus, people have been pathologized not only because of the biological sex of their sexual partners but also because their behavior, attitudes, ways of moving, tones of voice, and so on have been considered the *opposite* of what is proper for members of their sex. In fact, however, they may be complementary, different hues of the same color, different levels on a scale, different points on a continuum. Or, instead of dividing the population into those attracted to members of the "same" sex and those attracted to people not of the "same" sex, one could distinguish between *people* who are attracted to women (gynosexuals) and those who are attracted to men (androsexuals). And, as noted, the belief that all human beings belong to one of only two biological sexes is wrong (Fausto-Sterling 2000); about 1.7 of 100 people fall into various classes of non-dimorphic sexual categories and are called intersex. But no matter how many biological sexes there are, the biological sex(es) of the people with whom one has sex is only one aspect of what could more accurately be called not sexual orientation but rather a sexual profile, unique to an individual and composed of their locations on many dimensions. A sexual profile is a meaningful way to begin to describe a person's sexuality and can incorporate, in principle, all potentials and possibilities that bear on sexuality. A person's sexual profile is their combination of feelings, impulses, motivations, tastes, preferences, inclinations, practices, and experiences that relate to their sexual aspects. A few possible dimensions of a sexual profile include:

- Gender and Sex, including *manifestations* such as appearance, dress, mannerisms, movements; genital and chromosomal makeup; and feelings, attitudes, beliefs, thoughts, and spirituality
- Libido, including *range* of response (asexual to monosexual to ambisexual to polysexual); *level* of response (intensity and frequency, from celibate to "supersexual"); *potential* of response (including primal or conditioned, conscious or unconscious); and *fluidity or consistency* of response
- Preferences, including *with whom* (alone or not, and if not, the biological sex of the person, their gender, style, and preferences, as well as their age, physical attributes such as eyes, legs, hair, smell, shape); *what* (specific sexual activities, parts of body one likes to touch on another person or have touched on themselves, what one likes to have done with or do to parts of the other person's body or one's own); *where and when* (time of day, time of year) one has sex; *how* one has sex (e.g., tenderly, energetically, acrobatically, whimsically)
- Style, including *activity level* (from celibate to promiscuous); *types of relationships* (bonded, open or closed, monogamous or polygamous, other combinations); *elements of relationship formation* (the individual and their partner or partners are complementary or supplementary to each other or provide opposing aspects of sexuality and personality, and/or they provide mutuality); and *duration of relationships*

A person's sexual profile is determined by four main *conditions*:

- Psychological
- Physical
- Familial
- Larger environmental

There are at least three sources of *motivation* behind sexual drives, impulses, or whatever one chooses to call them. These are:

- Affection
- Lust
- Procreation

Thinking of people's sexuality using the sexual profile framework illustrates how difficult it would be to figure out what is "the norm" and what one *might*, therefore, consider "deviant." Furthermore, sexual profiles are not static. Sexuality is fluid; it grows, changes, recedes, broadens, extends, withdraws, and changes course and direction with changes in the person's circumstances, information, and attitudes, as well as events and possibilities in their life. Within this framework, how in the world would mental health professionals decide which squares in the matrix should be designated as forms of psychopathology?

REFERENCES

American Psychiatric Association. (2000). *Diagnostic and statistical manual of mental disorders-IV-TR* . Washington, DC.
——— . (1994). *Diagnostic and statistical manual of mental disorders-IV*. Washington, DC.
——— . (1987). *Diagnostic and statistical manual of mental disorders-III-R*. Washington, DC.
——— . (1980). *Diagnostic and statistical manual of mental disorders-III*. Washington, DC.
Caplan, Paula J. (1995). *They say you're crazy: How the world's most powerful psychiatrists decide who's normal.* Reading, MA: Addison-Wesley.
Fausto-Sterling, Anne. (2000). *Sexing the body*. New York: Basic Books.
Martinez, Julia. (1994). Doctor sues for disability money. *Philadelphia Inquirer*, July 14, p. B01.
Moser, C. (2001). Paraphilia: A critique of a confused concept. Pp. 91–108 in P. J. Kleinplatz, ed. *New Directions in Sex therapy: Innovations and alternatives.* Philadelphia, PA: Brunner-Routledge.

Chapter 16

Gender Bias and Sex Distribution of Mental Disorders in *DSM-IV-TR*

Lisa Cosgrove and Bethany Riddle

Community surveys, hospital admissions, and statistics on outpatient treatment, both medical and psychological, all concur: adult women report
more mental health problems than men, and are more likely to be diagnosed and treated for madness.

J. M. Ussher, "Women's madness:
A material-discursive-intrapsychic approach," 207

There has been a dramatic increase in the number of diagnoses from the first
edition of the *Diagnostic and Statistical Manual of Mental Disorders* (*DSM*)
to the most recent one (American Psychiatric Association 1952, 2000). Advocates of the empiricist-positivist tradition upon which mainstream psychology is based regard such expansion as progress. According to this model,
which is used to promote the idea that there are disorders that are just wait-
ing to be "discovered," the tools of modern science have allowed researchers
to sharpen the definitions of certain categories of mental illness. Researchers
who function within the framework of the dominant model believe that with
each new edition of the *DSM* we approach a greater degree of "accuracy" and
"truth" with regard to the disorders that are being described. Thus, disorders
that are either exclusively developed for women, such as Premenstrual Dysphoric Disorder (PMDD), or applicable to anyone in principle but in practice
given far more often to women, such as Borderline Personality Disorder
(BPD), are regarded as signs of medical progress. The authors of the *DSM* do
not problematize or even question the growing numbers of women who are
being given psychiatric diagnoses such as PMDD or BPD, for they believe
that women are finally getting the diagnoses and help they need for their mental illness. In the cases of some labels, when used wisely by clinicians, this is
no doubt true, but in many cases it is not.

"GETTING HELP"—OR BEING PATHOLOGIZED?

In what ways do our efforts to liberate actually perpetuate relations of dominance?

> Patti Lather, *Getting Smart: Feminist Research*
> *and Pedagogy within the Postmodern, 16*

Researchers who work from a more critical perspective recognize that the reification of mental disorders has less to do with bringing us any closer to the "truth" than it has to do with the connections among power, knowledge, and the normalizing and regulatory mechanisms of biopsychiatric discourse. Although mainstream psychological researchers claim to be objective, supposedly value-free research is in fact influenced by assumptions about what constitutes normative behavior and by gendered (and many other) stereotypes. As many chapters in this volume demonstrate, the *DSM*'s diagnostic categories do not represent value-free truths—they are socioculturally and sociohistorically specific ways of defining behavior, and their construction involves masculine privilege. Hence, women as a group are at great risk of being pathologized, especially poor, racialized, and non-heterosexual women. From a critical psychology perspective, the ever-growing number of *DSM* categories sustains a view of mental disorder as "[d]iscrete, consistent, homogeneous, clinical entities which further have an identifiable etiology and *cause* the symptoms women report. *This acts to deny the social and discursive context of women's lives, as well as the gendered nature of science, which defines how women's bodies are studied*" (Ussher 2000, 210, emphasis added; see also, Keller 1985).

Moreover, there are both subtle and overt ways in which a male norm is assumed by many of those who conduct experimental and clinical studies. Tavris (1992), for example, noted that numerous studies have been conducted to determine why women are "less self-confident" than men in describing their performance on a task. She wondered what the research would have looked like if the original question was why men are *over*confident in describing their performance. Women's "poor self-esteem" is often invoked as an explanatory variable for understanding their "dsyfunctional attributions" on performance tasks. As Javed and Gerrard (chapter 20 in this volume) discuss, the use of the diagnostic term "poor self-esteem" decontextualizes women's experience from the sociopolitical context of their lives, thus trivializing the poverty, abuse, violence, harassment, and discrimination to which large numbers of women are subjected. Indeed, "poor self-esteem" is one of the main diagnostic criteria for many of the gender-biased Personality Disorders (e.g., Borderline Personality Disorder, Dependent Personality Disorder, etc.)

In terms of clinical research, the proposed category of Self-Defeating Personality Disorder (SDPD) was widely criticized for issues of both validity and reliability. Scientific studies could not support the efficacy of this diagnostic category—in fact, SDPD seemed to be a description not so much of a pattern of intrapsychic pathology as a cluster of traits that is typically associated with cultural expectations of "being a good woman." It was also a description of patterns of behavior typical of individuals who have experienced violence at the hands of their partners, and thus it has been noted that such a category of mental illness is tantamount to pathologizing or even blaming the victim (Brown 1994; Caplan 1992). This is why particular attention has been paid to gender bias with regard to the personality disorders, for "[p]ersonality disorders . . . seem to represent social conventions more than medical diseases" (Walsh 1997, 337). The personality "traits" which comprise a number of the personality disorders are those which are often "associated with (stereotypically) feminine gender" (Lindsay, Sankis, and Widiger 2000). Caplan summed this up, writing that "[a]fter a woman has conscientiously learned the role her culture prescribes for her, the psychiatric establishment calls her mentally disordered" (1992, 74).

BECOMING AN INFORMED CLINICIAN: EXAMINING THE *DSM* SEX DISTRIBUTION WITH A CRITICAL EYE

> What they think about how the world works shapes the knowledge that scholars produce about the world.
>
> *Fausto-Sterling, Sexing the Body:*
> *Gender Politics and the Construction of Sexuality, 20*

It is not only the more egregious sex and gender bias noted in the Personality Disorders category that is of concern but also the larger issue of articulating a more explicit critique of the sexism *inherent* within the *Diagnostic and Statistical Manual of Mental Disorders* (APA 2000) itself.[1] Following Orr, we regard the medical model as a "discursive straitjacket which forces psychic disease to speak itself in the grammar of individualized, biologized disorder" (2000, 68). This way of speaking is enormously costly and oppressive, for it silences groups, individuals, communities; indeed, it silences conversations about the connection between social injustice based on sex and gender and emotional distress (see, for example, Cosgrove 2000; Fine 1992; Hare-Mustin and Marecek 1997; Layton 1998; Wilkinson and Kitzinger 1995). The authors of the latest edition of the *DSM* (APA 2000), include the following statistics but present them as if they existed in a sociopolitical vacuum:[2] women are two to three times more likely than men to be diagnosed with Dysthymia (a chronic depressive disorder); Major Depressive Disorder is two times more common in women than in men; Panic Disorder is diagnosed three times more often in women than in men; more than 90 percent of individuals diagnosed with Anorexia Nervosa and Bulimia are women.[3] A wealth of interesting and important information is embedded in the sex distribution table included below. Along those lines, Tavris makes a helpful suggestion:

> [I]f a mental disorder reliably and stereotypically fits a narrow category of people, then we should be looking at what is wrong with the conditions of people in that category, not exclusively at their individual pathologies. For example instead of asking, "What's wrong with women that makes them excessively dependent in marriage?" we could be asking, "What's wrong with marriage that makes so many women excessively dependent?" (or "why are we always labeling the caring work that women do as evidence of dependency?"). (Tavris 1992, 186)

NOTES

1. It is important to note that researchers have examined sexist biases at the clinical level (Bertakis, Helms, Callahan, Azari, Lehigh, and Robbins 2001) and they have provided useful information about the practical ramifications of such biases. Although we recognize and applaud their efforts, we are addressing the issue of bias in psychiatric diagnosis from a larger epistemological perspective—one that challenges the very ground upon which the *DSM* is built.

2. The *DSM* uses a multiaxial system, that is, the authors promote the view that they are providing a 'biopsychosocial approach" to diagnosis. Although it is true that there are separate axes for "psychosocial stressors" and "medical conditions," and a rating scale for an individual's "Global assessment of functioning," the *DSM* is not an instrument designed in any way to acknowledge the sociopolitical context of people's lives. For example, while a clinician can record the "stressor" of "loss of job," there is no place to acknowledge discrimination due to homophobic attitudes, economic injustice, institutionalized racism, and so forth. As Levenson wryly noted, Antisocial Personality Disorder makes no reference to "such practices as despoiling the environment and destroying other species for personal profit," "manipulating others to their detriment in the conduct of management," or "using deceptive practices to obtain public office" (cited in Parker, Georgaca, Harper, McLaughlin, and Stowell-Smith 1995, 79).

3. It should be noted that what the *DSM* authors present as the prevalence rates in general and the gender ratios in particular are matters of controversy, with some clinicians and researchers saying that various rates and ratios are higher and others saying they are lower than those given in the manual.

REFERENCES

American Psychiatric Association. (2000). *Diagnostic and statistical manual of mental Disorders-IV-TR*. 4th edition. Washington, DC.

————. (1952). *Diagnostic and statistical manual of mental disorders.* 1st edition. Washington, DC.

Bertakis, K. D., L. J. Helms, E. J. Callahan, R. Azari, P. Lehigh, and J. A. Robbins. (2001). Gender differences in the diagnosis of depression in primary care. *Journal of Women's Health and Gender Based Medicine* 10 (7), 689–98.

Brown, L. S. (1994). *Subversive dialogues: Theory in feminist therapy.* New York: Basic Books.

Caplan, P. J. (1992). Gender issues in the diagnosis of mental disorder. *Women and Therapy* 12 (4), 71–82.

Cosgrove, L. (2000). Crying out loud: Understanding women's emotional distress as both lived experience and social construction. *Feminism and Psychology* 10, 247–67.

Fausto-Sterling, A. (2000). *Sexing the body: Gender politics and the construction of sexuality.* New York: Basic Books.

Fine, M. (1992). *Disruptive voices: The possibilities of feminist research.* Ann Arbor: University of Michigan Press.

Hare-Mustin, R. T., and J. Marecek. (1997). Abnormal psychology and the politics of madness. Pp. 104–20 in D. Fox and I. Prilleltelsky, eds. *Critical psychology: An introduction.* Thousand Oaks, CA: Sage.

Keller, E. F. (1985). *Reflections on gender and science.* New Haven, CT: Yale University Press.

Kupers, T. (1997). The politics of psychiatry: Gender and sexual preference in *DSM-IV.* Pp. 340–47 in M. R. Walsh, ed. *Women, men, and gender.* New Haven, CT: Yale University Press,

Lather, P. (1991). *Getting smart: Feminist research and pedagogy within the postmodern.* New York: Routledge.

Layton, L. (1998). *Who's that girl? Who's that boy? Clinical practice meets postmodern gender theory.* Northvale, NJ: Jason Aronson.

Levenson, M.R. (1992). Rethinking psychopathy. *Theory and Psychology* 2, 51–71.

Lindsay, K. A., L. M. Sankis, and T. A. Widiger. (2000). Gender bias in self-report personality disorder inventories. *Journal of Personality Disorders* 14 (3), 218–32.

Orr, J. (2000). Performing methods: History, hysteria, and the new science of psychiatry. Pp. 49–73 in D. Fee, ed. *Pathology and the postmodern: Mental illness as discourse and experience.* Thousand Oaks, CA: Sage.

Parker, I., E. Georgaca, D. Harper, T. McLaughlin, and M. Stowell-Smith. (1995). *Deconstructing psychopathology.* Thousand Oaks, CA: Sage.

Tavris, C. (1992). *The mismeasure of woman.* New York: Simon & Schuster.

Ussher, J. M. (2000). Women's madness: A material-discursive-intrapsychic approach. Pp. 207–30 in D. Fee, ed. *Pathology and the postmodern: Mental illness as discourse and experience.* Thousand Oaks, CA: Sage.

Walsh, M. R., ed. (1997). *Women, men, and gender.* New Haven, CT: Yale University Press.

Wilkinson, S., and C. Kitzinger, eds. (1995). *Feminism and discourse: Psychological perspectives.* Thousand Oaks, CA: Sage.

APPENDIX 16.1: DSM-IV-TR REPORTS OF
SEX DISTRIBUTION FOR MENTAL DISORDERS

The following prevalence rates are based exclusively on the reports in the *DSM-IV-TR*.

Disorders Usually First Diagnosed in Infancy, Childhood, or Adolescence	Sex Distribution (where information given in *DSM*)[1]
Mental Retardation	Male:female ratio: 1.5:1
Learning Disorder (General)	
Reading Disorder	60–80% male
Mathematics Disorder	
Disorder of Written Expression	
Developmental Coordination Disorder	
Expressive Language Disorder	More males
Mixed Receptive Expressive Language Disorder	More males
Phonological Disorder	More males
Stuttering	Male:female ratio 3:1
Autistic Disorder	4–5x more males
Rett's Disorder	Only reported in females
Childhood Disintegrative Disorder	More males
Asperger's Disorder	At least five times as many males
Attention Deficit Hyperactivity Disorder	Male:female range 2:1 to 9:1, less pronounced sex difference in predominantly inattentive type, with more boys in clinic-referred groups
Conduct Disorder	More males
Oppositional Defiant Disorder	More males before puberty, apparently no difference after puberty
Pica	
Rumination Disorder	More males
Feeding Disorder of Infancy or Early Childhood	Equal
Tourette's Disorder	May be as high as 3 to 5 times more males, but in community samples, male: female ratio as low as 2:1

Disorders Usually First Diagnosed in Infancy, Childhood, or Adolescence	Sex Distribution (where information given in *DSM*)
Encopresis	More males
Enuresis	
Separation Anxiety Disorder	In epidemiological samples, more females; in clinical samples, no difference
Selective Mutism	Slightly more females
Reactive Attachment Disorder of Infancy or Early Childhood	
Stereotypic Movement Disorder	Head-banging: more males (3:1); self-biting may be more females

Delirium, Dementia, and Amnestic and Other Cognitive Disorders	Sex Distribution
Delirium	Male sex independent risk factor for delirium in elderly
Dementia of the Alzheimer's Type	Slightly more females
Vascular Dementia	More males
Amnestic Disorders	

Mental Disorders Due to a General Medical Condition	Sex Distribution
Catatonic Disorder	
Personality Change Due to a General Medical Condition	

Substance-Related Disorders	Sex Distribution
Alcohol-Related Disorders	More males, with male:female ratio as high as 5:1
Amphetamine-Induced Disorders	Intravenous use, male:female ratio 3 or 4:1; more evenly divided in nonintravenous use
Caffeine-Induced Disorders	More males
Cannabis-Related Disorders	More males
Cocaine-Related Disorders	More males, with male: female ratio of 1.5–2:1

(continued)

Substance-Related Disorders	**Sex Distribution**
Hallucinogen-Related Disorders	3x more common in males
Inhalant-Related Disorders	Males account for 70–80% of inhalant-related ER visits
Nicotine-Related Disorders	Slightly more males; smokeless tobacco, male:female ratio 8:1
Opioid-Related Disorders	Typical male:female ratio 1.5:1 for opioids other than heroin; 3:1 for heroin
Phencyclidine-Related Disorder	Three-quarters of ER visits are by males
Sedatives-, Hypnotic-, Anxiolytic-Induced Disorders	Maybe more women

Schizophrenia and Other Psychotic Disorders	**Sex Distribution**
Schizophrenia	Slightly more males
Schizophreniform Disorder	
Schizoaffective Disorder	More women, due mostly to increased incidence of Depressive Type among women
Delusional Disorder	Delusional disorder, jealous-type, more men than women, apparently no difference in overall frequency of Delusional Disorder
Brief Psychotic Disorder	
Shared Psychotic Disorder	More women
Psychotic Disorder Due to a General Medical Condition	
Substance-Induced Psychotic Disorder	

Mood Disorders	**Sex Distribution**
Major Depressive Disorder	Lifetime risk in community samples varies from 10–25% of women and 5–12% of men; twice as common in adolescent and adult females as males. In prepubertal children, boys and girls equally diagnosed

Mood Disorders	**Sex Distribution**
Dysthymic Disorder	More than two to three times as many women
Depressive Disorder NOS This category includes disorders with depressive features that do not meet the criteria for Major Depressive Disorder, Dysthymic Disorder, Adjustment Disorder with Depressed Mood or Adjustment Disorder with Mixed Anxiety and Depressed Mood. The first example given is premenstrual Dysphoric Disorder (p. 381)	PMDD can only be diagnosed in females
Bipolar I Disorder	Equally common in men and women, but first episode in females more likely to be depressive, first episode in males more likely to be manic. Men have as many manic as depressive cpisodes or more manic ones; women have more depressive ones. Mixed or depressive symptoms during manic episodes may be more common in women. Rapid cycling more common in women
Bipolar II Disorder	More common in women. In men, number of hypomanic episodes equals or exceeds number of major depressive episodes; in women, major depressive episodes predominate
Cyclothymic Disorder	Equal
Mood Disorder Due to a General Medical Condition	
Substance Induced Mood Disorder	

(*continued*)

Anxiety Disorders	Sex Distribution
Panic Disorder	Panic Disorder without Agoraphobia twice as common and Panic Disorder with Agoraphobia three times as common in women
Agoraphobia without History of Panic Disorder	Far more women
Specific Phobia	Female:male ratio 2:1 but varies by type: approximately 75–90% with Animal and Natural Environment type phobias are female (except fear of heights, where percentage of females is 55–70%). Approximately 75–90% with Situational type are female. Approximately 55–70% with Blood-Injection-Injury type are female
Social Phobia (Social Anxiety Disorder)	
Obsessive-Compulsive Disorder	No difference for adults, more common in boys
Post-traumatic Stress Disorder	
Acute Stress Disorder	
Generalized Anxiety Disorder (includes Overanxious Disorder in Childhood)	In clinical settings, about 55–60% are women; in epidemiological studies, approximately two-thirds female
Anxiety Disorder due to a General Medical Condition	
Substance-Induced Anxiety Disorder	

Somatoform Disorders	Sex Distribution
Somatization Disorder	Lifetime prevalence rates range from .2% to 2% among women, less than .2% among men
Undifferentiated Somatoform Disorder	
Conversion Disorder	Female:male ratios ranging from 2:1 to 10:1

Somatoform Disorders	Sex Distribution
Pain Disorder	Women more migraine and tension-type headaches and musculoskeletal pain
Hypochondriasis	
Body Dysmorphic Disorder	Equal

Factitious Disorders	Sex Distribution
Factitious Disorder	More women, but most chronic and severe type (Munchausen's) more common in males
Factitious Disorder NOS	

Dissociative Disorders	Sex Distribution
Dissociative Amnesia	
Dissociative Identity Disorder (DID)	3 to 9 times more females; in childhood, the female:male ratio more even
Depersonalization Disorder	In clinical samples, at least twice as common in women

Sexual and Gender Identity Disorders	Sex Distribution
Hypoactive Sexual Desire Disorder	
Sexual Aversion Disorder	
Female Sexual Arousal Disorder	Females only
Male Erectile Disorder	Males only
Female Orgasmic Disorder	Females only
Male Orgasmic Disorder	Males only
Premature Ejaculation	Males only
Dyspareunia (Not Due to a General Medical Condition)	
Vaginismus (Not Due to a General Medical Condition)	Females only
Sexual Dysfunction Due to a General Medical Condition	
Substance-Induced Sexual Dysfunction	
Exhibitionism	

(continued)

Sexual and Gender Identity Disorders	Sex Distribution
Fetishism	
Frotteurism	
Pedophilia	
Sexual Masochism	
Sexual Sadism	
Transvestic Fetishism	
Voyeurism	
Gender Identity Disorder	Male:female ratio 2–3:1

Eating Disorders	Sex Distribution
Anorexia Nervosa	More than 90% of cases are females
Bulimia Nervosa	Female:male ratio at least 9:1

Sleep Disorders	Sex Distribution
Primary Insomnia	More women
Primary Hypersomnia	Kleine-Levin syndrome three times as many males
Narcolepsy	No difference
Breathing-Related Sleeping Disorder	In adults, male:female ratios of obstructive sleep apnea syndrome range from 2:1 to 4:1. No sex difference prepubertally. In adults, central apneic events more prevalent in males but less difference after menopause
Circadian Rhythm Sleep Disorder	
Nightmare Disorder	Female:male ratio 2–4:1
Sleep Terror Disorder	Among children, more common in males. Among adults, no difference.
Sleepwalking Disorder	More females during childhood; more males during adulthood.
Sleep Disorders Related to Another Mental Disorder: Insomnia Related to Another Mental Disorder Hypersomnia Related to Another Mental Disorder	More prevalent in females

Sleep Disorders	Sex Distribution
Sleep Disorder Due to a General Medical Condition	
Substance-Induced Sleep Disorder	

Impulse-Control Disorders Not Elsewhere Classified	Sex Distribution
Intermittent Explosive Disorder	Episodic violent behavior more common in males
Kleptomania	In clinical samples, female:male ratio 2:1
Pyromania	Many more males
Pathological Gambling	One-third are females, but in different geographic areas and cultures, the gender ratio can vary considerably
Trichotillomania	Among children, no difference; among adults, many more females

Adjustment Disorders	Sex Distribution
Adjustment Disorders (The following is for the entire category, no specific prevalence or gender ratios are given based on subtype, e.g., Adjustment Disorder with Depressed Mood)	In clinical samples of adults, female:male ratio 2:1; in clinical samples of children and adolescents, no sex difference

Personality Disorders	Sex Distribution
Paranoid Personality Disorder	In clinical samples, more males
Schizoid Personality Disorder	Slightly more males
Schizotypal Personality Disorder	May be slightly more males
Antisocial Personality Disorder	In community sample, rates of 3% in men and 1% in women
Borderline Personality Disorder	Female:male ratio approximately 3:1
Narcissistic Personality Disorder	50–75% males
Histrionic Personality Disorder	In clinical settings, diagnosed more frequently in females than in males.

(continued)

Avoidant Personality Disorder   Equal

Dependent Personality Disorder   DPD has been diagnosed more frequently in females, although some studies have reported similar prevalence rates among men and women

Obsessive-Compulsive Personality Disorder   Male:female ratio about 2:1

NOTE

1. Often, information in the *DSM* is unclear or confusing, so we have erred on the side of caution by only reporting sex distribution information that was clear.

Chapter 17

Mislabeling Anxiety and Depression in Rural Women

Nikki Gerrard

Extensive work with farmwomen in the Canadian province of Saskatchewan provides an excellent illustration of the ways that governments' action and inaction can combine with ongoing social organization and traditions to cause severe anxiety and depression. It is valuable to understand this process, because anxiety and depression are two of the emotions most commonly cited as evidence of mental illnesses, and mental illnesses are widely considered as having individual and intrapsychic origins, not social and political ones. Although some things called mental illnesses may have intrapsychic causes, it is troubling that the vast majority of interventions designed to help very anxious or very depressed people are based on the assumption that all severe emotional problems begin within the individual.

In a large, interview-based study (Gerrard and Russell 2000), rural women described their provincial government's and federal government's practices—which are followed by many other Canadian provincial governments and U.S. federal and state governments—of neglecting the needs of farmwomen and their families, implementing programs and then soon ending them, or even conducting research to identify the women's needs but then failing to provide funding or staff to meet the needs thereby identified. Before describing some of these programs, it is helpful to consider the conditions under which many farmwomen live.

Decreasing numbers of family farms are viable (currently probably fewer than half), a fact which produces intense fear and anxiety. Many women live thirty miles from the nearest neighbor, store, or doctor, so many essential tasks take a long time to execute. Because of the dire straits of most family farmers, women work in the fields and run heavy equipment. In addition, they prepare three meals a day for everyone and deliver them into the fields. There is little or no day care, and it is extremely dangerous for infants and children to be around farm equipment, so many parents leave their babies and young children in the charge of the older children or even alone for long periods of time. Because women are seen as responsible for the children, mothers especially feel ashamed and afraid about this. When ten-year-olds are brought into service driving trucks so work can be completed, mothers have another cause to feel frightened and sad. They worry about what is happening to their children, and many develop sleep disturbances, increasing their exhaustion. To address these concerns, the Liberal government of Canada introduced the National Coalition for Rural Childcare, and during a three-year period, they mobilized rural women and women's organizations to do needs assessments across the country. Three years later, the government ended the program *without having brought in any rural childcare.*

Further, many farmwomen suffer from the "daughter-in-law issue." Farms are patrilineal, and the son may marry a woman from another farm or from a town or city. Everyone lives in the same farmyard, the parents-in-law often moving into a trailer and the young adults taking over the farmhouse. As a newcomer, the daughter-in-law often has no power and no say in the running of the farm. If she was not raised on a farm, she loses credibility in the eyes of her in-laws because she knows nothing about running a farm. If, as often happens, the parents do not share the power evenly with their son and also underpay him, the daughter-in-law is regarded as having no right to express concern. She often has no financial security, because the parents-in-law often retain ownership of the farm. The father-in-law might watch for their son's bedroom light to go on at 5:00 in the morning and then phone to talk to *him* about the farm, so the daughter-in-law feels she has no privacy. The parents-in-law feel they have no other options if the daughter-in-law knows nothing about running a farm.

A program designed to promote professionalism and leadership for farmwomen and to lower barriers to their participation in leadership roles, the Farm Women's Advancement Program (FWAP), was started in 1988. Provincial farmwomen's organizations sent representatives to a national group that met regularly to plan for change. The women's participation included lobbying, publishing newsletters or books, designing and carrying out research, conducting workshops, education, policy formation, and international development. The participants said that this program helped them to feel strong, confident, and connected to others. Eight years after it began, the government of Canada ended the program, and many women returned to their previous states of isolation, hopelessness, and depression.

Another program was introduced through the Farm Women's Bureau with the stated purpose of providing up to $150,000 per year in grants to assist farmwomen's organizations achieve legal and economic equality for farmwomen, promote their participation in policy making and management of the agricultural sector, and encourage recognition of their contributions. The grants were awarded, but when the women made proposals about policy and management, they were ignored. They are always ignored. The agriculture ministers said they would help but did not. This added to the farmwomen's feelings of being invisible and unimportant. They felt devalued because the message to the women was, in effect, "You do not matter to either a Liberal or a Progressive Conservative government. You are not important to this province or to society."

Farmwomen report that involvement in programs designed for them is, as one said, "very good for your mental health and your physical health." Another said, "The benefit to my health is feeling strong, feeling confident about myself and my position as a farm woman." A third reported, "My involvement has been one of the best antidotes to depression. . . . If there is something you can do about a situation, it is the best way to get undepressed, because instead of being focused on how grim things are, you focus on how you can impact the situation." Another referred to the boosting of confidence and "sense of accomplishing something and making a significant contribution" that result from "the collective power and support of working with other women" in a specific program or project. But always comes the same pattern: The women's hopes are raised, the women follow through, but the government ends the programs. This results in "expectation exhaustion," because those who run the political system repeatedly tell them that things will get better, and sometimes things do get a little bit better, but then that improvement turns out to be transitory. This kind of treatment has long been known to produce anxiety and depression. As one woman said, "If we're not involved, and we remain peripheral and voiceless, it's very detrimental to our psychological health, to our physical health." A psychological destabilization of the women also results from this pattern and disempowers them at the level of decision making and policy formation. As Thurston, Crow, and Scott (1998) point out, it is through women's organizations that a great deal of their public voice is heard and through which policies are implemented and disseminated.

Although anxiety and depression are disturbing for anyone, for farmwomen these emotional states that result from the combination of ongoing factors in the women's lives and those resulting from government-created expectation exhaustion can be disastrous. Many of the women are given psychotropic medication, often anxiolytics and/or antidepressant medication, by their family doctors or by psychiatrists when they have access to them. Anxiolytics can reduce anxiety but often leave people with no ability to feel alive and passionate, and they do not solve the underlying problems. The same is true of medication for depression. The depression may lift, but often the woman feels flat, lethargic, and uninspired. Their emotional flatness affects the whole family, especially in the not infrequent cases when the mother becomes minimally functional. Her already over-worked husband continues the farming and also feels that he has to take care of her because she doesn't go out any more, participate in the social life of the community, or attend whatever programs might be still active at the time. She may no longer be able to drive, and this is particularly serious because a rural woman has to drive long distances for so many things. If her husband drives her on errands, the farmwork suffers, since the driving time alone is likely to take at least an hour. If a neighbor can be enlisted to do the driving, that neighbor will likely drive 120 miles for a single errand, by the time she drives to the other woman's farm, takes her on the errand, re-turns the passenger home, and returns to her own farm. This makes it diffi-cult to get help, and the risk of causing resentment in the helper is high. As a result, the farmwoman's isolation and consequent anxiety and depression are likely to increase even further.

In research about factors that contribute to their resiliency, farmwomen named the chance to talk with other women about problems in their lives as a major factor (Gerrard 2000). But there are few such chances, and they have been reduced by the withdrawal of government programs. They report that while these programs were operating, they temporarily felt connected to the world, important in the world, part of the bigger picture. Then this ended.

Clearly, the problems of depression and anxiety for many farmwomen result not from intrapsychic conditions but from the environment in which they live. Isolation, lack of financial viability or security, powerlessness on family-run farms, and lack of support from government policies and programs to ensure that these women are consulted and have opportunities to participate in all as-pects of agricultural life contribute to expectation exhaustion and/or depres-sion and/or anxiety. As therapist Gretchen Grinnell (1985) has stated, their emotional state is "a normal reaction to a crazy world." To diagnose them as mentally ill not only draws their own and society's attention from the causes of their problems but also, often, leads to further harm.

REFERENCES

Gerrard, N. (2000). What doesn't kill you makes you stronger: Determinants of stress resiliency in rural people in Saskatchewan. Unpublished manuscript.

Gerrard, N., G. Russell, and the Saskatchewan Women's Agricultural Network. (2000). An exploration of health-related impacts of the erosion of agriculturally focussed support programs for farm women in Saskatchewan: Executive summary. Unpublished manuscript.

Grinnell, Gretchen. (1985). Personal communication.

Thurston, W., B. Crow, and C. Scott. (1998, December). *The role of women's organizations in health policy development, implementation, and dissemination.* Report prepared for Health Canada. Available from W. Thurston, University of Calgary.

Part IV

SPECIFIC LABELS

Chapter 18

Bias and Schizophrenia

Jeffrey Poland

The concept of schizophrenia is an icon of contemporary psychiatry: Most clinicians and laypeople have been led to believe that it is an indisputably real mental illness and that solid scientific research has led to a body of well-established knowledge about schizophrenia, what it is, what causes it, and how best to treat it. Most clinicians have been taught some version of the following "received view":

1) Schizophrenia is a brain disease. The specifics of its pathology and etiology are not fully known, although:
   * Schizophrenia has stable prevalence rates across cultures and over time (e.g., approximately 1 percent prevalence).
   * It is well established that schizophrenia has a genetic component in its etiology.
   * Schizophrenia is associated with a number of environmental stressors that might play a role in its etiology (e.g., prenatal exposure to famine, viral infection, and stress; birth trauma).
   * There are a number of compelling findings and promising leads concerning the pathophysiology of schizophrenia (e.g., dopaminergic dysregulation, ventriculomegaly, hypofrontality, hypertemporality, a variety of neurocognitive deficits).
2) Schizophrenia has a characteristic, identifiable clinical picture and can be reliably diagnosed using criteria found in the American Psychiatric Association's *Diagnostic and Statistical Manual of Mental Disorders, Fourth Edition-TR* (*DSM:* American Psychiatric Association 2000).
3) Schizophrenia has harmful psychological and social consequences, and it constitutes a serious public health problem.

4) Schizophrenia is *primarily* treatable with psychotropic drugs, and there have been significant improvements in such treatment in the past decade (e.g., the atypical antipsychotics). Schizophrenia is managed (palliation, support, relapse prevention, rehabilitation) with a combination of the primary pharmacological treatment and appropriate ancillary techniques (e.g., individual psychotherapy, psychosocial interventions).
5) Schizophrenia is unjustifiably stigmatized, and such stigma can be reduced through teaching that schizophrenia is a disease.

There is little doubt that millions of people suffer from severe mental illness and experience a wide range of problems, including: cognitive impairments, hallucinations and delusions, negative emotions such as fear and unhappiness, behavioral and social skills deficits, dysfunctional social identities and roles, demoralization, poverty, inadequate housing, no friends, nothing to do. And it is well established that there are effective ways of helping people with the various problems falling under the label "severe mental illness." The subject of this chapter is whether the concept of schizophrenia and the associated received view have anything useful to add to clinical practice concerned with severe mental illness. They do not.[1] The accepted beliefs about "schizophrenia" lack scientific credibility because they are not supported by high-quality research, and they lead to a simplistic view of severe mental illness and to harmful distortions of clinical practice.

THE RECEIVED VIEW OF SCHIZOPHRENIA IS A STEREOTYPE

The full case for the claim that the received view of schizophrenia lacks scientific credibility involves detailed examination of the research record (Boyle 1990; Bentall 1990; Heinrichs 2001) along with a close critical scrutiny of the research program associated with the received view, including its standards of evidence and potential for progress (Poland, in press), the intactness and integrity of the scientific community engaged in this research (Poland and Spaulding, forthcoming), and the practical utility of the received view even if its claims are not supported. But even short of such a comprehensive assessment, it is informative to consider some widely acknowledged problems with what most clinicians and laypeople believe to be true about schizophrenia.

First, the concept of schizophrenia has never actually been shown to have either *construct validity or predictive validity*. That is, there has never been sufficient scientific evidence that its putative signs and symptoms are intercorrelated and hence constitute a genuine syndrome; the fact that the *DSM* listing for Schizophrenia stipulates certain features as criteria does not prove that those features constitute a syndrome. This raises serious doubts about the scientific credibility of all instances of schizophrenia research.[2]

Further, the research record concerning schizophrenia is replete with findings that are methodologically flawed, negative, unreplicated, inconsistent, weak, nonspecific, or uninterpretable.[3] Such findings do not provide support for scientific hypotheses about schizophrenia, although they do comprise massive amounts of data that lead some to talk as if various hypotheses have been tested and supported. However, it is doubtful that any hypothesis about schizophrenia has ever been *rigorously* tested and supported. Thus, in addition to problems of construct validity, the concept of schizophrenia does not have any well-established predictive validity either. Although some would consider it heretical to say so, there has been no substantial improvement in scientific knowledge about schizophrenia over the past one hundred years.[4]

A second widely acknowledged problem with clinical and research use of the diagnostic category of schizophrenia concerns its well-documented *heterogeneity* with respect to criterial features, associated features, biological and psychological processes, and contextual features and processes (Heinrichs 1993; 2001). Thus, individuals diagnosed as schizophrenic are likely to differ from each other even with respect to the clinical features that provide the basis for the diagnosis (i.e., the *DSM* criteria), as well as with respect to biological, psychological, behavioral, and social processes that operate both internally and externally. Such "process heterogeneity" means that the clinical dynamics (course, outcome, response to intervention) of the condition also vary widely, as clinicians and researchers have repeatedly discovered (Poland et al. 1994). Although this massive heterogeneity is widely acknowledged, there is substantial disagreement about its significance. Those who are firmly committed to the existence of schizophrenia suggest that there is heterogeneity because schizophrenia is a disease (or multiple diseases) that is embedded in widely varying biological, psychological, or social contexts with which it interacts. They believe that, with time and research progress, such heterogeneity will become better understood and managed. Those who have no commitment to the belief that "schizophrenia" picks out a well-defined disease[5] suggest that the heterogeneity is part of the evidence that the category is scientifically and clinically meaningless, that schizophrenia does not, in fact, exist.[6]

At the very least, it should not be *assumed* that one or the other of the interpretations of diagnostic heterogeneity is correct. This issue should be resolved on scientific grounds, and, prior to such resolution, the scientific credibility of the diagnostic category is, at least, in doubt. Given its lack of established validity, that doubt is a serious one, since all that we know for sure is that many individuals have been grouped together under the label "schizophrenia," that these individuals exhibit massive heterogeneity at all levels of functioning, and that there is no current understanding regarding what (if anything) unites them. Thus, it would appear that the received view is nothing more than a set of unsupported (if meaningful at all) beliefs about a putative disease called "schizophrenia" and about the people supposedly afflicted with this "disease." Because of this, when clinicians classify individuals as having schizophrenia there is a substantial *loss of information* with no compensatory gains in either understanding of a person's condition or predictive power.[7] As we shall see below, the schizophrenia label actually obscures the complexity that must be managed if clinical goals are to be pursued effectively. The received view is a stereotype that provides a simplistic understanding of the people who are the subjects of clinical practice, and this introduces a substantial risk of error and harmful treatment.

THE SCHIZOPHRENIA STEREOTYPE
LEADS TO HARMFUL BIASES

In the case of severe mental illness, bias can result from any component of the received view of schizophrenia, and it can arise in at least five general areas of clinical practice: processing information, the making of inferences, clinical understanding, intervention, and clinical identities, roles, and relationships. Together, such biases undermine clinical practice and harm both the clinician and (especially) the people who seek help for severe mental illness.

Information Processing

Information processing includes, among other things, observation, attention, information search, memory, and information recording. Such processes determine what information is available for clinical reasoning, judgment, and decision making and, as a consequence, play a strong role in shaping clinicians' feelings, attitudes, and motivations. When information processing is influenced by the schizophrenia stereotype, the following bias is promoted:

> *Bias 1*: The tendency to observe, attend to, collect, record, remember, and highlight primarily a narrow range of information concerning pathological, clinically identifiable features (e.g., hallucinations, delusions, bizarre behavior, disorganized behavior, "negative symptoms"[8]).

In diagnostic practice guided by the schizophrenia stereotype, the kinds of information deemed to be of most clinical interest tend to be the pathological clinical features listed in the *DSM*. This increases the salience of such features, the categorizing of ambiguous events as instances of such features, the effort expended in systematically identifying them, and the recording of them in clinical records. Thus, bias 1 leads to the *creation of a body of clinical information that is heavily weighted with respect to a narrow and impoverished range of features* that are readily identifiable and negatively valued by the clinician and are the primary currency in psychiatric discourse about schizophrenia. They are sought for in dyadic clinical diagnostic interviews, highlighted in clinical records, and considered sufficient for diagnosis.

The focus on these features is maintained at the expense of a much wider range of features not included in *DSM* criteria and not deemed of *primary diagnostic significance*. Thus, many types of information either are not attended to or collected or are relegated to a secondary or irrelevant status for the purposes of a diagnostic assessment (e.g., information regarding the person's functional capacities along a wide range of biological, psychological, behavioral, and social dimensions; or regarding the person's specific functioning in a wide range of personal and social contexts; or regarding the person's view of their life history, projects, goals, plans, outlook, and positive relationships). Those in the grip of the received view of schizophrenia tend to minimize the importance of such information when it comes to figuring out *what is wrong with the person*. Either such information is not collected at all, or, if it is collected, its primary significance concerns figuring out what is an appropriate *DSM* diagnosis. This applies to the clinician's taking of the person's medical and social histories, as well as use of psychological tests and skills assessments. For example, such ancillary information is often used to corroborate a clinical diagnosis, using such investigative questions as: What is the person's diagnostic history? What is the person's family history with respect to mental illness? Was the Minnesota Multiphasic Personality Inventory profile consistent with a diagnosis of schizophrenia? Was there a recent decline in functioning? Is there clinically significant impairment in functioning? Thus, even when information other than the *DSM* criteria for schizophrenia is collected, the operation of the stereotype tends to lead to the minimizing of its role in diagnosis and to locating it in a pathology-oriented framework.

Why are these consequences of bias 1 harmful? The building of a narrow, pathology-oriented database poorly equips the clinician to understand what is wrong and what sorts of causal processes are in play in the person's world or the clinical setting. In addition, an impoverished, pathology-oriented body of information fails to provide the basis for an adequate understanding of the person's life, goals, and values. The sense that there is something wrong with the person dominates, rather than being one part of, clinical activity. As a result, the individual whose life is at the center of clinical practice loses status and is disempowered, giving cause for alarm, because the agency of the person is one of the most important factors in successful clinical practice.

Inferential Practices

The schizophrenia stereotype leads to clinical inferential practices that exhibit the following bias:

> *Bias 2*: The tendency to infer the existence of a core disease process that explains the presence of, and relationships among, clinical features, and to interpret events and features of the person as the manifestations of an individual biological disease condition.

Thus, whenever information deemed relevant to diagnosis is evaluated, the clinician in the grip of the schizophrenia stereotype is primed to see groups of clinical features and events as intercorrelated and all being manifestations of a single, underlying disease. In addition, essentially ambiguous features and events (e.g., a report of an hallucination, a delusional statement, a bizarre act) are likely to be interpreted as manifestations of a brain disease.[9]

Some defenders of the schizophrenia stereotype acknowledge that schizophrenia might be not a unitary disease but rather a spectrum disease that varies along a number of dimensions or "multiple diseases" (the term "schizophrenia" is applied to different disease processes in different individuals). In individual cases, nevertheless, it is invariably assumed that some disease process causes the clinical manifestations. However, there is no scientific evidence of what that disease process might be or of how the disease might be causally related to its alleged clinical manifestations. Clinicians who exhibit bias 2 tend to ignore or minimize the importance of causal hypotheses not involving a core brain disease: direct environmental impact or environment-individual feedback loops; complex biological, psychological, and social interactions; and "normal" psychological processes involving choice, social learning, and attributional processes. Since individual features and events that gain clinical attention quite possibly result from such alternative sorts of causal process, a rigid, stereotypic, disease hypothesis tends to obscure the real causes of a person's problems.

Bias 2 also leads clinicians to ignore the distinct possibility that the clinical features they see are *independent* of each other (e.g., a person's hallucinations are related to a biochemical dysregulation, while their delusional speech reflects a complex social learning history), or that they are *interrelated in some other way* (e.g., escalating arousal that makes it hard for a person who already has social skills deficits to manage a distressing social conflict), both of which are regularly discovered to exist.[10]

The common assumption among clinicians and laypeople that hallucinations and delusions form a meaningful pair and that they are the essential features of schizophrenia is an instance of the profound impact that the nonscientific clinical psychiatric tradition has exerted. But not even the *DSM* requires that hallucinations and delusions be present in schizophrenia, and it certainly doesn't require that they be present together. No careful scientific investigations have established that delusions and hallucinations are empirically correlated with each other, and they are well known not to be specific to a diagnosis of schizophrenia. Thus, the belief that such features are intercorrelated and the consequence of the same core brain disease in schizophrenia can only reflect deeply held ideological commitments. Why would one *assume* that hallucinations and delusions form a meaningful cluster just because they happen to co-occur in some cases?

Clinical Understanding

Clinical understanding affected by the schizophrenia stereotype leads to the following bias:

> *Bias 3*: The tendency to view people diagnosed with schizophrenia in terms of a disease model, according to which a core disease process drives the perception, thought, feeling, and behavior of the person, and, hence, to view persons as the victims of a brain disease over which they have no control.

As just discussed, biased inferential practices under the influence of the schizophrenia stereotype tend to promote *a simplistic causal understanding* of the condition of the person as involving a core disease process and the pathogenic cascades to which it leads: all pathological features of the person will tend to be understood as downstream causal consequences of the core disease process. Within such a framework, the person's perception, thought, feeling, and behavior are considered to be driven by an internally located, pathological process,[11] and thus, they tend to be viewed as the psychologically meaningless causal fallout of a diseased brain. The alternative causal hypotheses mentioned above (viz., independence of problems, environmental causes, complex interactional feedback loops, normal psychological processes) tend to be ignored or minimized, and a pathology-oriented view of the person as the passive victim of a brain disease tends to predominate.[12] In this way, the schizophrenia stereotype compromises clinical practice by misleading clinicians about the character and complexity of the circumstances in which individuals are embedded and with which they are attempting to cope.

Bias 3 also tends to promote a *simplistic understanding of the people* (not just the causal nexus in which they are embedded) who suffer from severe mental illness. A view of the person as the passive victim of a brain disease leads to a substantial loss of understanding of both the *perspective* of the person and their *agency*. If a clinician tends to regard the person's perception, thought, feeling, and behavior as essentially the "psychologically meaningless causal fallout of a diseased brain," then both the person's perspective and their actions will be dismissed as manifestations of the core brain disease process, things to be eradicated by treatment rather than to be grasped as essential components of clinical understanding. Such a dismissal will lead the clinician to lose sight of such things as:

- the ways in which the person apprehends what is happening in a clinical setting
- how the person reacts to being classified and treated in certain ways by clinicians and by others
- the social roles that the person occupies, or the ways in which a person might resist pressures to occupy such roles (e.g., the role of "mental patient")[13]
- the person's outlook on their life: their values, goals, aspirations, plans, prospects, historical understanding, and understanding of their current circumstances
- the operation of the person's cognitive architecture and of normal psychological and social processes in the production of behavior
- the ways in which a person's actions may be quite legitimate in the light of their circumstances, their limitations, and the ways they are treated

Without such understanding, much of what the person does will be unintelligible to the clinician, especially given the limitations of looking at only a narrow range of factors and assuming that a core brain disease causes the trouble. Without a genuine appreciation of the person's predicament from their own point of view, effective and respectful clinical relationships are difficult to establish, and that creates further impediments to the kind of understanding that should underlie diagnosis.

There are two further biases (concerning intervention practices and clinical identities, roles and relationships) that the schizophrenia stereotype tends to promote, and which I shall mention but not discuss in detail. Each is intimately bound up with diagnostic practice and interacts with the other biases introduced by the stereotype.

Intervention Practices

Good clinical practice leaves no room for an impoverished or pathology-oriented database, skewed inferences, or simplistic understanding. Unfortunately, these biases, in conjunction with various components of the schizophrenia stereotype, lead to a fourth bias in clinical practice, one that concerns the design and implementation of clinical interventions:

> *Bias 4*: The tendency to target the putative brain disease and its manifestations as the *primary* object of intervention and to monitor symptoms as the principal measure of treatment success or failure.

Within the framework induced by the schizophrenia stereotype, the brain disease status of the person's condition occupies center stage, subordinating all intervention to its control and management. For these purposes, psychotropic drug therapy is the first and foremost form of intervention, and symptom monitoring is the first and foremost form of assessment regarding treatment success or failure. As a consequence of this bias, the wide variety of possible alternative causal processes alluded to earlier will tend to go unidentified and unaddressed. Bias 4 is dangerous because it tends to short-circuit serious clinical thought regarding intervention, leading to rote and ill-conceived intervention plans and leaving the clinician without adequate resources for understanding why a chosen intervention fails to be effective.

Clinical Roles, Identities, and Relationships

The last area in which the schizophrenia stereotype exerts a biasing influence concerns the social infrastructure of clinical processes and practices (the ways in which clinical identities, roles, and relationships are shaped):

> *Bias 5*: The tendency to create a social infrastructure for clinical activity in which the person's *identity* is that of a victim of disease beyond control, the person's *role* is that of a patient whose primary responsibility is to comply with treatments prescribed by the clinician, and the person's *relationships* involve occupying inferior status and authority relative to others.

Clinicians under the influence of the schizophrenia stereotype will tend to interact with persons labeled schizophrenic as if they were passive victims of a disease process, needing to be treated by a physician using essentially biomedical intervention strategies and techniques. As a critical part of this interaction, such clinicians will educate the persons in their care to embrace the same view of themselves: persons diagnosed with schizophrenia ought to come to believe that they are the passive victims of a brain disease. Such clinicians will also tend to educate everyone else, including the family and friends of the person and other members of a hospital staff, along the same lines.[14] This creation of a shared understanding among all principal parties leads to a rigid structuring of the person's social world, in which their first- and third-person *identity* is that of the passive victim of a brain disease, in whom pathological features and behavior occupy a dominant focus of attention. Consequently, the person's status, roles, and relationships in this social world are powerfully and negatively influenced. Specifically, the impact resulting from this bias includes: the demeaning of the person, the promotion of a passive orientation of the person toward their problems, the disempowerment of the person in their life, the undermining of the person's engagement in their own treatment, the creation of flawed clinical relationships, and, as a result, the promotion of harmful and unproductive clinical and social processes.

WHAT CAN BE DONE?

The received view of schizophrenia, then, is a stereotype that leads to a number of biases that influence and undermine the diagnostic process and all other critical dimensions of clinical practice and promote a variety of harms. This stereotype and the biases it promotes are deeply rooted within the culture: the broad socioeconomic infrastructure in which mental health care is embedded; the reimbursement practices, specifically regarding the financing of mental health care; the current zeitgeist within mental health practice, and the training and socioeconomic reward structure of the clinical professions (Poland and Caplan, chapter 2 in this volume). Nonetheless, there are some things that individual clinicians can do, difficult though they are likely to be.

Assuming one is in the grip of the schizophrenia stereotype and, hence, the biases it promotes, one might commit to the idea of divesting oneself of that stereotype, to identifying and counteracting the biases, and to adopting different beliefs and practices. Even if one works in a place where diagnostic labels are required, one can expand the range of information one collects for assessment purposes, introduce more sophisticated causal analyses of a person's functioning and problems, and embrace a less pathology-oriented, disease-minded understanding of the person one is trying to help.

For example, to the extent that one tends to interpret ambiguous events as signs of pathology, one would consider alternative interpretations, such as that a person's distress or behavior reflects a normal response to stressful circumstances (e.g., an individual who starts to experience "symptoms" while beginning a new job). And, instead of assuming that all features of a clinical picture provide support for choosing a particular diagnosis, one can consider that such features may be relatively independent of each other and have independent causes, including environmental ones.

A specific kind of alternative practice concerns "patient education": rather than attempting to indoctrinate a person into the harmful schizophrenia stereotype in an effort to increase the person's (apparently deficient) insight into their situation or to increase the likelihood that they will comply with treatment recommendations, one can frame one's concerns about either insight or compliance more directly, without employing the language of brain disease (e.g., a problem-solving formulation that appeals to the person's capacities and the challenges they face).

Above all, humility, respect for the people one is trying to help, appreciation of the enormous difficulty of providing meaningful assistance, and recognition of the possibility that stereotypes and biases are operating in one's clinical practice are the beginnings of any effective response to the problems identified here.

NOTES

Thanks to Paula J. Caplan and Barbara Von Eckardt for helpful comments on earlier drafts of this chapter.

1. See Spaulding, Sullivan, and Poland (2003) for a framework in which the problems of severe mental illness are comprehensively identified and addressed, without reliance upon psychiatric diagnostic labels such as "schizophrenia."

2. See Boyle (1990) for important discussion of this line of critical discussion. See also Poland (in press).

3. See Heinrichs (2001) for a review of a wide range of research hypotheses concerning schizophrenia.

4. Those in the grip of the received view of schizophrenia see the significance of this fact in terms of the immaturity of current science and the complexity of the disease: with more time and resources, they believe research will produce an understanding of the brain disease called "schizophrenia." However, the alternative hypotheses, that there is no such thing as schizophrenia and that the concept is scientifically meaningless, seem better confirmed by the research record to date than are the received view and this optimistic outlook for the associated research program.

5. This is not to say that there are no brain diseases at all; it is to say that a commitment to the idea that the concept of schizophrenia picks out a brain disease is currently groundless. Certainly it is possible that some individuals who happen to fall into a category defined by *DSM-IV* criteria for schizophrenia have, as part of their condition, some brain disease or other. But this in no way vindicates the category as a brain disease, and, in any event, it should be kept in mind that not just any condition that leads to problems is a disease.

6. The claims that the category of schizophrenia is scientifically and clinically meaningless and that schizophrenia does not exist inevitably strike those who are

firmly committed to the concept as obviously false or at least overstated, since they believe that the category has proven useful in clinical and research practice and that people with serious problems meeting the diagnostic criteria for schizophrenia exist. How could the category be meaningless? How could the condition not exist? But being puzzled in this way is largely a reflection of an a priori and empirically unsubstantiated commitment to the hypothesis that schizophrenia exists.

7. For example, if a person reports hallucinations that are distressing and disruptive, a clinician might consider prescribing an antipsychotic drug known to be helpful in managing hallucinations. However, a diagnosis of schizophrenia is not required for predicting that the drug might be effective, and it adds nothing to understanding what is going on in such a case.

8. The so-called "negative symptoms" of schizophrenia include: flat affect, lack of motivation, poverty of thought, and poverty of speech.

9. The report of an hallucination or the making of a delusional statement, for example, are essentially ambiguous because, although hallucinations are real phenomena, not every report of an hallucination is an accurate report, and, although delusional statements are often made, they can have very different sorts of clinical significance, ranging from putative pathophysiological dysregulations to complex social learning histories and outright manipulations.

10. See Spaulding, Sullivan, and Poland (2003) for a clinical approach to severe mental illness in which just such fine-grained causal analysis is pursued.

11. A particularly important consequence of the bias involved here is a tendency to "decontextualize" the person's problems. The schizophrenia stereotype implies that a core disease process exists within the individual and that (1) it is perhaps partially caused by factors in an environmental context, (2) it can have consequences in an environmental context, but (3) neither causal antecedents nor causal consequences of the disease nor any other features of the context are parts of the disease process itself. That is, the context can be completely detached from an understanding of what is wrong with the person.

12. See Spaulding, Sullivan, and Poland (2003) for discussion of why a decontextualized view of severe mental illness leads to serious misunderstanding of the nature of a person's problems and of why according causal privilege to core disease processes within an individual's brain is quite misguided (i.e., causation can move in all directions, it can involve features and processes at *any* level of causal analysis, and it can involve "normal" as well as pathological processes).

13. The fact that traditional psychiatric practices have tended to reinforce dysfunctional roles, identities, and behavior through a focus on pathology, a lack of personal respect, and treatment that reinforces disability, makes such resistance quite poignant.

14. From the point of view of the clinician, building appropriate relationships based upon a shared understanding of the person is critical to implementing effective clinical intervention plans and to supporting the patient in their efforts to manage their disease. But, of course, such a point of view makes a number of questionable assumptions.

REFERENCES

American Psychiatric Association. (2000). *Diagnostic and statistical manual of mental disorders IV-TR*. Washington, DC.

Bentall, Richard, ed. (1990). *Reconstructing schizophrenia*. London: Routledge.

Boyle, Mary. (1990). *Schizophrenia: A scientific delusion?* London: Routledge.

Heinrichs, Walter. (2001). *In search of madness: Schizophrenia and neuroscience*. Oxford: Oxford University Press.

———. (1993). Schizophrenia and the brain: Conditions for a neuropsychology of madness. *American Psychologist* 48, 221–33.

Poland, Jeffrey. (in press). How to move beyond the concept of schizophrenia. In M. Chung, W. Fulford, G. Graham, eds. *The philosophical understanding of schizophrenia*. Oxford: Oxford University Press.

Poland, Jeffrey, and William Spaulding. (forthcoming). *Crisis and revolution: Toward a reconceptualization of psychopathology*. Cambridge, MA: MIT Press.

Poland, Jeffrey, Barbara Von Eckardt, and William Spaulding. (1994). Problems with the *DSM* approach to classification of psychopathology. Pp. 235–60 in George Graham and Lyn Stephens, eds. *Philosophical psychopathology*. Cambridge, MA: MIT Press

Spaulding, William, Mary Sullivan, and Jeffrey Poland. (2003). *Treatment and rehabilitation of severe mental illness*. New York: Guilford Press.

Chapter 19

The Truth about "False Memory Syndrome"

Karen A. Olio

Because it includes the word "syndrome," many people may assume that False Memory Syndrome (FMS), a term used in both popular and professional literatures, is a scientifically validated diagnostic category. However, often new constructs including terms like "syndrome" or "disorder" have simply been created by an individual or group which may not have offered empirical data to prove that it (1) exists and (2) has the characteristics and etiology that it claims (Caplan 1995). In fact, the name FMS was coined in 1992, not by any mental health organization or research group but rather by a lay advocacy group—the False Memory Syndrome Foundation (FMSF)—that represents parents who claim that they have been falsely accused of sexual abuse by their now adult children.

WHAT IS THE SUPPOSED FALSE MEMORY SYNDROME?

In a FMSF pamphlet, John Kihlstrom suggests that FMS is:

> A condition in which a person's identity and interpersonal relationships are centered around a memory of traumatic experience which is objectively false but in which the person strongly believes. Note that the syndrome is not characterized by false memories as such. We all have memories that are inaccurate. Rather, the syndrome may be diagnosed when the memory is so deeply engrained that it orients the individual's entire personality and lifestyle, in turn disrupting all sorts of other adaptive behaviors. The analogy to personality disorder is intentional. False Memory Syndrome is especially destructive because the person assiduously avoids confrontation with any evidence that might challenge the memory. Thus it takes on a life of its own, encapsulated, and resistant to correction. (False Memory Syndrome Foundation 1994, 3)

Kihlstrom's definition highlights one of the essential difficulties in confirm-
ing a diagnosis of FMS, in that the individual's memory must be documented
to be objectively false. Just as it may be difficult to prove the veracity of an
individual's memory, so it is also difficult, perhaps in many cases impossible,
to prove that the entirety of a person's memory is objectively false.

It is important to consider the political and historical context of childhood
sexual abuse. The sexual abuse of women and children has been a starkly political issue for hundreds of years. In both professional and public arenas, the
character and credibility of the victims have been questioned and disparaged.
Often we wish to find alternative explanations for the wrenching stories of
childhood abuse that our clients relate. It may be that FMS offers a more comfortable and familiar way to "explain" these disclosures. The notion of FMS
taps into deeply held stereotypes of women as hysterical, naive, highly sug-
gestible, and easily manipulated. Popular embrace of the concept of FMS—
and the rush to interpret reports of child sexual abuse as false—may indicate
a need to locate the source of such violation outside of our own families and
neighborhoods, and to minimize our society's propensity for violence, rather
than a thoughtful review of scientific findings and the specific details for each
individual case.

The coining of the term False Memory Syndrome and the dissemination of
information by the False Memory Syndrome Foundation on this supposed
phenomenon seems to have had a significant impact on the popular press reports of childhood sexual abuse and the credibility given to the recollection of
survivors of sexual abuse. Stanton (1997) noted that a recent study revealed a
dramatic shift in how four major popular press magazines (*Time*, *Newsweek*,
U. S. News & World Report, and *People*) treated the topic of sexual abuse. In
1991 more than 80 percent of the coverage was weighted toward stories of survivors of sexual abuse, but by 1994 more than 80 percent of the coverage focused on false accusations, often involving supposedly false memory.

To put the topic of FMS in perspective, it is useful to review documented
prevalence rates for both childhood abuse and FMS. Until the past twenty
years, instances of child sexual abuse were believed to be infrequent. For
example, the authors of one of the most widely read professional texts—
Comprehensive Textbook of Psychiatry—reported that the incidence rate for
incest was about 1.1 to 1.9 per million people (Henderson 1975). However,
data collected since the late 1970s show this not to be the case. Although
the rate of abuse varies due to differing methodologies, populations, and
definitions of abuse, some researchers found instances of sexual abuse to be
as high as 16 percent for boys (Finkelhor et al. 1990) and 1 in 3 for girls
(Russell 1983). These figures suggest that many millions of adults in the
United States have had childhood histories of sexual abuse.

Documentation of the occurrence of FMS seems more difficult to substantiate. Rhetorical claims, such as although "it is hard to form even a rough idea of the number of persuaded clients, a conservative guess would be a million persons since 1988 alone" (Crews 1995, 160), do not seem to be based on empirical data. For example, Wright asserted that what happened in the Paul Ingram (a man who was accused of sexually abusing his two daughters; for a review see Olio and Cornell 1998) case "is actually happening to thousands of other people throughout the country" (1993, 76). However, when asked how many cases of false accusation he had actually documented, Wright conceded that he had documented only one (Herman 1994).

In an effort to quantify the occurrence of FMS, Wakefield and Underwager have suggested that "the empirical data the FMS Foundation" has collected constitute "good support and high certainty for the concept of a false memory syndrome" (1994, 98). However, no criteria for determining that the alleged abuse did not occur (one of the diagnostic criteria of FMS defined by Kihlstrom) are given. Rather, these represent anecdotal cases in which parents accused of abuse say that they did not do it. The portion of these claims that actually reflect false accusations cannot be ascertained, and the etiology of such false accusations has not been determined. The existence of false accusations, in and of themselves, does not document or validate the existence of a False Memory *Syndrome*.

Kihlstrom's specification that the FMS does not simply refer to an inaccurate memory offers a helpful distinction. The term "false memory" (referring to a report of an inaccurate memory) is frequently used in the cognitive literature to describe the results from a wide variety of research paradigms that demonstrate instances in which some "false memories" may be easy to "create" (e.g., changes in the peripheral details in the misinformation research). It does not follow from these studies, however, that entire false memories of childhood abuse are equally easy to create in adults with no history of childhood trauma. Most researchers who attempt to create false memories have chosen "memories" of far less traumatic and secrecy-laden experiences than repeated sexual abuse of a child. For example, at the clemency hearings for Paul Ingram, in order to support her claim that Ingram was an innocent man and the victim of false memories, Loftus referred to a study by Kassin and Kiechel, asserting that it "shows that you can under certain circumstances get ninety percent of a sample of normal adults to confess to committing an act that they didn't do (Clemency and Pardons Board 1996, 6). However, as Freyd noted, the Kassin and Kiechel report was about a single study in which participants were accused of damaging a computer by pressing the wrong key, and FMS advocates seemed to "equate accidentally and fleetingly hitting the wrong key while typing with a father repeatedly and intentionally raping his daughter over several years" (Freyd 1996, 8).

Similar criticisms have been made regarding the application of conclusions from studies like Loftus's (1993) "lost-in-the-mall" experiment to the creation of false memories of childhood sexual abuse (for a more detailed critique, see Pope 1995 and 1996; Crook and Dean 1999; see also http://kspope.com, which can be found at http://users.owt.com/crook/memory). For example, Pezdek (1995; 1996) was able to convince some participants that they had been lost in a mall as children, but she had a 0 percent success rate when trying to create false memories for a rectal enema, a memory more analogous to childhood sexual abuse. Although the concept of FMS has successfully been presented on behalf of alleged abusers (Brown, Scheflin, and Hammond 1998) in criminal trials and civil suits, it is difficult to find scientific validation for the existence or extent of a supposed FMS based on independently conducted studies published in peer-review scientific or professional journals that include adequate control groups for traumatic memories in the therapeutic setting and the assessment of other confounding variables.

In an effort to establish the validity of FMS, one of the claims frequently made by the false memory proponents is that amnesia for memories of childhood sexual abuse cannot occur or rarely occurs; as Wakefield and Underwager describe it, "People who undergo severe trauma remember it" (1994, 182). Similar claims have been made by the FMSF as early as 1992: "Psychiatrists advising the Foundation members seem to be unanimous in the belief that memories of such atrocities cannot be repressed. Horrible incidents of childhood are remembered" (False Memory Syndrome Foundation 1992, 2). In an argument to the court, the FMSF claimed that: "Although a broad range of mechanisms are known to produce various kinds of memory disturbance and have been examined by memory researchers and theorists, none are, at present, considered capable of contributing to a supposed amnesia for traumatic events" (1995, 17). As Harrison Pope and Hudson summarized, "traumatic experiences are memorable" (1995, 715).

Interestingly, however, a review of empirically based studies supports a very different conclusion. According to Courtois (1999), more than thirty-five scientific studies have been published, and corroborated case reports (descriptions and citations of documented cases can be found at www.brown .edu/Departments/Taubman_Center/Recovmem/Archive.html) have been compiled that document various degrees of amnesia/forgetting for experiences of child sexual abuse (for further discussion, also see Pope and Brown 1996; Brown et al. 1998).

It seems that perhaps when considering the validity of a False Memory Syndrome construct it is important to keep Ken Pope's caution in mind: "Although there seems to be a never ending stream of popular books whose titles use the word "syndrome" preceded by some fictional character's name or some scientific language, psychological science requires more. Psychology requires that diagnostic categories be empirically validated" (1997, 998). "Each scientific claim should prevail or fall on its research validation and logic" (Pope 1996, 971).

REFERENCES

Articles, abstracts, research, and resources in psychology: Therapy, ethics, malpractice, forensics. http://kspope.com.

Brown, D., A. W. Scheflin, and D. C. Hammond. (1998). *Memory, trauma treatment, and the law: An essential reference on memory for clinicians, researchers, attorneys, and judges*. New York: W. W. Norton.

Caplan, P. J. (1995). *They say you're crazy: How the world's most powerful psychiatrists decide who's normal*. Reading, MA: Addison-Wesley.

Clemency and Pardons Board, Office of the Governor, State of Washington. (1996). Minutes from June 8, 1996, meeting. Available from the Office of the Governor, P.O. Box 40002, Olympia, WA 98504-0002.

Crews, F. (1995). *The memory wars: Freud's legacy in dispute*. New York: New York Review of Books.

Courtois, C. (1999). *Recollections of Sexual Abuse; Treatment principles and guidelines*. New York: W. W. Norton.

Crook, L. S., and M. C. Dean. (1999). "Lost in a shopping mall"—A breach of professional ethics. *Ethics & Behavior* 9, 39–50. Also found at http://users.owt.com/crook/memory.

False Memory Syndrome Foundation. (1995). Amicus curiae brief filed with the Supreme Court for the State of Rhode Island in the cases of *Heroux v. Carpentier* (Appeal No. 95–39) and *Kelly v. Marcantonio* (Appeal No. 94–727).

——. (1992). *Legal aspects of False Memory Syndrome*. Philadelphia.

——. (1994). Frequently asked questions. Pamphlet.

Finkelhor, D., G. Hotaling, I. A. Lewis, and C. Smith. (1990). Sexual abuse in a national survey of adult men and women: Prevalence, characteristics, and risk factors. *Child Abuse & Neglect* 14, 19–28.

Freyd, J. (1996). The science of memory: Apply with caution. *Traumatic Stress Points* 10, 4, and 18.

Freyd, J. J., and D. H. Gleaves. (1996). "Remembering" words not presented in lists: Relevance to the current recovered/false memory controversy. *Journal of Experimental Psychology: Learning, Memory, and Cognition* 22, 811–13.

Henderson, D. J. (1975). Incest. Pp. 1530–39 in A. M. Freedman, H. I. Kaplan, and B. J. Saddock, eds. *Comprehensive textbook of psychiatry*. Baltimore: Williams & Wilkins.

Herman, J. (1994). Presuming to know the truth. *Nieman Reports* 48 (1), 43–45.

Loftus, E. F. (1993). The reality of repressed memories. *American Psychologist* 48, 518–37.

Olio, K., and W. Cornell. (1998). The façade of scientific documentation: A case study of Richard Ofshe's analysis of the Paul Ingram case. *Psychology, Public Policy, and Law* 4, 4, and 1182–97.

Pezdek, K. (1995). What types of false childhood memories are not likely to be suggestively implanted? Paper presented at the annual meeting of the Psychonomic Society, Los Angeles.

Pezdek, K., K. Finger, and D. Hodge. (1996). False memories are more likely to be planted if they are familiar. Paper to be presented at the annual meeting of the Psychonomic Society, Chicago.

Pope, H. G., and J. I. Hudson. (1995). Can individuals "repress" memories of childhood abuse? An examination of the evidence. *Psychiatric Annals* 25, 715–19.

Pope, K. S. (1997). Science as careful questioning: Are claims of a false memory syndrome epidemic based on empirical evidence? *American Psychologist* 52, 997–1006. http://kspope.com.

———. (1996). Memory, abuse, and science: Questioning claims about the false memory syndrome epidemic. Invited address for the American Psychological Association's award for Distinguished Contributions to Public Service delivered at the 103rd Annual Convention of the American Psychological Association. *American Psychologist* 51, 957–74. http://kspope.com.

———. (1995). What psychologists better know about recovered memories, research, lawsuits, and the pivotal experiment. *Clinical Psychology: Science and Practice* 2, 304–15. http://kspope.com.

Pope, K. S., and L. Brown. (1996*). Recovered memories of abuse: Assessment, therapy, and forensics*. Washington, DC: American Psychological Association.

Russell, D. (1983). *The prevalence of intrafamilial and extrafamilial sexual abuse of female children*. New York: Basic Books.

Stanton, M. (1997). U-Turn on memory lane. *Columbia Journalism Review*, July/August, 44–49.

Wakefield, H., and R. Underwager. (1994). *Return of the furies: An investigation into recovered memory therapy*. Chicago: Open Court.

Wright, L. (1993). Remembering Satan, Part II. *The New Yorker* 69 (14), 54–76.

ADDITIONAL READINGS

Brown, D. (1995). Pseudomemories: The standard of science and standard of care in trauma treatment. *American Journal of Clinical Hypnosis* 37, 1–24.

Davies, J. M., and M. G. Frawley. (1994). *Treating the adult survivor of sexual abuse: A psychoanalytical perspective*. New York: Basic Books.

Gleaves, D. H. (1996). The evidence for "repression": An examination of Holmes (1990) and the implications for the recovered memory controversy. *Journal of Child Sexual Abuse* 5, 1–19.

Herman, J. L. (1992). *Trauma and recovery.* New York: Basic Books.

Lindsay, D. S., and J. D. Read. (1994). Psychotherapy and memories of childhood sexual abuse: A cognitive perspective. *Applied Cognitive Psychology* 8, 281–338.

Loftus, E. F., and K. Ketcham. (1994). *The myth of repressed memory: False memories and allegations of sexual abuse.* New York: St. Martin's Press.

Ofshe, R., and E. Watters. (1994). *Making monsters: False memories, psychotherapy, and sexual hysteria.* New York: Scribners.

Olio, K. (1996). Are 25% of clinicians using potentially risky therapeutic practices? A review of the logic and methodology of the Poole, Lindsay, et al. study. *Journal of Psychiatry & Law* 24, 277–98.

Olio, K., and W. Cornell. (1994). Making meaning not monsters: Reflections on the delayed memory controversy. *Journal of Child Sexual Abuse* 3, 77–94.

———. (1994). Truth in memory: Comments on Elizabeth Loftus's "Reality of repressed memory." *American Psychologist* 37, 442–43.

Pezdek, K., K. Finger, and D. Hodge. (1997). Planting false childhood memories: The role of event plausibility. *Psychological Science* 8, 437–41.

Salter, A. C. (1997). *Truth, lies, and sex offenders.* (Videotape No. 81492 of the series *Listening to Sex Offenders* available from Specialized Training Services, San Diego, CA. www.specializedtraining.com

Chapter 20

Reclaiming the Meanings of "Self-esteem"

Nayyar Javed and Nikki Gerrard

Jane[1] is a 45-year-old woman who is depressed and suffering from low self-esteem. She has been physically and emotionally abused by her husband for twenty years.

Marilyn is a 27-year-old student who has had to drop out of university because her self-esteem is so low she cannot function. She was sexually abused by an uncle from when she was age six through age twelve.

—Common descriptors from referrals to a
community-based mental health service

As practicing psychologists we have met many women whose presenting problem is "low self-esteem" (LSE). Some have been told they have "LSE," and some labeled themselves after having internalized this label from the self-esteem discourse from therapists or the media. They regard low self-esteem as their personal deficit and believe they need to change themselves. They identify their low self-esteem as a major cause of their anxiety and depression, whereas the real sources of their anxiety and depression are often abuse, oppression, or loss. Since abuse and oppression are external sources of anguish, for these women to be reinforced in the belief that the problem comes from within them is both misleading and damaging, often leading to more depression and shame.

"Self-esteem" refers to "the extent to which one values, prizes, approves, and likes oneself" (Blascovich and Tomaka 1991, 115). Valuing, prizing, and approving oneself does not occur in a social vacuum. Individuals *learn* from family and the wider society how to feel about themselves. Privileged and underprivileged groups, for instance, have different experiences that affect how they feel about themselves, because members of the latter group are by definition more oppressed than members of the former. This is not to say that members of marginalized groups have weaker systems of support or strength among themselves, for they often come together and resist oppressive treatment, as well as providing other important positive experiences for each other. Consider just two examples: rural women have described their opportunities to meet together and form a group identity as having profoundly positive effects on their health, including lowering depression and anxiety (Gerrard 2000); and in large meetings of women, such as the United Nations Conference on Women's Equality attended by one of us (NJ) in Beijing in 1995, women valued, prized, approved of, and liked themselves better as a result of *together* describing international and universal problems, developing solutions, and communicating those solutions to the UN and governments all over the world. But mistreatment of marginalized people by those who are privileged is damaging and certainly can lead to "low self-esteem." In *both* kinds of cases the level of an individual's "self-esteem" and depression and anxiety result from their different kinds of treatment by groups of people, whether their own or another. The collective self-concept is a significant determinant of, as Blascovich stated, valuing, prizing, approving, and liking oneself (Blascovich and Tomaka 1991). And both good and bad effects of treatment by one's own group or another one are virtually ignored in the current self-esteem literature.

There are many who benefit from the use of the label of "LSE" and the presentation of it as a problem that originates from the individual. First are perpetrators of physical, sexual, or emotional abuse. If the victim is diagnosed as having low self-esteem, the abuser's role in causing psychological harm is too often minimized or even ignored (Armstrong 1993). The focus on low self-esteem as the outcome of abuse, with consequent lack of focus on the *cause* of the abuse, has resulted in a huge market for the self-help industry, which capitalizes on the label of "LSE" to sell books, tapes, workshops, and other paraphernalia purportedly to assist the victim. (Of course, sometimes they are helpful, or sometimes they are helpful in some ways, but too often they leave the reader or participant believing that the problem of her LSE comes from within her.) "LSE" is a convenient term that has become a "catch-all" for professionals who look simplistically at clients' lives and do not address the many complexities associated with the label of "low self-esteem" or the social context in which the concept of self-esteem is embedded. The "LSE" label needs to be explored in a framework that includes the economic, political, and social context of women's lives.

Another beneficiary of the "LSE" concept is the global market economy, which depends on dichotomizing humanity and reinforcing the "otherness" of disempowered people, because this strategy makes their labor available at a lower cost. We have witnessed the development of many new mechanisms for constructing and perpetuating "otherness" (or treating people as objects), such as economic sanctions, limitation of access to technology and services for health, and so forth.[2] The "otherness" of women is a worldwide phenomenon and is a dominant theme in mainstream psychology. Men can be treated as "others," too, especially working-class, racialized men, but because they still have the power of patriarchy behind them, this article is focused on women, who are targeted, internationally and universally, because of sexism.

In our work with clients who are labeled with "LSE," we try to shift their focus from seeing themselves as people with "LSE" to people who have strengths that have enabled them to survive loss, abuse, or oppression. Reframing this is not easy, for two reasons. First, they continue to live in damaging systems, whether due to abuse, sexism, racism, ageism, poverty, or other forms of oppression, and it can be difficult to help them change social connections to help fill empty spaces left by losses; and second, their notion of themselves as the source of the problem continues to be reimposed on multiple levels, often including their interaction with other mental health practitioners.

Feminist scholars and researchers in the mental health field have begun to unpack "self-esteem" by identifying the problems in conceptualizing and measuring it (Chatham-Carpenter and DeFrancisco 1997). Lykes (1985; 1994) says that "self-esteem" is conceptualized within a Western context and reflects a Euro-centric bias. It is individualistic, classist, and, to some extent, capitalist. People who use "LSE" with an individualistic slant tend to focus on self-reliance and positive self-projection as the major features of self-esteem and to ignore both the good and the bad effects of groups. This focus tends to mask the salience of interdependence and the ability to relate to and with others as a source of self-esteem. Further, an assumption that this world is a level playing field is obvious in the traditional theories and conceptualizations of self-esteem. These assumptions reflect capitalist, colonialist, and masculinist biases because they are sustained by those who ignore the everyday lives of the disadvantaged.

As "others," women are locked in circumscribed social territories with clearly defined borders. Crossing these borders can be dangerous (Javed 1997), and the fear of these dangers has been totally obscured by the conceptualization of self-esteem. Groups and individuals struggling with this issue are not going to "esteem self" for independence and self-assertion. "Esteeming self" cannot be separated from survival, which may depend on interdependence and compliance with social expectations rather than on individualistic self-assertion. Members of privileged classes can more easily afford to focus on independence and material achievement for themselves, without needing to subordinate their own needs for the sake of survival of the family or the larger group. In contrast, subordination of personal needs in order to provide services, including emotional services, is expected of members of subordinate groups. That is reflected in the gender difference incorporated in tests of "self-esteem," which many clinicians use in deciding whether or not to apply the "LSE" label to patients. According to Rosenberg (1965), using these instruments one computes overall "self-esteem scores," but the designers of most of the scales based them on traditional expectations of males and on male samples and did not take into account what qualities of self women are taught to value (Stake 1992; Nugent 1994). As a result, women's scores tend to be low.

Chathan-Carpenter and DeFrancisco (1998, 472) asked women how they define "self-esteem" and what characteristics they associate with it. Their participants considered self-esteem as "much more complex" than it is popularly assumed to be and "seemed very aware that self-esteem is dynamic rather than static and that it varies according to the context." The women associated self-esteem with high levels of self-confidence, ability to express opinions, risk-taking in order to live fulfilling lives, concerns for others, and they especially considered concern for others as important in building self-confidence. However, this concern for others is not given credence in the labeling or measuring of "self-esteem" in the psychological literature.

When women are said to have "LSE," they tend to be regarded as deficient, and this renders invisible the strong things women have done. For instance, in the face of repression, "men retreat and . . . instead women come out in their traditional roles as nurturers and as protectors. . . . It is the women who negotiate with the security forces and administration" (Manchanda 1999, 30). For instance, Afghan women in refugee camps provided services to the sick and wounded, education to girls and boys, and income-generating opportunities to women, and under the Taliban regime, they took horrendous risks to support underground schools for girls and medical services for women (Gailani 1999). Jewish and Arab women and women in Rwanda and Burundi, respectively, come together actively to build peace. In 2000, the United Nations Security Council passed the groundbreaking Resolution 1325, an acknowledgment of women's incredible strength to take charge under the worst circumstances.

Women and members of other oppressed groups seem to survive oppression and treatment as inferior by developing and hanging on to a belief in our personal strength. We may or may not be aware of this belief, but we use it as a coping mechanism, as is evident in the superhuman tasks women complete and the interpersonal, familial, and social minefields we often negotiate without giving ourselves credit for it or even acknowledging to ourselves the strength, courage, and resilience it takes to do that. Women often shoulder burdens unquestioningly, needing to assume we are strong enough to cope with anything. When one is powerless to change one's circumstances, the belief that one can handle them can be comforting (Gerrard 1990). In consequence, convincing women that the solution to our problems lies in raising "self-esteem" is easy, because it fits into our view of self as capable of handling even life's hardest challenges: A so-called expert says that women have low self-esteem, we decide to raise ours, and we embark on that task. Unfortunately, many professionals who talk about patients with "LSE" fail to identify this belief and ignore the fact that it is a strength. The seductive nature of this discourse has made "LSE" a profitable commodity. Women consumers buy it, use it, believe it, without questioning how it is used to obscure who we are.

We believe that self-esteem requires nurturance and that many women are deprived of nurturing at various levels. For instance, Chesler (1994) points out that as girls, many women are starved all across the globe. Can "LSE" be attributed solely to individual factors when they are struggling for psychological and even physical survival? If the survival instinct is fundamental to psychological development, then the level of self-esteem depends on the level of security a woman feels, and lack of this security does not constitute an internal, individually caused problem.

Labeling often becomes a tool of social control of women (Caplan 1995), and the label "LSE" is used to control women; it obscures the sources of their oppression and renders invisible their strength and resilience. Any use of "self-esteem" as a label or a concept without these considerations does a major disservice not only to women but also to society as a whole. The label is at best uninformative and at worst dangerous. To disassociate self-esteem from the social context is to contemplate it abstractly and without meaning.

NOTES

1. All names have been changed, and circumstances are composites of real situations.

2. The topic of how "otherness" is constructed and perpetuated is extensive. Literature about racism provides a good analysis of this (Miles 1992).

REFERENCES

Armstrong, Louise. (1993). *And they call it help: The psychiatric policing of America's children.* Reading, MA: Addison-Wesley, 1993.

Blascovich, B. L., and J. Tomaka. (1991). Measures of self-esteem. Pp. 115–60 in J. P. Robinson, P. R. Shaver, and L. S. Wrightsman, eds. *Measures of personality and social psychological attitudes.* San Diego, CA: Academic Press.

Caplan, Paula J. (1995). *They say you're crazy: How the world's most powerful psychiatrists decide who's normal.* Reading, MA: Addison Wesley

Chatham-Carpenter, A. and V. DeFrancisco. (1998). Women construct self-esteem in their own terms: A feminist qualitative study. *Feminism and Psychology* 8, 467–89.

———. (1997). Pulling yourself up again: Women's choices and strategies for recovering and maintaining self-esteem. *Western Journal of Communication* 61, 164–87.

Chesler, P. (1994). Extracts from *Women and madness*. *Feminism and Psychology* 4, 261–67.

Gailani, F. (1999). History of political participation erased: The plight of Afghani women. Pp. 32–33 in International Alert's Conference Proceedings, *Women, violent conflict, and peacebuilding: Global perspective.* May 5–7.

Gerrard, Nikki. (1990). Racism and sexism in the mental health system: Voices of women of color. Unpublished Ph.D. dissertation. Ontario Institute for Studies in Education, University of Toronto.

Gerrard, Nikki, G. Russell, and the Saskatchewan Women's Agricultural Network. (2000*).* An exploration of health-related impacts of the erosion of agriculturally focused support programs for farm women in Saskatchewan. Unpublished manuscript.

Javed, N. S. (1997). Border crossing on a racist terrain. Pp 83–90 in M. Hill, ed. *More than a mirror: How clients influence therapists' lives.* New York: Haworth Press.

Lykes, M.B. (1994). Speaking against the silence: One Maya woman's exile and return. Pp. 97–114 in C. E. Franz and A. J. Stewart, eds. *Women creating lives: Identities, resilience, and resistance.* Boulder, CO: Westview Press.

———. (1985). Gender and individualistic vs. collective bases for notions about self. *Journal of Personality* 53, 356–83.

Manchanda, R. (1999). Trapped by extremism: Women in the Kashmiri conflict. Pp. 30–31 in International Alert's Conference Proceedings, *Women, violent conflict and peacebuilding: Global perspective.* May 5–7.

Miles, R. (1989). *Racism.* London and New York: Routledge.

Nugent, W. (1994). A differential validity study of the self-esteem rating scale. *Journal of Social Service Research* 19, 71–86.

Rosenberg, M. (1965). *Society and the adolescent self-image.* Princeton, NJ: Princeton University Press.

Stake, J. E. (1992). Gender differences and similarities in self-concept within everyday life context. *Psychology of Women Quarterly* 16, 349–63.

Chapter 21

Agoraphobia

Maureen McHugh and Lisa Cosgrove

AGORAPHOBIA DEFINED

The authors of the *Diagnostic and Statistical Manual of Mental Disorders* (*DSM IV-TR*: American Psychiatric Association 2000) acknowledge that agoraphobia is far more common in women than in men. They note that agoraphobia can include the experience of panic, the inability to travel freely, and the "irrational" fear of public places, but they present these experiences as forms of pathology that reside "in" patients. As a result, they fail to recognize the connections between agoraphobic reactions and the everyday experiences that make so many women feel unsafe. This failure severely limits therapists' ability to help women with these "symptoms."

It is also interesting to note that agoraphobia is not a "codable" *DSM* disorder *in and of itself* (APA 2000, 433). Where it appears in the manual, they list it under 300.22, Agoraphobia without a history of Panic Disorder; 300.01, Panic Disorder without Agoraphobia; and 300.21, Panic Disorder with Agoraphobia (APA 2000). In the last two categories, then, Agoraphobia (its presence or absence) is a primary *symptom* of something else, not a disorder on its own.

The *DSM* authors define Agoraphobia as "anxiety about being in places or situations from which escape might be difficult (or embarrassing) or in which help may not be available" (APA 2000, 432). The anxiety then leads to persistent avoidance whereby individuals restrict their behavior, thus impairing their ability to "travel to work or to carry *out homemaking responsibilities (e.g., grocery shopping, taking children to the doctor)*" (APA 2000, 432, emphasis added). Despite the seemingly gender neutral diagnostic criteria, homemaking activities are listed as one of the most significant domains in which behavior may be restricted, and both examples the *DSM* authors give

177

as indications of "impaired ability" are activities performed far more frequently by women. Interestingly, however, the *DSM IV-TR* authors make only a passing reference to an important epidemiological finding: Panic Disorder with Agoraphobia is diagnosed *three times as often* in women as it is in men (APA 2000, 436). Although no ratios are given, the *DSM IV-TR* also notes that Agoraphobia without History of Panic Disorder "is diagnosed *far more often in females* rather than males" (APA 2000, 442).

IMPLICATIONS FOR THE DIAGNOSTICIAN

> If a mental disorder reliably and stereotypically fits a narrow category of people, then we should be looking at what is wrong with the conditions of people in that category, not exclusively at their individual pathologies.
>
> C. Tavris, *The Mismeasure of Woman*, 186

The inclusion of a multiaxial system in the *DSM* in 1980 was heralded (by the *DSM* committee) as a "methodological innovation" insofar as it represented an attempt to increase the complexity and fullness of the picture of an individual's distress. However, including an axis to code psychosocial stressors does not do justice to the complex sociopolitical context in which behavior—"disordered" or not—is manifest. The fact that the overwhelming majority of individuals diagnosed with agoraphobia are women, and that difficulty going grocery shopping is provided as one of the main examples of how quality of life is diminished, reflects an underlying sexism. Women are diagnosed with agoraphobia if they restrict their travel to a significant degree or if their anxiety prevents them from going to work, but mental health professionals may pay greater attention to agoraphobic symptoms when women cannot perform their traditional roles. It is when women's anxieties inconvenience family members—when women can no longer grocery shop or chauffeur their children—that we assign a diagnosis and recommend an intervention for reducing their fears (McHugh 1996). Women who are afraid to go out alone at night unescorted or to work on Wall Street are not as likely to be regarded as suffering from irrational fear. Thus, gender-based expectations figure significantly in our assessments about the rationality or pathology of women's fears.

In contrast to traditional approaches, advocates of a feminist perspective on agoraphobia encourage clinicians to regard agoraphobia (and other sex-linked disorders) not as an individual pathology but in the context of women's experience in general. A number of scholars have argued persuasively that the gender-role training of women leads to their socialization into a prescribed role that promotes fearfulness and agoraphobic behavior (Brehoney 1983;

Chambless 1982; Fodor 1992; Franks 1986). Seen in this light, the assumption that the agoraphobic individual's fears are unrealistic or irrational needs to be closely examined; the agoraphobic's anxiety is unrealistic only to the extent that the streets are objectively safe and public places are comfortable for women (Gelfond 1991). In fact, there is considerable evidence that women generally restrict their behavior and are expected to restrict their behavior because they fear rape (Rozee 2004). Fodor (1992) notes that, following rape, some women reported fearfulness and panic. Women's fear of and previous experience with men's violence may result in anxiety, depression, stress reactions, and a reluctance to go out in public. Agoraphobia has developed in teens as a reaction to physical abuse (Flisher, Kramer, Hoven, and Greenwald 1997) and was an early precursor of Post-traumatic Stress Disorder in rape victims (Darves-Bornoz, Lepine, Choquet, Berger, Degiovanni, and Gaillard 1998). Based on the research demonstrating that marital conflict is a precursor of agroraphobia, McHugh (1996, 2004) has hypothesized that a significant number of agoraphobic women may be battered. Despite years of research about relationship conflict and distress and about patterns of (husbands') dominance and (wives') dependence, researchers have not examined the incidence of battering or abuse among individuals with agoraphobia (see McHugh 2004). What has been found is that marital discord increases as the wife's agoraphobia abates (Hafner 1984). Published case studies (e.g., Hafner 1982) show that the marital interactions of recovering agoraphobic women and their husbands involve jealousy, interrogation, and surveillance. These descriptions correspond to the experiences reported for battered women (McHugh 2004). Unfortunately, we do not have the requisite quantitative or qualitative data that would help clinicians understand the etiological role that domestic violence may play in the development of agoraphobia, because even in the research documenting marital conflict for women with agoraphobia, questions about violence have not been asked. Psychologists who do not consider these factors may be inadvertently contributing to the possible harm inflicted on agoraphobic women.

Interestingly, when Gelfond (1991) compared women diagnosed as agoraphobic with highly independent and average women, she found that 55 percent of the average women scored at or near the clinical range for agoraphobia. Clearly, women diagnosed with agoraphobia share characteristics and behavior with much of the female population. Thus, it is imperative that clinicians develop awareness of the pervasive and realistic fears that are parts of women's everyday lives. A focus on intraindividual factors, regarding agoraphobia as a discrete disorder residing in the person, undermines a clinician's ability to recognize and appreciate the sociocultural context in which anxiety is manifest.

RECOMMENDATIONS

Clinicians must recognize the limits of the *DSM IV-TR*'s intra-individual focus and offer a corrective to its sexist underpinnings with regard to the diagnosis of agoraphobia. Although the literature on domestic violence and agoraphobia has not traditionally intersected (agoraphobic women are not typically questioned about violence, and battered women are not typically asked if they have agoraphobic symptoms), it should become standard practice to include questions about violence when gathering psychosocial histories of individuals with agoraphobia. Women with histories of being targets of violence should be given the opportunity to integrate that experience into their treatment for agoraphobia. In other words, the therapist must not assume that past or present violence is a separate treatment issue. Also, although psychopharmacological interventions are frequently used in the treatment of anxiety, the prescribing provider must think carefully about the appropriateness and ethical issues involved in the use of drug therapies for agoraphobic women, especially if a woman has been subjected to violence. For example, benzodiazapines may provide symptom relief, but in prescribing them, we may be complicit with the gendered power dynamics that allow for the development of fear-based behavior in women. In addition, in light of the fact that agoraphobia is considered a female disorder, clinicians need to be aware of a tendency to overlook or dismiss agoraphobic behavior in men.

In terms of the possible relationship between agoraphobia and battering, it is imperative that clinicians working in battered women's shelters be trained to assess for agoraphobic behavior. Women should be given the opportunity to answer open-ended questions and/or symptom checklists for agoraphobic behavior during their initial shelter interview. An important area for future research includes the systematic assessment of the incidence of violence in marriages and partnerships of women diagnosed with agoraphobia. When the relationship involves serious conflict and possible violence, the husband should not be engaged as a co-therapist or coach. Finally, we all need to work toward the development of public spaces that are free of intimidation, ridicule, and violence so that women's fear of public places would indeed be unwarranted.

REFERENCES

American Psychiatric Association. (2000). *Diagnostic and statistical manual of mental disorders-IV-TR*. Washington, DC.

Brehoney, K. A. (1983). Women and agoraphobia: A case for the etiological significance of the feminine sex role stereotype. Pp. 112–28 in V. Franks and E. D. Rothblum, eds. *The stereotyping of women: Its effects on mental health*. New York: Springer.

Brown, T. A., and T. F. Cash. (1990). The phenomenon of non-clinical panic: Parameters of panic, fear, and avoidance. *Journal of Anxiety Disorders* 4, 15–29.

Chambless. D. (1982). Characteristics of agoraphobes. Pp. 1–8 in D. L. Chambless and A. J. Goldstein, eds. *Agoraphobia: Multiple perspectives on theory and treatment*. New York: Wiley.

Fodor, I. G. (1992). The agoraphobic woman: From anxiety neurosis to panic disorder. Pp. 177–205 in. L. Brown and M. Ballou, eds. *Personality and psychopathology: Feminist reappraisals*. New York: Guilford.

Franks, V. (1986). Sex role stereotyping and diagnosis of psychopathology. *Women and Therapy*. Special issue: The dynamics of feminist therapy 5, 219–32.

Gelfond. M. (1991). Reconceptualizing agoraphobia: A case study of epistemological bias in clinical research. *Feminism & Psychology* 1, 247–62.

McHugh, M. C. (1996/2004). A feminist approach to agoraphobia: Challenging traditional views of women at home. Pp. 339–57 in J. C. Chrisler, C. Golden, and P. D. Rozee, eds. *Lectures on the psychology of women*. New York: McGraw Hill.

Tavris, C. (1993). *The mismeasure of woman*. New York: Simon & Schuster.

Chapter 22

Depression in Women

Sarah McSweeney

Research suggests that women suffer from depression more than men (e.g., Heneghan 2000; Jack 1999a; Lerman 1996; McGrath, Keita, Strickland, and Russo 1990). In fact, several researchers have cited a rate of depression twice as high for women as for men in the United States and in most Western societies (Bhatia and Bhatia 1999; Jack 1991; Preboth 2000).

There is considerable debate regarding the true difference between men and women's rates of depression, but, to date, researchers have not found a satisfactory explanation for this gender difference (Bhatia and Bhatia 1999; Jack 1999a; Kornstein 1997; Stoppard 1993). One explanation is that depression is considered an illness more consistent with femininity than masculinity. This view is used to explain why women are more willing than men to acknowledge and discuss their depressive symptoms. According to this argument, if men are masking their true feelings, they may be at least as depressed as women but not reporting their conditions. However, careful review of the current research suggests that, although social norms may grant women more permission to talk about their problems, women in Western societies also have greater vulnerability than men to depression (Heneghan 2000; Silverstein and Perlick 1995; Stoppard 1993).

Although some women, like some men, may become depressed due to physical/chemical factors, social factors and gender-role influences are seen as the most salient contributors to women's vulnerability (Jack 1991; Joiner, Coyne, and Blalock 1999; Miller 1986; Stoppard 1993; Women and Mental Health Committee 1987). The American Psychological Association's National Task Force on Women and Depression (McGrath et al. 1990) identified possible contributors to women's high rate of depression, including reproductive events, family roles and intimate relationships, work roles, sexual and physical abuse, and poverty. Major points of the task force's report regarding these risk factors include:

- Women are at greater risk for depression due to a number of social, economic, biological, and emotional factors and therefore must be studied from a biopsychosocial perspective.
- The percentage of sexual and physical abuse of females is very high. Estimates suggest that two to three million women in the United States are physically assaulted by male partners each year and that 21–34% of all women will be assaulted by an intimate male partner as an adult (Browne and Bassuk 1997). Browne and Bassuk (1997) state that this research, like other national survey findings, likely represents minimum estimates.
- Marriage confers a greater protective advantage on men than on women. Women in unhappy marriages were three times as likely to be depressed as married men and single women (McGrath et al. 1990; Steinem 1993). Mothers of young children are also found to be highly vulnerable to depression, with the presence of additional children in the house being correlated with more reported depression.
- Poverty is labeled "a direct pathway to depression" (McGrath et al. 1990, xii). In 1995, the poverty rate for female-headed families with children under eighteen was 44.5%, which was six times the rate for married couple families (7.8%) (U.S. Census Bureau 1996). Over half of Black (56.1%) and Hispanic (58.2%) female-headed households live on incomes below the poverty level (Salomon, Bassuk, and Brooks 1996).
- Racialized women, elderly women, chemically dependent women, lesbians, and professional women are high-risk groups for depression, requiring special attention and support.

For decades, traditional strategies aimed at improving women's mental health have not included consideration of the principal link between women's health and their actual social circumstances, and thus it was often assumed that their depression was intrapsychic in origin.

In Western societies, autonomy and individuation are regarded as signs of "maturity," but girls and women are socialized to care about human connections (Jordan et al. 1991). Caring about feelings and relationships is considered antithetical to autonomy and individuation, is often mislabeled "dependency," and is regarded as pathological (Siegel 1988). Interpersonal connection is devalued in a patriarchal culture, where boys are made to feel that they must separate from their mothers to become men, and traditionally masculine socialized behavior is held up as the norm for all (Miller 1986; Surrey 1984).

Researchers who focus on women's developmental issues, such as some of those from the Stone Center (Jordan et al. 1991; Miller and Stiver 1997) and Rachel Josefowitz Siegel (1988), say that as a result of socialization many women's sense of self is relational, and thus relationships to others are integral to the identity of many women. This is why many women feel so threatened when they feel alienated from others. Their developmental experience has been "a move from attachment to continued connection, always developing in the context of relationships" (Stiver 1984, 7). Many women, therefore, experience society's goal of "independence" as lonely and isolating. Women's positive feelings/attitudes about connection are viewed as detrimental in the workplace because they seem counter to the revered qualities of ambition, drive, and competitiveness. Wanting to succeed both at work and in their relationships, women perform delicate balancing acts that are often stressful, and the resulting sense of powerlessness and hopelessness can lead to depression.

Listening to what women need and value is imperative for understanding how to treat them when they are depressed (Jack 1999a; 1999b). Dana Crowley Jack (1999b) explains that clinicians must hear how social factors (such as quality of relationships and beliefs about gender roles and responsibilities) are structured in their clients' thoughts and how these factors affect depressive conflict. For example, women frequently feel that they must minimize their needs to preserve harmony in their close relationships. They understand being "good" to mean self-sacrificing, and when they sacrifice so much that they feel less valued, angry, and no closer to the significant others in their lives, they become depressed (Jack 1999a).

Understanding the importance of hearing women's stories, therefore, is crucial to being able to diagnose their ailments accurately. Too often women's reports of problems are dismissed as behavior expected of women (e.g., crying, self-blame, sadness), who are viewed as weak or somaticizing (Preboth 2000; Stoppard 1993). Based on misinformation, these sex differences in socialization render diagnosis of the nature of the problem, and thus intervention, less effective. Even the authors of the most recent edition of the most widely used diagnostic manual, the *Diagnostic and Statistical Manual of Mental Disorders* (DSM), fail, like their predecessors, to focus much on the role that contextual factors play in women's depression. With each new edition of the manual, they claim that they have introduced large numbers of important changes. For instance, in the current edition of the *DSM*, in a special appendix titled "Highlights of Changes in *DSM-IV Text Revision*," the authors list at great length changes they made between the previous edition and the current one. With respect to depression, they take the positive step of pointing out that not all sadness following childbirth should be regarded as a mental disorder. This is encouraging because it allows room for conscientious therapists to consider a contextual factor; that is, a certain amount of sadness and fear are understandable reactions to the isolation in which so many North American women find themselves postpartum. However, they continue to ignore sex-differential contextual factors by using the same diagnostic criteria for depression for both sexes, even though women with depression more frequently experience guilt, anxiety, increased sleep, appetite, weight gain, and co-morbid eating problems (Bhatia and Bhatia 1999). Furthermore, Lopez and Guarnaccia (2000) argue that the *DSM* does not adequately reflect the context of cultural differences, keeping differences in culture and gender marginalized rather than infused throughout the *DSM*'s presentation of all disorders among all people.

In a *Harvard Mental Health Letter* article, "Women and Depression," an unnamed author highlights the importance of context as it relates to depression, stating that despite gains in the field, "unmet needs remain" (Miller 2004, 4) and recommending that more attention be given to the effects of sex and gender in clinical trials, to the study of genetic and hormonal influences on depression, and to the kinds of stresses that are linked to depression for women. The article includes a call for better screening tests, easier access to services, and an increase in the development of preventive measures for children of depressed mothers. This article is tremendously important. Indeed, unless our professional society undergoes a diagnostic paradigm shift from strict classification to a more contextualized approach, it is unlikely that newer knowledge about the psychology of women will ever be fully integrated into the understanding of the nature and causes of women's depression.

REFERENCES

American Psychiatric Association. (2000). *Diagnostic and statistical manual of mental disorders-IV-TR*. Washington, DC.

———. (1994). *Diagnostic and statistical manual of mental disorders-IV.* Washington, DC.

Bhatia, S. C., and S. K. Bhatia, S. K. (1999). Depression in women: Diagnostic and treatment considerations. *American Family Physician* 60 (1), 225–34 and 239–40.

Brown, A., and S. Bassuk. (1997). Intimate violence in the lives of homeless and poor housed women: Prevalence and patterns in an ethnically diverse sample. *American Journal of Orthopsychiatry* 67 (2), 261–78.

Jack, D. C. (1999a). Silencing the self: Inner dialogues and outer realities. Pp. 221–46 in J. Coyne and T. Joiner, eds. *The interactional nature of depression:*

Advances in interpersonal approaches. Washington, DC: American Psychological Association.

———. (1999b). Ways of listening to depressed women in qualitative research: Interview techniques and analysis. *Canadian Psychology* 40 (2), 91–101.

———. (1991). *Silencing the self: Women and depression*. Cambridge, MA: Harvard University Press.

Joiner, T., J. C. Coyne, and K. J. Blalock. (1999). On the interpersonal nature of depression: Overview and synthesis. Pp. 3–19 in J. Coyne and T. Joiner, eds. *The interactional nature of depression: Advances in interpersonal approaches*. Washington, DC: American Psychological Association.

Jordan, J., A. G. Kaplan, J. B. Miller, I. P. Stiver, and J. L. Surrey. (1991). *Women's growth in connection: Writings from the Stone Center.* New York: Guilford.

Kornstein, S. G. (1997). Gender differences in depression: Implications for treatment. *Journal of Clinical Psychiatry* 58 (Suppl. 15), 12–18.

Lerman, H. (1996). Pigeonholing women's misery: A history and critical analysis of the psychodiagnosis of women in the twentieth century. New York: Basic Books.

Lopez, S. R., and P.J.J. Guarnaccia. (2000). Cultural psychopathology: Uncovering the social world of mental illness. *Annual Review of Psychology* 51, 571–98.

McGrath, E., G. P. Keita, B. R. Strickland, and N. F. Russo, eds. (1990). *Women and depression: Risk factors and treatment issues. Final report of the American Psychological Association Task Force on Women and Depression*. Washington, DC: American Psychological Association.

Miller, J. B. (1976). *Toward a new psychology of women.* Boston: Beacon Press.

Miller, J. B., and I. Stiver. (1997). *The healing connection: How women form relationships in therapy and in life.* Boston: Beacon Press.

Miller, M. C., ed. (2004, May). Women and depression. *Harvard Mental Health Letter 20* (11).

Salomon, A., S. Bassuk, and M. Brooks. (1996). Patterns of welfare use among poor and homeless women. *American Journal of Orthopsychiatry* 66 (4), 510–25.

Siegel, R. J. (1988). Women's "dependency" in a male-centered value system: Gender-based values regarding dependency and independence. *Women and Therapy* 7, 113–23.

Silverstein, B., and D. Perlick. (1995). *The cost of competence: Why inequity causes depression, eating disorders, and illness in women.* New York: Oxford University Press.

Steinem, G. (1993). *A revolution from within: A book of self-esteem.* Boston: Little, Brown & Co.

Stiver, I. (1984). The meaning of "dependency" in female-male relationships. Work in progress paper #11. Wellesley, MA: Stone Center Working Paper Series, Wellesley College.

Stoppard, J. M. (1993). Gender, psychosocial factors, and depression. Pp. 121–29 in Philippe Cappeliez and Robert John Flynn, eds. *Depression and the social environment: Research and intervention with neglected populations*. Montreal: McGill-Queen's University Press.

Surrey, J. (1984). The "self-in-relation": A theory of women's development. Work in progress paper #13. Wellesley, MA: Stone Center Working Paper Series, Wellesley College.

U.S. Census Bureau. (1996). *Current Population Reports*, series P60–194, Poverty in the United States: 1995. Washington, DC: U.S. Government Printing Office.

Women and Mental Health Committee. (1987). *Women and mental health in Canada: Strategies for change*. Toronto, Canada: Canadian Mental Health Association.

Chapter 23

The "Eating-Disordered" Patient

Judith R. Rabinor

I am sitting in my office with Amanda. She is twenty-one years old and has struggled with anorexia and bulimia since she was twelve. Although Amanda weighs eighty-nine pounds, she is plagued with "fat" feelings and is unable to eat. This is our second session. She is filling me in on all she has learned in her three previous courses of being a psychotherapy patient. Her eating disorder developed when her parents divorced. Following her father's departure and the economic decline that ensued, she and her mother went on a diet. In the beginning, both gained a sense of empowerment and hope, which were short-lived. Her mother proceeded to gain fifty pounds, and Amanda developed a life-threatening case of anorexia. "This is my way of telling my father to fuck off and separating from my overbearing mother," Amanda tells me. As she speaks, I become increasingly distressed, frustrated, angered, and hopeless. Amanda is simply feeding back what she has learned from our culture about parents supposedly being responsible for all of their children's problems, including eating disorders.

This thumbnail sketch speaks volumes about how sexist values lead therapists to silence women's voices, damage their bodies, create pejorative psychiatric diagnoses, and then blame mothers, while ignoring the role of the culture in creating these problems. The enormous pressure on women to achieve an unachievable standard of thinness leads to a host of eating disorders—obesity at one end of the spectrum and anorexia and bulimia nervosa at the other—which affect between five and ten times as many women as men and are the only psychiatric diagnoses (other than Premenstrual Dysphoric Disorder) to be so disproportionately to applied women and men (www .NationalEatingDisordersAssociation.org; Shisslak, Crago, and Estes 1995). Despite a growing consciousness of the damaging effects of dieting, the vast majority of women of all ages and backgrounds continue to diet and judge their own bodies harshly.

From birth, little girls absorb societal messages that to be valued as females, they must be impossibly thin. From observing their mothers' lives, they learn that a woman's appearance is often the most obvious or the only socially condoned form of power openly afforded her. In perfecting their bodies by dieting, daughters mirror their mothers' attempts to be powerful. And it is poignant that when a woman does become consumed by fear about how her body looks and is so afraid it will not be perfect that she can no longer accurately see how she looks, she may be diagnosed with Body Dysmorphic Disorder (BDD) (even if she does not develop serious eating problems). The BDD label carries the implication that the problem comes from within her. Indeed, under the BDD listing in *DSM-IV-TR* the only caveat is that one should not assign this diagnosis if the person has another mental illness (American Psychiatric Association 2000), but there is no mention of the role played by a society obsessed with women's appearance in causing distress. Although dieting does not cause eating disorders, starving is a precipitant of bingeing, often the first step in developing anorexia, bulimia, and obesity.

Amanda's experience in therapy reflects a worrisome practice of some therapists who ignore the role that cultural expectations play in the development of eating disorders, implying that such disorders have only intrapsychic origins and are passed down from neurotic, dysfunctional mothers to their daughters. This approach furthers another sexist trend: mother-blaming.

We live in a culture that promotes rather than prevents eating and body image disorders and then blames the sufferers and their mothers. Therapists have often blamed mothers as a matter of course (Caplan 2000), failing to account for the social context in which a girl's or a woman's control over her appearance is often the most obvious or the only socially condoned form of power available to her. Generations of women have struggled with female powerlessness passed down from mother to daughter that lives on in the present generation in the symptoms of anorexia and bulimia, today's "chains of human misery" (Bassoff 1991).

Mothers who diet need to be understood in the context of their cultural milieu. Referring to centuries of gender-specific arrangements that have given rise to economic dependence and inequality, sexual violence, and emotional and physical subordination of females (all precursors of eating disorders), Jean Baker Miller (1976) reminds us that blaming mothers allows us to ignore how society has restricted women.

Throughout time, different roles and expectations have been attached to gender. Males have been reinforced for their achievements, while females have been praised for being accommodating and attractive. Although beauty has always been a woman's most powerful tool, today beauty is defined by an *unachievable* number on the weight scale, and this has fueled a relentless pursuit of thinness and spawned an epidemic of eating disorders.

In striving to "perfect" her body by dieting, the eating-disordered girl or woman may indeed be mirroring attempts by her mother or other women to be powerful, but therapists using a feminist reformulation will broaden this lens rather than criticizing the mother as though the problem began with her. It is a reflection of an ongoing, sexist preoccupation with women's thinness that some mothers either exemplify this preoccupation or actively urge their daughters to diet persistently. Mothers who feel negatively about their own bodies cannot help but communicate their body image dissatisfaction to their daughters, who internalize the powerlessness and self-deprecation they observe. Motivated by a desire to remain connected to their mothers, daughters remain consciously or unconsciously loyal to their mothers' values and lifestyles.

To understand each person who suffers with eating problems, a therapist must have a broad lens. She must be alert to the cultural pressures that create, encourage, and perpetuate eating disorders, while remaining carefully attuned to the ways each person plays out unique psychological issues in a battle with food and struggles with the body. Actively engaging the father as well as the mother in therapy affirms the importance of relating to *both* parents. The therapist can help all family members appreciate how women are harmed by the norm of extreme thinness, how the drive to fit that norm damages their bodies and their relationship, and how they can all support each other in challenging the norm. Through healing her relationships with her parents, a daughter expands her capacity to develop healing connections with others — ultimately a source of strength, growth, and power.

REFERENCES

American Psychiatric Association (2000). *Diagnostic and statistical manual of mental Disorders-IV-TR*. Washington, D.C.
Bassoff, E. (1991). *Mothering ourselves*. New York: Dutton.
Miller, J. B. (1976). *Toward a new psychology of women*. Boston: Beacon Press.

BIBLIOGRAPHY

Benjamin, J. (1988). *The bonds of love*. New York: Pantheon.
Bloom, C., A. Gitter, S. Gutwill, L. Kogel, and L. Zaphiropoulos. (1994). *Eating problems: A feminist psychoanalytic treatment model*. New York: Basic Books.

192 *Judith R. Rabinor*

Brown, L. M., and C. Gilligan. (1992). *Meeting at the crossroads: Psychological theory and women's development.* Cambridge, MA: Harvard University Press.

Brownell, K. D., and J. Rodin. (1994). The dieting maelstrom: Is it possible and desirable to lose weight? *American Psychologist* 49, 781–91.

Caplan, P. (2000). *Don't blame mother: Mending the mother-daughter relationship.* New York: Routledge.

Chernin, K. (1985). *The obsession: Reflections on the tyranny of slenderness.* New York: Harper & Row.

Gilligan, C. (1982). *In a different voice: Psychological theory and women's development.* Cambridge, MA: Harvard University Press.

Hancock, E. (1989). *The girl within.* New York: Ballantine.

Havas, E., and D. Bonnar. (1999). Therapy with adolescents and families: The limits of parenting. *American Journal of Family Therapy* 27, 121–35.

Jordan, J., A. Kaplan, J. B. Miller, I. Stiver, and J. Surrey. (1991). *Women's growth in connection.* New York: Guilford Press.

Miller, J. B., and I. P. Stiver. (1997). *The healing connection.* Boston: Beacon Press.

Orbach, S. (1986). *Hunger strike.* New York: Norton

——. (1982). *Fat is a feminist issue II.* New York: Berkley Books.

——. (1978). *Fat is a feminist issue.* New York: Paddington Press.

Rabinor, J. (2002). *A starving madness: Tales of hunger, hope, and healing in psychotherapy.* Carlsbad, CA: Gurze Press.

——. (2000). Collaborating with parents. *AABA Newsletter* (summer).

——. (1993). Mothers, daughters, and eating disorders: Honoring the mother-daughter relationship. Pp. 272–87 in P. Fallon, M. Katzman, and S. Wooley, eds. *Feminist perspectives on eating disorders.* New York: Guilford Press.

Shisslak, C. M., M. Crago, and L. S. Estes. (1995). The spectrum of eating disturbances. *International Journal of Eating Disorders* 18 (3), 209–19.

Siegel, M., J. Brisman, and M. Weinschel. (1997). *Surviving an eating disorder: Strategies for families, friends, and loved ones.* New York: Harper Perennial.

Stice, E. (1994). Review of the evidence for a sociocultural model of bulimia nervosa and an exploration of the symptomatology: An examination of mediation mechanisms. *Journal of Abnormal Psychology* 103, 836–40.

Surrey, J. (1991). Eating patterns as a reflection of women's development. Pp. 237–50 in Jordan et al., eds. *Women's growth in connection.* New York: Guilford Press.

Women's Health Advocate Newsletter. (December 1997), 4, wellwoman@barnard.columbia.edu.

Zerbe, K. (1993). *The body betrayed.* Washington, DC: American Psychiatric Press.

Chapter 24

The Fine Line between Clinical and Subclinical Anorexia

Emily Cohen

Although there is understandable concern about psychiatric overdiagnosis, multitudes of people cry out for help and do not receive it. They deserve help and support, and they should not have to be labeled "mentally ill" in order to get it. Not only those in the "abnormal" range need and deserve treatment but also a whole category of others who could greatly benefit from receiving help and support as well. An extraordinary amount of information is available regarding eating disorders, but little research is available about the actual diagnostic process. One usually comes to medical or psychological attention when a family member, friend, or a doctor finally recognizes that there is a problem, usually only after the person has lost significant weight. As a result, the eating problems of countless, suffering people go undetected, so there is no reliable estimate of those with subclinical eating difficulties. Like all diagnostic labels, "eating disorder" (ED) is a construct, and it is difficult to define "normal" eating, due to the frequency of dieting in Western society and people's ability to hide or dismiss problems early on. The way a patient is regarded depends on the clinician's subjective judgments, and the ED term incorrectly suggests a clear-cut dichotomy between mental illness and mental health (Fernald and Gettys 1980). In fact, at least some phenomena that are called "disorders" blend into common human experiences, making it hard to determine who needs help, professional or otherwise.

The authors of the *Diagnostic and Statistical Manual of Mental Disorders-IV-TR* selected four criteria for "anorexia nervosa": "(A) Refusal to maintain body weight at or above a minimally normal weight for age and height (e.g., weight loss leading to maintenance of body weight less than 85% of that expected, or failure to make expected weight gain during period of growth, leading to body weight less than 85% of that expected). (B) An intense fear of gaining weight or becoming fat, even though underweight.

(C) A disturbance in the way in which one's body weight or shape is experienced, undue influence of body weight or shape on self-evaluation, or denial of the seriousness of the current low body weight. (D) In postmenarcheal females, amenorrhea, i.e., the absence of at least three consecutive menstrual cycles" (American Psychiatric Association 2000, 589). The *DSM-IV-TR* criteria for bulimia nervosa are: "(A) Recurrent episodes of binge eating. An episode of binge eating is characterized by both of the following: (1) eating, in a discrete period of time (e.g., within any 2-hour period), an amount of food that is definitely larger than what most people would eat during a similar period of time and under similar circumstances. (2) a sense of lack of control over eating during the episode (e.g., feeling that one cannot stop eating or control what or how much one is eating). (B) Recurrent inappropriate compensatory behavior in order to prevent weight gain, such as self-induced vomiting, misuse of laxatives, diuretics, enemas, or other medications, fasting, or excessive exercise. (C) The binge eating and inappropriate compensatory behaviors both occur, on average, at least twice a week for 3 months. (D) Self-evaluation is unduly influenced by body shape and weight. (E) The disturbance does not occur exclusively during episodes of anorexia nervosa" (APA 2000, 594). The focus of this chapter is on anorexia, but many similar concerns about diagnosis of anorexia apply to bulimia. Problems can arise when one relies solely on these strict criteria; the criteria can be too exclusive, making it easy to miss significant problems. The *DSM* authors fail to acknowledge other significant features of eating difficulties, and they fail to recognize that not everyone who suffers will fit their criteria.

The term "subclinical eating disorder" will be used to describe problematic eating patterns that do not fit *DSM-IV-TR* descriptions. This would include people with eating problems whose symptoms fail to reach the severity level specified in the *DSM*, many of whom will eventually meet those criteria (Herzog, Hopkins, and Burns 1993). People with subclinical anorexia might not be sufficiently emaciated to meet the *DSM* criterion but might exhibit problematic eating habits, ways of thinking, self-criticism, and physical health deficiencies.

The National Institute of Mental Health reports that an estimated 0.5 to 3.7 percent of females suffer from anorexia nervosa in their lifetime, but this figure includes only those who fit the *DSM* diagnosis. The mortality rate of anorexics is about twelve times higher than the annual death rate due to all causes of death among females ages fifteen to twenty-four in the general population (Spearing 2001). In a study of 682 undergraduate women, Mintz and Betz (1988) found that, although 3 percent of women were diagnosable as "bulimic" according to the *DSM*, an astonishing 61 percent had intermediate eating problems; only 33 percent displayed "normal" eating habits, defined as three balanced meals a day. In that study, 82 percent of women reported daily dieting, defined as vigilance about food intake, and 33 percent admitted to serious forms of weight control, such as purging and substantial food restriction. More recently, Tylka and Subich (1999) found that large percentages of high school and college women display similar behavior patterns: 59 percent skip meals frequently, 37 percent significantly restrict their dietary intake, 7 percent use laxatives, 6.6 percent use diuretics, and 5 percent vomit after eating in order to control their weight. People located at different points on the wide, continuous dimension of disordered eating differ in degree, not kind.

Nearly every woman in industrialized society has been on a diet at some point in her life (Horwitz 2002). Watching one's weight by being fully aware of what is consumed, concern about body size, and relentless attempts to change one's body have been deemed "normal" by American society (Polivy and Herman 1987; Mintz and Betz 1988). Food restriction is often seen in a positive light, and one is frequently inundated with compliments after losing weight. Western culture is a breeding ground for anorexia; thinness has become associated with autonomy, success, and especially beauty. Because extreme standards of attractiveness are nearly impossible for the average individual to achieve, what actually is "normal" is often mistakenly seen as overweight, and this can trigger disordered eating behavior (Polivy and Herman 1987). Concerns about weight are not causes for alarm unless they are pervasive and severe. On college campuses, there is a strikingly high incidence of eating problems (Klemchuk, Hutchinson, and Frank 1990; Kitsantas, Gilligan, and Kamata 2003; Hart and Kenny 1997), with 60 percent of college women saying they engage in dysfunctional eating behavior, such as frequent dieting and avoiding particular foods, and 70 percent of those using extreme measures to control their weight (Tylka and Subich 2002).

Few researchers have considered the concept of a continuum of eating problems (Mintz and Betz 1988; Schmidt 2000; Cooley and Toray 2001), although Franko and Omori (1999) found support for the existence of a disordered eating spectrum, with "dieters-at-risk" at one end and "non-dieters" at the other. Individuals who self-report eating-disordered behavior have greater psychological distress than those who fall at the "normal" end of the continuum (Holt and Espelage 2002). There are many shared characteristics found in those with any eating problems, including resistance to maintaining body weight (with varying success), intense fear of being fat, extreme dissatisfaction with one's body, and perceptual disturbance of body shape and weight. Even for many who do not meet the *DSM* criteria, eating is an obsession; one cannot be too thin. Because of their weakening bodies, people who diet chronically can damage their health even before they meet *DSM* criteria. For many, when the problems are finally addressed, it is often too late; they are fully consumed by extreme and harmful eating behavior. By the time most individuals are brought to professional attention, their average weight is 25–30 percent below "normal" (Hsu 1990). Because treatment is most successful when administered early, treating subclinical eating problems immediately can minimize the chance that one will plummet into a full-fledged, irreversible problem (Polivy and Herman 1987; Herzog, Dorer, and Keel 1999; Spearing 2001).

Polivy and Herman (1987) attempted to differentiate between "a person with anorexia" and "an average dieter." According to them, a dieter aspires to achieve the positive goal of improved appearance and health, whereas the person with anorexia suffers from severe body and cognitive distortions. Although casual dieters and people with disordered eating share concerns about weight and appearance and a drive for thinness, the distorted body image, depression, and problems with control and self-esteem are confined to a more restricted segment of the population (Polivy and Herman 1987). People diagnosed with anorexia and those who frequently count calories and monitor their weight were found not to differ on several eating-related scales.

The person who has sub-*DSM* problems struggles with the confusion of suffering but not suffering enough to get help, certainly not help for which health insurance pays. Unfortunately, insurance does not cover nutritional counseling or preventive measures but only the treatment deemed necessary if one meets *DSM* criteria. Clinicians who depend more on codified systems than on the amount the person suffers disregard the fact that each individual suffers in a unique way. How much suffering need one experience in order to cross the line from a subclinical problem to a "clear mental disorder"? In the *DSM*, no distinction is made between someone with zero symptoms of anorexia and someone with only three of the four in their list (Mintz, O'Halloran, Mulholland, and Schneider 1997). A person who binges and purges between one and seven times a month is not bulimic, according to the *DSM-IV-TR* (2000) criteria for bulimia. Does the eighth purge make a significant difference? Similarly, how did the *DSM* authors decide that a body weight below 85 percent is abnormal? The *DSM* does not include guidelines about what is a "normal" weight, so clinicians use varying standards or may estimate what a person should weigh. A person displaying anorexic tendencies who maintains her weight at 85 percent of what the *DSM* authors indicate is normal would not meet the requirements for the diagnosis. In an interview (2002), a twenty-year-old college student who has struggled with chronic dieting for three years says she has had "rigid food rituals about the amount I ate, compensating exercise, and extreme anxiety about gaining weight. Even though I lost twenty pounds in less than two months, my weight never dropped below normal, and my doctor never formally recognized my condition. No one realized how much I suffered, including me."

Patients seeking treatment for a complaint that results from eating problems may be assessed and treated only for purely physical problems. For example, a not-yet-underweight patient who is consistently lightheaded from malnourishment is often subjected to a medical examination, perhaps for anemia or a neural or optic problem, but not investigated for serious eating problems. Similarly, one might seek treatment for a psychiatric symptom such as depression, because malnourishment can cause depression and other negative emotions (Wilcox and Stattler 1996). The college student says defiantly, "How could I have a problem? I'm only 5'5". The scale has never dropped below 110 pounds, my BMI [body mass index] never went below 18.5" (personal interview, 2002). She suffered constant psychological pain but was never diagnosed because she did not realize or admit that there might be a problem, and the numbers did not add up.

Another major problem is the fourth *DSM-IV-TR* criterion of "anorexia nervosa": absence of at least three consecutive menstrual cycles in females. Why specifically three? And that criterion cannot be applied to men, prepubescent girls, or menopausal women, making it impossible for members of these groups to meet that criterion and thus making it more difficult for them to meet enough criteria to qualify for the diagnosis. Further, menstruating women are used as the "norm" for this "abnormal" group. Anorexia in males has often been overlooked because of the extremely rare prevalence rates on record, and this criterion would keep the rates misleadingly low. A common distinction between so-called clinical and subclinical anorexia is that if one belongs to the latter category, one exhibits all of the symptoms but still menstruates. However, Kim and Ahn (2002) found that clinicians thought that amenorrhea rarely causes other symptoms of anorexia and should not be accorded much diagnostic importance. It is generally assumed that periods stop when one goes below a certain weight (Rock, Gorenflo, Drewnowski, and Demitrack 1996). However, continuation of menstruation should not be used to minimize the severity of the problem, because some girls and women can reach very low body weights yet never miss a period; only about half of the women meeting the other disordered eating criteria develop amenorrhea or very irregular periods (Treasure and Szmukler 1995). This also is an unreliable criterion, due to the nature of the menstrual cycle. The peak time for the onset of anorexia is between fourteen and eighteen years of age. The earlier onset is close to the time of one's first period, and it often takes a couple of years for the menstrual cycle to become "regular." In fact, some women never have completely dependable cycles. For certain groups, such as children, the weight loss required in the *DSM* is too great: For an eighteeen-year-old woman and a twelve-year-old girl, losing twenty pounds may have very different significance because of their probably unequal starting points.

Even a person who does not have all of the signs and symptoms of a particular disorder may have enough to make their lives miserable. My interviewee describes her past three years as "an endless fixation with calorie counting . . . a vicious cycle of dieting. I lost countless friends from my mood changes and my complete obsession with food" (personal interview, 2002). "Even to get to the psychiatrist one must be suspected of being mentally ill, and therefore the labeling process has at least already started. If in any case it is necessary to see a psychiatrist to become labeled 'mad;' there cannot, by definition, be a 'mad' person who has never seen a psychiatrist . . . the most important difference is that not everybody can see or knows about the label" (Bowers 1988, 21). Those with maladaptive eating patterns and body image problems who fall short of the current *DSM* criteria may nevertheless experience enough distress and interference with daily life from these problems to warrant attention, help, and support, including therapy. Like anorexia nervosa and bulimia, subclinical eating problems are accompanied by related psychological symptoms, such as low self-esteem, high self-criticism, perfectionism, depression, anxiety, social isolation, and anhedonia (Mintz and Betz 1988; Geller, Zaitsoff, and Srikameswaran 2002). Psychotherapists, as well as family and friends, could be quite helpful to people with these problems.

In light of the unclear lines between "eating disorders" and "problems with eating and body image," several factors need to be used to determine who should be able to receive help, whether formal treatment or support from family and friends. These are preoccupation with food and body shape; distorted body image; intense, unwarranted fear of gaining weight or becoming fat; and severe food restrictions and/or excessive exercise (Kim and Ahn [2002] found that clinicians considered distorted body perception and denial of the problem to be important characteristics of eating problems and to cause related symptoms). Just one or two of these symptoms can cause psychological distress and warrant getting help. In order to enable people at all points on the continuum to be identified, *DSM* requirements of amenorrhea, a particular amount of weight loss, and a specific frequency of purging should not be considered essential for acknowledging a problem. Bowers (1998) recommends a dimensional scale for each symptom in diagnosing various mental disorders. This would be effective with eating disorders, because there is a wide range of distress, and a person who is high on a scale for one symptom may be low on another but still be suffering. The *DSM* authors do not distinguish among levels of individual dysfunction.

Prevention and treatment can keep subclinical symptoms from becoming *DSM*-diagnosable (Herzog et al. 1999). Greater efforts need to be made to include people at all levels of the continuum, so that they may receive help before it is too late.

REFERENCES

American Psychiatric Association. (2000). *Diagnostic and statistical manual of mental disorders-IV-TR*. Washington, DC.

Bowers, L. (1998). *The social nature of mental illness*. New York: Routledge.

Cooley, E., and T. Toray. (2001). Disordered eating in college freshmen women: A prospective study. *Journal of American College Health* 49 (5), 229–35.

Fernald, C. D., and L. Gettys. (1980). Diagnostic labels and perceptions of children's behavior. *Journal of Clinical Child Psychology* 9 (3), 229–33.

Franko, D. L., and M. Omori. (1999). Subclinical eating disorders in adolescent women: A test of the continuity hypothesis and its psychological correlates. *Journal of Adolescence* 22, 389–96.

Geller, J., S. L. Zaitsoff, and S. Srikameswaran. (2002). Beyond shape and weight: Exploring the relationship between nonbody determinants of self-esteem and eating disorder symptoms in adolescent females. *International Journal of Eating Disorders* 32 (3), 344–51.

Hart, K., and M. Kenny. (1997). Adherence to the super woman ideal and eating disorder symptoms among college women. *Sex Roles* 36, 461–78.

Herzog, D. B., D. J. Dorer, and P. K. Keel. (1999). Recovery and relapse in anorexia and bulimia nervosa: A 7.5-year follow-up study. *Journal of the American Academy of Child and Adolescent Psychiatry* 38, 829–37.

Herzog, D. B., J. D. Hopkins, and C. D. Burns. (1993). A follow-up study of 33 subdiagnostic eating disordered women. *International Journal of Eating Disorders* 14, 261–67.

Holt, M. K., and D. L. Espelage. (2002). Problem-solving skills and relationship attributes among women with eating disorders. *Journal of Counseling and Development* 80 (3), 345–55.

Horwitz, A.V. (2002). *Creating mental illness*. Chicago: University of Chicago Press.

Hsu, L.K.G. (1990). *Eating disorders*. New York: Guilford Press.

Kim, N. S., and W. Ahn. (2002). Clinical psychologists' theory-based representations of mental disorders predict their diagnostic reasoning and memory. *Journal of Experimental Psychology* 131 (4), 451–76.

Kitsantas, A., T. D. Gilligan, and A. Kamata. (2003). College women with eating disorders: Self-regulation, life satisfaction, and positive/negative affect. *Journal of Psychology* 137 (4), 381–95.

Klemchuk, H. P., C. B. Hutchinson, and R. I. Frank. (1990). Body dissatisfaction and eating-related problems on the college campus: Usefulness of the Eating Disorder Inventory with a nonclinical population. *Journal of Counseling Psychology* 37 (3), 297–305.

Mintz, L. B., and N. E. Betz. (1988). Prevalence and correlates of eating disordered behavior among undergraduate women. *Journal of Counseling Psychology* 35 (4), 463–71.

Mintz, L. B., M. S. O'Halloran, A. M. Mulholland, and P. A. Schneider. (1997). Questionnaire for eating disorder diagnoses: Reliability and validity of operationalizing

DSM-IV criteria into a self-report form. *Journal of Counseling Psychology* 44, 63–79.

Polivy, J., and C. P. Herman. (1987). Diagnosis and treatment of normal eating. *Journal of Consulting and Clinical Psychology* 55 (5), 635–44.

Rock, C. L., D. W. Gorenflo, A. Drewnowski, and M. A. Demitrack. (1996). Nutritional characteristics, eating pathology, and hormonal status in young women. *American Journal of Clinical Nutrition* 64, 566–71.

Scarano, G. M., and C. R. Kalodner-Martin. (1994). A description of the continuum of eating disorders: Implications for intervention and research. *Journal of Counseling & Development* 72 (4), 356–61.

Spearing, Melissa. (2001). *Eating disorders: Facts about eating disorders and the search for solutions.* Bethesda, MD: National Institute of Mental Health.

Treasure, J., and G. I. Szmukler. (1995). Medical complications of chronic anorexia nervosa. Pp. 197–220 in G. I. Szmukler, C. Dare, and J. Treasure, eds. *Handbook on eating disorders: Theory, treatment, and research.* Chichester, UK: Wiley.

Tylka, T. L., and L. M. Subich. (2002). Exploring young women's perceptions of the effectiveness and safety of maladaptive weight control techniques. *Journal of Counseling & Development* 80, 101–10.

———. (1999). Exploring the construct validity of the eating disorder continuum. *Journal of Counseling Psychology* 46, 268–76.

Wilcox, M., and D. N. Stattler. (1996). The relationship between disorders and depression. *Journal of Social Psychology* 136, 269.

Chapter 25

Histrionic Personality

Pamela Reed Gibson

The diagnostic category of Histrionic Personality Disorder (hysteria re-named) has been invested with legitimacy through a variety of channels. However, one could question whether hysteria was "discovered" to have been an a priori category awaiting the genius of the likes of Charcot and Freud or whether it was created through the collusion of some observers of women's behavior who found it in their interests to characterize women in this specific way. I shall address four points. First, Hysteria, or Histrionic Personality Disorder, is an amorphous category having neither historical continuity nor contemporary reliability. Second, the diagnosis has served the status quo from its politically motivated construction to its socially constructed present. Third, there is ample evidence that biases operate when women are observed. Fourth, our culture actually exerts pressure upon women to adopt and exhibit histrionic behavior but labels them mentally ill if they do so.

A review of the history of the concept of hysteria clearly illustrates that what were said to be manifestations of this "disease" changed over time in accordance with beliefs about etiology and methods of treatment. Although they lacked a full understanding of the female anatomy, early Greek physicians attributed "hysterical" symptoms primarily to physiology. For example, in Plato's writing, the womb is portrayed as an animal which longs to generate children and which, when barren for too long, becomes upset and roams through the body, making it difficult to breathe, causing the sufferer great anguish and many diseases (Veith 1965).

As Christianity began to influence scientific thought, women's behavior came to be described as evil, and their symptoms suddenly were assumed to stem from alliance with the devil rather than from wandering anatomy. Augustine saw physically distressed individuals as "willfully possessed, be-witched, in league with the devil and even heretical" (cited here from Veith

1965, 47). Sexual abstinence went from being considered the cause of illness to a prescription for women's complaints. The beginnings of the progression of philosophies from physiological to psychological etiology are apparent in the thought of the nineteenth-century physician Samuel Carter. He referred to emotions in terms of their causal capabilities but still ultimately blamed outbursts on faulty sexual organs, allowing the disease to continue to be regarded as an affliction of women. It is also apparent in his writings that women considered hysterical were viewed with contempt, seen as conniving, greedy, and self-serving. This exemplifies the fact that the ever-changing diagnostic criteria for hysteria were repeatedly warped to mirror the social structures that were characteristic of the prevailing zeitgeist (Veith 1965).

Second, the ways in which the diagnosis has served the status quo have been documented by feminists who have written critiques regarding the role of the medical establishment in social control through diagnosis (Showalter 1987). It may be relevant here that an electronic literature search (using the database called UNCOVER) for the word "hysteria" produced 121 references, twelve of which referred to persons with concerns about the environment. The following were represented: "hysteria" over waste incineration, gas oil contamination, carbon dioxide, malathion, VDTs, Lyme disease, pesticides, the greenhouse effect, and recycling. Other topics included police brutality hysteria and hysteria over the drug crisis, cholesterol, computer viruses, child abuse, and AIDS, among others. It seems that when citizens have serious concerns or fears, they are characterized as hysterical by those with vested interests in the status quo. Similar attributions are made about women when they seek help and make the mistake of showing strong emotion to a clinical observer.

The following incident occurred in a university psychology-training clinic and demonstrates both the ways that biases operate when observers perceive women and the ways our culture exerts pressure on women to exhibit histrionic behavior. A female graduate student was in the initial stages of working with a client, a thirty-year-old woman who was anxious and depressed and had experienced considerable childhood trauma. As a precaution, the student arranged for the client to have a medication evaluation with the staff psychiatrist. In the evaluation, the psychiatrist inquired about the client's childhood, during which she had witnessed domestic violence and experienced sexual abuse by her father. The client cried and became somewhat agitated. It seemed to the student that the psychiatrist was unduly pressuring the client about the abuse, considering that this was their first meeting. Later, the student asked him why he had "pushed" her client to that extent. He responded that he was looking for histrionic indications and informed the student that, in fact, her client was "a little histrionic" because of her emotional reactivity and her "subtle seductiveness" toward him. What went wrong in this situation?

1. The psychiatrist admittedly went into the situation looking for histrionic characteristics in a female client.
2. The psychiatrist overlooked the level of pain involved in discussing childhood trauma.
3. The psychiatrist may have been mistaken or projecting when describing the woman as sexually seductive.

What does the research say about what can and does go wrong in the diagnosis of Histrionic Personality Disorder (HPD)? Following are five questions to ask before diagnosing a female client as histrionic. Based on psychological research, they are designed to help avoid overdiagnosis.

Question 1: If exaggerated emotional expressiveness seems to be present, is it more salient to me because the client is a woman?

Research shows that people look for emotion in women more than in men and make more references to emotion—either its presence or its absence—in women than in men (Shields and MacDowell 1987). Our culture associates emotions and emotional expression with women. As observers, we seem to be primed to look for emotion in women. Ask yourself, "Would I be considering this diagnosis if this client were male?"

Question 2: If I think that I sense sexual seductiveness, am I projecting it onto the client?

The criterion for HPD that has received the most attention has been sexual seductiveness. Hysterical/histrionic behavior has been described as flirtatious and provocative but "usually unaccompanied by genuine feelings of sexual or personal interest" (Wolowitz 1972, 312). But research suggests that men often project seductiveness onto women's friendly behavior. Abbey (1982) found that men perceived women's friendly behavior as flirtatious and sexual. Lest we conclude that the women were actually being flirtatious, the men in Abbey's study also saw other men as more flirtatious and sexual than did women participants. We live in a culture that has trained men to seek out and respond to real or imagined sexual cues as part of their masculine identity. Certainly, clinicians observing patients/clients are subject to actor/observer bias (Jones and Harris 1967; Jones 1979), and clinicians must take pains to be aware of this.

Question 3: Am I really following the symptoms, or am I leaping to judgment about diagnosis because of sex-role stereotypes?

Clinicians are not immune to cultural sex-role stereotypes (Broverman, Broverman, Clarkson, Rosenkrantz, and Vogel 1970). We know that the

"Histrionic" diagnosis is given primarily to women (Kass, Spitzer, and Williams 1983) and is likely to be given to a female client even when her presenting symptoms are of a mixed disorder (Warner 1978) and even when the description is specifically written to reflect another disorder (Ford and Widiger 1989). Hamilton, Rothbart, and Dawes (1985) found that licensed psychologists rated females as significantly more histrionic than males who exhibited the same symptoms. Loring and Powell found that male clinicians diagnosed women as histrionic "even though the case studies give little indication of this disorder" (1988, 18). Interestingly, Loring and Powell found that giving any information about race or gender to clinicians in an analogue study reduced the likelihood of the participants choosing the diagnostic criteria upon which the case description was based. When case descriptions were written to reflect Dependent Personality Disorder, clinicians diagnosed Caucasian women as histrionic and African American women as paranoid.

Some standardized testing instruments may contribute to the overdiagnosis of women as histrionic. Reich (1987) found that more female patients were diagnosed as "Histrionic" when evaluated through use of the Millon Clinical Multiaxial Inventory than through the Structured Interview for *DSM-III* Personality Disorders. Both clinical judgment and testing results must be subjected to scrutiny in order to avoid the tendency to assign diagnoses on the basis of cultural biases.

Question 4: If I am seeing a lot of emotion with pressure for expression, might it be due to underlying trauma?

Persons with HPD are said to display "pervasive and excessive emotionality" (American Psychiatric Association 2000, 714). Trauma clients frequently present with a tremendous amount of pent-up emotion that has had no outlet. Often it has not been safe for them to express anger at an abuser. Perhaps the client has not conceptualized what has happened as abuse (as in unacknowledged victims of acquaintance rape). Perhaps there has been no forum for discussion of these issues. If you see that the client needs to express a considerable amount of emotion, ask your client about loss, abuse, and other forms of trauma that tend to leave this kind of "signature." Therapists formerly believed that trauma was "outside the range of usual human experience" (APA 1987), but it is in fact quite common (Brown 1993). Because of this, in the course of the diagnostic process, it is appropriate to question clients about past or present abuse, much as one does about issues such as substance abuse.

Question 5: Is the client simply behaving the way our culture has taught women to behave?

In popular culture, women are portrayed as provocative and obsessed with appearance, and they are encouraged to behave in ways that are seductive and expressive and demand attention. In fact, the covers of women's magazines read like prescriptions for histrionic behavior (e.g., how to get him to notice you, how to dress for summer, whether you should sleep with your boss, how to have the perfect body). Women's magazines, how-to books, music videos, and other media have been studied and analyzed in recent years, and it is informative to see what scholars find about popular culture's depictions of women. Manipulative behavior such as playing hard-to-get is touted in *The Rules* (Fein and Schneider 1995) as appropriate for finding and catching a man. Recent advice from *Cosmopolitan* magazine suggests that a woman execute "an eye-catching stunt" to pick up a man, such as loudly proclaiming that she is up for anything and requesting suggestions from a nearby, good-looking man (Haber 2001, 136). Suggestions for coffee shop behavior include seductively licking mocha cream off one's lips and typing into a man's laptop computer "I'd love to take a closer look at the merchandise" (Haber 2001, 138). While some women may be impervious to or attempt to ignore these prescriptions, there is a great deal of input that encourages women to behave in ways that would qualify them for the diagnosis of Histrionic Personality Disorder.

CONCLUSION

Responsible clinical and counseling work must be based on an informed perspective that includes taking personal and cultural biases and context into account. Truly ethical work by clinicians requires confronting and processing their own internalized biases about gender, race, class, degree of disability, religion, and sexual orientation in order to understand their clients as persons in context (Brown 1994; Poland and Caplan, chapter 2 in this volume). In addition, clinicians must inform themselves regarding the limitations/state of current practice (e.g., the research on sex bias in diagnosis) rather than learning laundry lists of descriptors and matching them to clients' symptoms. Clients must be regarded as individuals in a social context that includes much more than whether they appear emotional in a fifteen-minute medical evaluation. Clinicians should be aware of both the lack of diagnostic specificity inherent in the diagnosis of Histrionic Personality Disorder and the research showing that sex bias often enters into clinicians' process of deciding whether to apply this label to their patients.

REFERENCES

Abbey, A. (1982). Sex differences in attributions for friendly behavior: Do males misinterpret females' friendliness? *Journal of Personality and Social Psychology* 42, 830–38.

American Psychiatric Association. (1987). *Diagnostic and statistical manual of mental disorders-III-R*. Washington, DC.

American Psychiatric Association. (2000). *Diagnostic and statistical manual of mental disorders-IV-TR*. Washington, DC.

Broverman, I. K., D. M. Broverman, F. E. Clarkson, P. Rosenkrantz, and S. R. Vogel. (1970). Sex-role stereotypes and clinical judgements of mental health. *Journal of Consulting Psychology* 34, 1–7.

Brown, L. S. (1993). Not outside the range: One feminist perspective on psychic trauma. *American Image* 48 (1), 119–33.

——. (1994). *Subversive dialogues*. New York: Basic Books.

Fein, E., and S. Schneider. (1995). *The rules*. New York: Warner Books.

Ford, M. R., and T. A. Widiger. (1989). Sex bias in the diagnosis of histrionic and antisocial personality disorders. *Journal of Consulting and Clinical Psychology* 57, 301–5.

Haber, H. (2001, July). 30 sexy conversation starters. *Cosmopolitan* 231 (1), 136–38.

Hamilton, S., M. Rothbart, and R. M. Dawes. (1985). Sex bias, diagnosis, and I. *Sex Roles* 15, 268–74.

Jones, E. E. (1979). The rocky road from acts to dispositions. *American Psychologist* 34, 107–17.

Jones, E. E., and V. A. Harris. (1967). The attribution of attitudes. *Journal of Experimental Social Psychology* 3, 1024.

Kass, F., R. L. Spitzer, and J.B.W. Williams. (1983). An empirical study of the issue of sex bias in the diagnostic criteria of *DSM-III* axis II personality disorders. *American Psychologist* 38, 799–801.

Loring, M., and B. Powell. (1988). Gender, race, and *DSM-III*: A study of the objectivity of psychiatric diagnostic behavior. *Journal of Health and Social Behavior* 29, 1–22.

Reich, J. (1987). Sex distribution of *DSM-III* personality disorders in psychiatric outpatients. *American Journal of Psychiatry*, 144, 485–88.

Shields, S. A., and K. A. MacDowell. (1987). "Appropriate" emotion in politics: Judgments of a televised debate. *Journal of Communication* (spring), 78–89.

Showalter, E. (1987). *The female malady: Women, madness, and English culture, 1830–1980*. New York: Viking Penguin.

Veith, I. (1965). *Hysteria: The history of a disease*. Chicago: University of Chicago Press.

Warner, R. (1978). The diagnosis of antisocial and hysterical personality disorders. *Journal of Nervous and Mental Disease* 166, 839–45.

Wolowitz, H. M. (1972). Hysterical character and feminine identity. Pp. 307–14 in J. M. Bardwick, ed. *Readings on the psychology of women*. New York: Harper & Row.

Chapter 26

Post-traumatic Stress Disorder

Dana Becker

Post-traumatic Stress Disorder (PTSD), as described in *DSM-IV-TR* (American Psychiatric Association 2000), is a constellation of symptoms that can arise in the aftermath of exposure to trauma. These include symptoms associated with reexperiencing the trauma (e.g., flashbacks), those associated with avoidance (e.g., of anyone or anything that evokes memories of the trauma), and increased arousal (e.g., hypervigilance).

Currently, PTSD is one of a very few diagnoses in *DSM-IV-TR* whose symptoms are attributed solely to situational causes. This has made the PTSD label particularly attractive to therapists and others seeking to find a "non-blaming" diagnosis whose criteria take into account the social/interpersonal context of the psychological problems of many women. The focus of PTSD is on the traumatic events and their effects rather than on alleged intrapsychic problems of the individual (Brown 1994; Carmen, Rieker, and Mills 1984; Courtois 1988). For this reason, PTSD has been considered a less stigmatizing diagnosis for women who have been sexually and/or physically traumatized than are diagnoses such as Borderline Personality Disorder (BPD). The BPD diagnosis, to which highly pejorative connotations continue to cling, has been shown in analogue studies to be applied more frequently to women than to men (Adler, Drake, and Teague 1990; Becker and Lamb 1994). Women diagnosed with BPD often receive considerably worse clinical and legal treatment than do those diagnosed with PTSD (Stefan 1998). Because many women to whom the BPD diagnosis has been applied have histories of sexual and/or physical abuse (Goodwin, Cheeves, and Connell 1990; Herman, Perry, and van der Kolk 1989; Ogata et al. 1990; Surrey, Swett, Michaels, and Levin 1990; Weaver and Clum 1993; Zanarini, Gunderson, Marino, Schwartz, and Frankenburg 1989), it was assumed that PTSD would provide a welcome diagnostic alternative. In some respects, this has proven to be the case, but there remain problems with the PTSD diagnosis that need to be addressed.

In the more than twenty years that have passed since PTSD was first introduced into *DSM-III* (APA 1980), the conceptualization of the diagnosis and its use have altered dramatically. Stressful events that might precipitate the disorder were described in *DSM-III* and *DSM-III-R* as needing to be "outside the range of human experience" (APA 1987, 236; 1980). This definition of stressful events excluded many traumatic phenomena that were well within the scope of women's experience, because abuse is so common, thus well within the range of human experience. In *DSM-IV-TR* (APA 2000), therefore, in acknowledgment of the fact that domestic violence, rape, physical abuse, and child sexual abuse are commonly experienced by girls and women, it is no longer stated that traumata resulting in PTSD must be "outside the range of human experience." However, they must pose "actual or threatened death or serious injury, or other threat to the physical integrity of self or others" and also have "involved intense fear, helplessness, or horror" (APA 2000, 467). Although this definition is helpful for female trauma victims who have been in danger of serious physical injury or death, it is not so useful for those adults for whom emotional events produce posttraumatic symptoms (although the *DSM-IV-TR* includes the note: "For children, sexually traumatic events may include developmentally inappropriate sexual experiences without threatened or actual violence or injury" [APA 2000, 464]). Lerman (1996) and others contend that battered women who kill their partners may be disadvantaged in court by not being able to claim self-defense if a direct and immediate threat to their persons must be proven. Although in the *DSM-IV-TR*, one does find the statement that "domestic battering" could be one of the interpersonal stressors leading to PTSD, the *DSM* criterion requiring that "the person experienced, witnessed, or was confronted with an event or events that involved actual or threatened death or serious injury or a threat to the physical integrity of self or others" (APA 2000, 467) would seem to disqualify women who experience even severe psychological abuse. Important consequences follow from opening up the PTSD diagnosis to millions of women who would not previously have been eligible for it (Kutchins and Kirk 1997). Broadening the criteria has contributed to the medicalization of women's problems, thereby detracting from the impetus to attack the problem of male-to-female violence on a sociostructural level (Becker 2000). Thus, attachment to the PTSD diagnosis may fail women clients in the very task that changes in the PTSD criteria were meant to accomplish—that is, to ensure that the individual would *not* be regarded as the pathological source of her own misery.

Although many feminist therapists have been able to use the existence of PTSD to advocate for female trauma victims, there is growing concern about the paradox of using PTSD—a diagnosis of mental disorder—to normalize women's responses to abuse. Marecek (1999) found that feminist therapists frequently call PTSD the only acceptable diagnosis for women clients. Marecek noted that in some cases PTSD was represented to clients as a diagnosis that, as one therapist put it, "says right in the definition that this is a normal response to trauma that most people would have" (Marecek 1999, 163). We can question why, if PTSD symptoms are not abnormal responses to abuse, we are calling them, in the aggregate, a mental disorder. Some would say that, since not every individual develops PTSD symptoms in response to a given stressful experience (Kessler, Sonnega, Bromet, Hughes, and Nelson 1995; Yehuda and Mcfarlane 1995), and because PTSD is not a universal response to abuse, its symptoms must be viewed as constituents of disorder (Lamb 1996), in a way that, for instance, symptoms in response to war experiences or natural disasters are not. It may prove important to give traumatized women support but refuse to give them a diagnosis of mental disorder; however, this option is made more difficult in the United States and some other countries by insurance companies' requirement of a *DSM* label for reimbursement.

There is also concern that use of the PTSD diagnosis may cause therapists to centralize issues of trauma and abuse at the expense of examining other salient problems in a woman's life (Haaken and Schlaps 1991). Another dilemma is posed by the invocation of biological science to justify the medicalization of PTSD (Andreason 1995), a trend that de-emphasizes the social context of abuse as it emphasizes the separation of mind and body. There has even been a suggestion that differences in the ways women and men respond to traumata may be hormonal (Wolfe and Kimerling 1997). A growing group of advocates suggests that abused women currently diagnosed with BPD might better be considered as suffering from a "complex" or chronic variant of PTSD (Alexander and Muenzenmaier 1998; Brown 1994; Courtois 1999; Herman, Perry, and van der Kolk 1989; Herman 1992; Lerman 1996; Zanarini et al. 1998). However, problems with the replacement of the diagnosis of Borderline Personality Disorder with PTSD are manifold.

First, not all women currently diagnosed as having BPD have been sexually or physically traumatized, and the various symptom constellations we currently call "borderline" are produced by the interaction of multiple factors (Becker 1997; Kroll 1988; 1993)—notably, chronic emotional invalidation (Linehan 1993). Individuals' responses to trauma differ, and only some of these responses are identifiable as posttraumatic symptoms (Graziano 1992; Lamb 1999). Second, it appears that the "borderline" label, with its attendant implications of chronicity, countertransference problems, and poor outcomes—whether merited or not—has not been vanquished by the increased use of the PTSD diagnosis. There are already indications in the treatment literature that, although some women with histories of clear-cut traumatic antecedents and PTSD symptoms are being removed from the "borderline" group, a group of women considered "true" borderlines is being left behind (Becker 2000). Thus, diagnosing greater and greater numbers of "borderline" women with PTSD will not, in the end, eliminate the pernicious BPD diagnosis.

Although the ways in which many women are traumatized in our society are structurally and socially determined, the sequelae of that traumatization are labeled "disorder." In the words of Paula J. Caplan: "In a sexist society, anything that *can* be used against women *will* be used against women" (Caplan 1993). Medicalization exists as one feature of the social control of women by expanding the definition of madness, leading to the pursuit of cures for the "disease" of PTSD rather than to the more energetic pursuit of correctives to the structural conditions that allow for the persistence of male-to-female violence in our society.

REFERENCES

Adler, D. A., R. E., Drake, and G. B. Teague. (1990). Clinicians' practices in personality assessment: Does gender influence the use of *DSM-III* Axis II? *Comprehensive Psychiatry* 31 (2), 125–33.

Alexander, M. J., and K. Muenzenmaier. (1998). Trauma, addiction, and recovery: Addressing public health epidemics among women with severe mental illness. Pp. 215–39 in B. L. Levin, A. K. Blanch, and A. Jennings, eds. *Women's mental health services: A public health perspective*. Thousand Oaks, CA: Sage.

American Psychiatric Association. (2000). *Diagnostic and statistical manual of mental disorders-IV-TR*. Washington, DC.

——. (1987). *Diagnostic and statistical manual of mental disorders-III-R*. Washington, DC.

——. (1980). *Diagnostic and statistical manual of mental disorders-III*. Washington, DC.

Andreason, N. (1995). Posttraumatic stress disorder: Psychology, biology, and the Manichean warfare between false dichotomies. *American Journal of Psychiatry* 152, 963–65.

Becker, D. (2000). When she was bad: Borderline personality disorder in a posttraumatic age. *American Journal of Orthopsychiatry* 70 (4), 422–32.

——. (1997). *Through the looking glass: Women and borderline personality disorder*. Boulder, CO: Westview.

Becker, D., and S. Lamb. (1994). Sex bias in the diagnosis of borderline personality disorder and posttraumatic stress disorder. *Professional Psychology: Research and Practice* 25 (1), 55–61.

Brown, L. S. (1994). *Subversive dialogues: Theory in feminist therapy*. New York: Basic Books.

Caplan, Paula J. (1993). *Lifting a ton of feathers: A woman's guide to surviving in the academic world*. Toronto: University of Toronto Press.

Carmen, E. H., P. R. Rieker, and T. Mills. (1984). Victims of violence and psychiatric illness. *American Journal of Psychiatry* 141, 378–83.

Courtois, C. A. (1999). *Recollections of sexual abuse: Treatment principles and guidelines*. New York: Norton.

———. (1988). *Healing the incest wound: Adult survivors in therapy*. New York: Norton.

Goodwin, J. M., K. Cheeves, and V. Connell. (1990). Borderline and other severe symptoms in adult survivors of incestuous abuse. *Psychiatric Annals* 20 (1), 22–31.

Graziano, R. (1992). Treating women incest survivors: A bridge between "cumulative trauma" and "post-traumatic stress." *Social Work in Health Care* 17, 69–85.

Haaken, J., and A. Schlaps. (1991). Incest resolution therapy and the objectification of sexual abuse. *Psychotherapy* 39, 39–46.

Herman, J. (1992). *Trauma and recovery*. New York: Basic Books.

Herman, J. L., J. C. Perry, and B. A. van der Kolk. (1989). Childhood trauma in borderline personality disorder. *American Journal of Psychiatry* 146 (4), 460–65.

Kessler, R. C., A. Sonnega, E. Bromet, M. Hughes, and C. B. Nelson. (1995). Post-traumatic stress disorder in the national comorbidity survey. *Archives of General Psychiatry* 52, 1048–60.

Kroll, J. K. (1988). *The challenge of the borderline patient: Competency in diagnosis and treatment*. New York: W. W. Norton.

———. (1993). *PTSD/borderlines in therapy: Finding the balance*. New York: W. W. Norton.

Kutchins, H., and S. A. Kirk. (1997). *Making us crazy: DSM: The psychiatric bible and the creation of mental disorders*. New York: The Free Press.

Lerman, H. (1996). *Pigeonholing women's misery: A history and critical analysis of the psychodiagnosis of women in the twentieth century*. New York: Basic Books.

Lamb, S. (1996). *The trouble with blame: Victims, perpetrators, and responsibility*. Cambridge, MA: Harvard University Press.

———. (1999). Constructing the victim: Popular images and lasting labels. Pp. 108–38 in S. Lamb, ed. *New versions for victims: Feminists struggle with the concept*. New York: New York University Press.

Linehan, M. M. (1993). *Cognitive-behavioral treatment of borderline personality disorder*. New York: Guilford.

Marecek, J. (1999). Trauma talk in feminist clinical practice. Pp. 158–82 in S. Lamb, ed. *New versions for victims: Feminists struggle with the concept*. New York: New York University Press.

Ogata, S. N., K. R. Silk, S. Goodrich, N. E. Lohr, D. Westen, and E. M. Hill. (1990). Childhod sexual and physical abuse in adult patients with borderline personality disorder. *American Journal of Psychiatry* 147 (8), 1008–13.

Stefan, S. (1998). Impact of the law on women with diagnoses of borderline personality disorder related to childhood sexual abuse. Pp. 240–78 in B. L. Levin, A. K.

Blanch, and A. Jennings, eds. *Women's mental health services: A public health perspective*. Thousand Oaks, CA: Sage.

Surrey, J., C. Swett, A. Michaels, and S. Levin. (1990). Reported history of physical and sexual abuse and severity of symptomatology in women psychiatric outpatients. *American Journal of Orthopsychiatry* 60 (3), 412–17.

Weaver, T. L., and G. A. Clum. (1993). Early family environments and traumatic experiences associated with borderline personality disorder. *Journal of Consulting and Clinical Psychology* 61 (6), 1068–75.

Wolfe, J., and R. Kimerling. (1997). Gender issues in the assessment of posttraumatic stress disorder. Pp. 192–237 in J. P. Wilson and T. M. Keane, eds. *Assessing psychological trauma and PTSD*. New York: Guilford.

Yehuda, R., and A. C. McFarlane. (1995). Conflict between current knowledge about posttraumatic stress disorder and its original conceptual basis. *American Journal of Psychiatry* 152, 1705–13.

Zanarini, M. C., J. G. Gunderson, M. F. Marino, E. O. Schwartz, and F. R. Frankenburg. (1989). Childhood experiences of borderline patients. *Comprehensive Psychiatry* 30 (1), 18–25.

Zanarini, M. C., F. R. Frankenburg, E. D. Dubo, A. E. Sickel, A. Trikha, A. Levin, and V. Reynolds. (1998). Axis I comorbidity of borderline personality disorder. *American Journal of Psychiatry* 155 (12), 1733–39.

Chapter 27

Some Gender Biases in Diagnosing Traumatized Women

Vincent Fish

When mental health professionals diagnose people as mentally disordered, we do so from within strong institutional, societal, and cultural contexts that systematically influence how clients' data are elicited, presented, and perceived and how we use these data to assign diagnostic labels. These contexts also help determine the burdens, risks, and opportunities our diagnostic judgments carry for clients. Some diagnostic labels are more pejorative than others, some lead to better or worse kinds of treatment, and some are simply more accurate than others when applied to people who have had certain life experiences, such as trauma.

One frequently harmful systematic shaper of diagnostic practice is gender bias. Females are misdiagnosed more than males with chronic, stigmatizing disorders such as Borderline Personality Disorder (BPD) and Schizophrenia, while more treatable posttraumatic conditions caused largely by overwhelming situational stress, such as Post-traumatic Stress Disorder (PTSD) and Dissociative Identity Disorder (DID), tend to be underdiagnosed in females.

Overdiagnosis of BPD. Becker and Lamb (1994) surveyed psychologists, clinical social workers, and psychiatrists about their diagnostic impressions of a fictitious client in a case formulated to include an equal number of criteria from the *Diagnostic and Statistical Manual of Mental Disorders* (*DSM*; American Psychiatric Association 1987; 1994) for both BPD and PTSD. They discovered that mental health clinicians were more disposed to diagnose BPD, particularly if the client was identified as a woman.

Underdiagnosis of PTSD. Since a history of some traumatic event is necessary to diagnose PTSD, therapists who fail to ask about a history of potentially traumatic events, such as abuse, will miss PTSD diagnoses. Despite the importance of inquiring about abuse history, many clinicians fail to do so (Young, Read, Barker-Collo, and Harrison 2001). Pruitt and Kappius (1992)

213

found that only slightly more than half (51 percent) of therapists routinely asked clients about sexual abuse. Reviewing medical records in a New Zealand general hospital, Read and Fraser (1998) determined that staff completed the section of an admission form about abuse history for only seventeen of the fifty-three patients with whom the form was used. In the same hospital, the records of one hundred consecutive admissions indicated a prevalence rate of abuse of 32 percent, but of the seventeen patients directly asked about abuse, fourteen (82 percent) answered affirmatively.

Craine, Henson, Colliver, and MacLean (1988) noted that 51 percent of 105 women patients at state hospitals reported a history of sexual abuse, and 66 percent of these abused women met the diagnostic criteria for PTSD. Nevertheless, none of these patients had been diagnosed with PTSD, and only 20 percent of those who had been abused felt that their sexual abuse had been adequately treated. Mueser et al. (1998) found that 98 percent of 275 severely mentally ill patients treated in public programs reported exposure to at least one traumatic event. Forty-three percent of the sample met criteria for PTSD, but only 2 percent (3 of 119) were given this diagnosis in their charts. Child sexual abuse was the second strongest predictor of PTSD in this sample, and the number of different types of trauma was the strongest predictor.

Underdiagnosis of DID; overdiagnosis of Schizophrenia and BPD. Several investigators have documented that DID and other dissociative disorders are more common in clinical populations than the recorded diagnoses would suggest (Boon and Draijer 1991; Dunn, Paolo, Ryan, and Van Fleet 1993; Graves 1989; McCallum, Lock, Kulia, Rorty, and Wetzel 1992; Ross, Anderson, Fleisher, and Norton 1992; Ross, Kronson, Koensgen, Barkman, Clark, and Rockman 1992; Ross and Norton 1988; Ross, Norton, and Wozney 1989; Schenck, Milner, Hurwitz, and Bundlie 1989). Ross, Norton, and Wozney (1989) noted that the patients with DID in their study had spent an average of nearly seven years in the mental health system before being diagnosed with DID and until then had been given other diagnoses, including Schizophrenia and BPD.

Greater impact on women of underdiagnosis of DID and PTSD. The tendency to underdiagnose posttraumatic disorders such as DID and PTSD no doubt adversely affects many males but probably disproportionately affects females. It is generally accepted in the psychiatric community that the ratio of adult women to adult men with DID is at least 2:1 (American Psychiatric Association 1994; 2000), and several studies suggest that females are more at risk to develop PTSD (Cottler, Compton, Mager, Spitznagel, and Janca 1992; Green, Korol, Grace, Vary, Leonard, Gleser, and Smitson-Cohen 1991; Palinkas, Petterson, Russell, and Downs 1993; Reinherz, Giaconia, Lefkowitz, Pakiz, and Frost 1993; Stein, Walker, and Forde, 2000; Steinglass and Gerrity 1990; Wolfe, Sas, and Wekerle 1994) or to develop more severe PTSD (Fitzpatrick and Boldizar 1993; Green et al. 1991). The routes to PTSD also vary somewhat by gender. For example, more men serve in the military and are traumatized in combat, while more females experience traumatic sexual abuse.

Understanding gender bias in diagnosing PTSD, DID, BPD, and Schizophrenia. Three explanations for gender bias in regard to these diagnoses are available. The first is focused on particular characteristics of clinicians. Characteristics that may incline clinicians to overdiagnose BPD and Schizophrenia and underdiagnose PTSD and DID include:

- a tendency to attribute dysfunctional behavior and experience to intrapsychic/constitutional variables, such as those that are presumed to occur in Schizophrenia and BPD, rather than to situational factors such as traumatic events;
- the underestimation (particularly by male therapists) of the effects of traumatic abuse;
- the popularity, as a result of training and other social processes, of the BPD diagnosis, especially applied to women; and
- a lack of familiarity with and/or acceptance of the PTSD and DID diagnoses on clinicians' part (see Becker and Lamb 1994; Kluft 1991).

These characteristics result in gender bias because more women enter therapy and are thus exposed at a higher rate to the characteristics; because more women in therapy have experienced sexual abuse, a situational factor which is strongly associated with a higher rate of PTSD and DID; and because women are at higher risk than men to develop PTSD.

A second, related explanation for the misdiagnosis of PTSD as BPD may be extrapolated from the recent discussion in the literature regarding the relationship, and even the equivalence, of these two diagnoses (Gunderson and Sabo 1993; Herman and van der Kolk 1987; Lonie 1993; Spitzer et al. 2000; Thorpe 1993; Watson 1989). Lonie argues that, as defined in the *DSM-III-R*, BPD is the equivalent of PTSD. In that vein, for example, in the *DSM-IV-TR*, the criteria for PTSD include "irritability or outbursts of anger" (APA 2000, 468), while the criteria for BPD include "inappropriate, intense anger or difficulty controlling anger" (although the "inappropriate" nature of the anger in the latter criterion is not distinguished from the plain "irritability or outbursts of anger" in the former) (APA 2000, 710). Similarly, there has been some debate about the relationship or equivalence between DID and BPD (Clary, Burstin, and Carpenter 1984; Fink and Golinkoff 1990; Horevitz and Braun 1984; Kemp, Gilbertson, and Torem 1988; Lauer, Black, and Keen 1993;

Marmer and Fink 1994). Individuals with these diagnoses frequently present with similar symptoms and similar responses to standardized personality tests (Kemp et al. 1988; Lauer et al. 1993; Marmer and Fink 1994). The addition in *DSM-IV* of "severe dissociative symptoms" to the criteria set for BPD further increased the potential for confusion of BPD with DID (APA 1994). (It is important to note, however, that beginning with *DSM-IV,* one of the general diagnostic criteria for *all* personality disorders—of which BPD is one—is that it is "an enduring pattern of inner experience and behavior" that "is not better accounted for as a manifestation or consequence of another mental disorder" (APA 1994, 633). Thus, forced with a choice between a personality disorder diagnosis and a non-personality-disorder diagnosis, either of which could account for the presenting symptoms and problems, clinicians should actually choose the non-personality-disorder diagnosis over the personality disorder diagnosis.

A third explanation for the misdiagnosis of DID as Schizophrenia was suggested by Nakdimen (1990), who observed that in *DSM-III-R*, Schizophrenia is included in the differential diagnosis for Multiple Personality Disorder (MPD, now called DID), but MPD is not included in the differential diagnosis for Schizophrenia. This would tend to increase the frequency with which Schizophrenia is diagnosed and decrease the frequency with which MPD (DID) is diagnosed. The same problem can be found in the *DSM-IV* and *DSM-IV-TR*. The difficulty in this stems from the fact that the clinical presentation of the active, floridly psychotic phase of some types of Schizophrenia and the presentation of DID are very similar in many patients. For instance, there is evidence that certain types of auditory hallucinations and delusions usually considered indicative of Schizophrenia are actually found as frequently, or more frequently, in patients with DID, although the underlying causes of these symptomatic manifestations are believed to differ for the two diagnostic groups (Coons 1988; Ross et al. 1990). Because of this frequent overlap in symptoms, the lack of reference to DID in both the criteria and the differential diagnosis for Schizophrenia creates a structural bias within the *DSM-IV* toward misdiagnosing DID as Schizophrenia.

Negative impact of misdiagnosis. The presence of PTSD or a dissociative disorder can complicate treatment of comorbid disorders, such as substance abuse (Brown 2000; Dunn et al. 1993), so underdiagnosis of these disorders can be harmful. The costs to women with PTSD or DID who are misdiagnosed as Schizophrenic or BPD can be severe, because the stigma for both disorders is extremely burdensome, including negative attitudes of mental health professionals (Calvert 1997; Chernomas, Clarke, and Chisholm 2000; Giacalone 1997; Nehls 1999). Further, those misdiagnosed with Schizophrenia are likely to receive medications with painful, debilitating, and, often, irreversible side effects. Despite progress in the treatment of these disorders, treatment outcomes are still uncertain and often poor for Schizophrenia and BPD (e.g., Paris 1993), even when diagnoses are presumed to be accurate.

Accurate diagnosis of PTSD and DID, and treatment. For women who suffer from PTSD, there is an array of efficacious treatments (see, for example, Williams and Sommer 1995), including cognitive-behavioral treatments with strong empirical support for their short-term and longer-term effectiveness compared to other treatments (Foa, Olasov-Rothblum, Riggs, and Murdock 1991; Hembree and Foa 2000).

Conclusion. In summary, there is evidence that women who already have been traumatized, resulting in conditions such as PTSD and DID, are being routinely misdiagnosed and given inadequate and, often, harmful treatment. Better training of therapists in the differential diagnosis of PTSD, BPD, Schizophrenia, and DID, as well as increased discussion of the institutional, societal, and cultural underpinnings that promote such systematic gender bias, are necessary to address this consequential issue.

REFERENCES

American Psychiatric Association. (2000). *Diagnostic and statistical manual of mental disorders-IV-TR*. Washington, DC.
———. (1994). *Diagnostic and statistical manual of mental disorders-IV*. Washington, DC.
———. (1987). *Diagnostic and statistical manual of mental disorders-III*. Washington, DC.
Becker, D., and S. Lamb. (1994). Sex bias in the diagnosis of Borderline Personality Disorder and Posttraumatic Stress Disorder. *Professional Psychology: Research and Practice* 25, 55–61.
Boon, S., and N. Draijer. (1991). Diagnosing dissociative disorders in the Netherlands: A pilot study with the structured clinical interview for *DSM-III-R* dissociative disorders. *American Journal of Psychiatry* 148, 458–62.
Brown, P. J. (2000). Outcome in female patients with both substance use and posttraumatic stress disorders. *Alcoholism Treatment Quarterly* 18, 127–35.
Calvert, P. D. (1997). Gender differences in clinician predictions of working alliance with borderline personality disordered and posttraumatic stress disordered clients. *Dissertation Abstracts International, Section B*, 57 (10B), 6561.
Chernomas, W. M., D. E. Clarke, and F. A. Chisholm. (2000). Perspectives of women living with schizophrenia. *Psychiatric Service*, 51, 1517–21.
Clary, W. F., K. J. Burstin, and J. S. Carpenter. (1984). Multiple personality and borderline personality disorder. *Psychiatric Clinics of North America* 7, 89–99.
Coons, P. M. (1988). Schneiderian first rank symptoms in schizophrenia and multiple personality disorder. *Acta Psychiatrica Scandinavica* 77, 235.

Cottler, L. B., W. M. Compton, D. Mager, E. L. Spitznagel, and A. Janca. (1992). Posttraumatic stress disorder among substance users from the general population. *American Journal of Psychiatry* 149, 664–70.

Craine, L. S., C. E. Henson, J. A. Colliver, and D. G. MacLean. (1988). Prevalence of a history of sexual abuse among female psychiatric patients in a state hospital system. *Hospital and Community Psychiatry* 39, 300–4.

Dunn, G. E., A. M. Paolo, J. J. Ryan, and J. Van Fleet. (1993). Dissociative symptoms in a substance abuse population. *American Journal of Psychiatry* 150, 1043–47.

Fink, D. L., and M. Golinkoff. (1990). MPD, borderline personality disorder, and schizophrenia: A comparative study of clinical features. *Dissociation: Progress in the Dissociative Disorders* 3, 127–34.

Fitzpatrick, K. M., and J. P. Boldizar. (1993). The prevalence and consequences of exposure to violence among African-American youth. *Journal of the American Academy of Child and Adolescent Psychiatry* 32, 424–30.

Foa, E. B., B. Olasov-Rothbaum, D. S. Riggs, and T. B. Murdock. (1991). Treatment of post-traumatic stress disorder in rape victims: A comparison between cognitive-behavioral procedures and counseling. *Journal of Consulting and Clinical Psychology* 59, 715–23.

Giacalone, R. C. (1997). A study of clinicians' attitudes and sex bias in the diagnosis of borderline personality disorder and posttraumatic stress disorder. *Dissertation Abstracts International: Section B* 57 (12-B), 7725.

Graves, S. M. (1989). Dissociative disorders and dissociatve symptoms at a community mental health center. *Dissociation: Progress in the Dissociative Disorders* 2, 119–27.

Green, B. L., M. Korol, M. C. Grace, M. G. Vary, A. C. Leonard, G. C. Gleser, and S. Smitson-Cohen. (1991). Children and disaster: Age, gender, and parental effects on PTSD symptoms. *Journal of the American Academy of Child and Adolescent Psychiatry* 30, 945–51.

Gunderson, J. G., and A. N. Sabo. (1993). The phenomenological and conceptual interface between borderline personality disorder and PTSD. *American Journal of Psychiatry* 150, 19–27.

Hembree, E. A., and E. B. Foa. (2000). Posttraumatic stress disorder: Psychological factors and psychosocial interventions. *Journal of Clinical Psychiatry* 61 (Suppl. 7), 33–39.

Herman, J., and B. van der Kolk. (1987). Traumatic antecedents of borderline personality disorder. Pp. 111–26 in B. van der Kolk, ed. *Psychological trauma*. Washington, DC: American Psychiatric Press.

Horevitz, R. P., and B. G. Braun. (1984). Are multiple personalities borderline? An analysis of 33 cases. *Psychiatric Clinics of North America* 7, 69–87.

Kemp, K., A. D. Gilbertson, and M. S. Torem. (1988). The differential diagnosis of multiple personality disorder from borderline personality disorder. *Dissociation: Progress in the Dissociative Disorders* 1, 41–46.

Kluft, R. P. (1991). Clinical presentations of Multiple Personality Disorder. *Psychiatric Clinics of North America* 14, 605–29.

Lauer, J., D. W. Black, and P. Keen. (1993). Multiple personality disorder and borderline personality disorder: Distinct entities or variations on a common theme? *Annals of Clinical Psychiatry* 5, 129–34.

Lonie, I. (1993). Borderline disorder and post-traumatic stress disorder: An equivalence? *Australian and New Zealand Journal of Psychiatry* 27, 233–45.

Marmer, S. S., and D. Fink. (1995) Rethinking the comparison of Borderline Personality Disorder and Multiple Personality Disorder. *Psychiatric Clinics of North American* 17, 743–71.

McCallum, K. E., J. Lock, M. Kulla, M. Rorty, and R. D. Wetzel. (1992). Dissociative symptoms and disorders in patients with eating disorders. *Dissociation: Progress in the Dissociative Disorders* 5, 227–35.

Mueser, K. T., L. B. Goodman, S. L. Trumbetta, S. D. Rosenberg, F. C. Osher, R. Vidaver, P. Auciello, and D. W. Foy. (1998). Trauma and posttraumatic stress disorder in severe mental illness. *Journal of Consulting and Clinical Psychology* 66, 493–99.

Nakdimen, K. A. (1990). Multiple personality. *Hospital and Community Psychiatry* 41, 566–67.

Nchls, N. (1999). Borderline personality disorder: The voice of patients. *Research in Nursing and Health* 22, 285–93.

Palinkas, L. A., J. S. Petterson, J. Russell, and M. A. Downs. (1993). Community patterns of psychiatric disorders after the Exxon Valdez oil spill. *American Journal of Psychiatry* 150, 1517–23.

Paris, J. (1993). The treatment of Borderline Personality Disorder in light of the research on its long-term outcome. *Canadian Journal of Psychiatry* 38, S28–S34.

Pruitt, J. A., and R. E. Kappius. (1992). Routine inquiry into sexual victimization: A survey of therapists' practices. *Professional Psychology Research and Practice* 23, 474–79.

Read, J., and A. Fraser. (1998). Abuse histories of psychiatric inpatients: To ask or not to ask? *Psychiatric Services* 49, 355–59.

Reinherz, H. Z., R. M. Giaconia, E. S. Lefkowitz, B. Pakiz, and A. K. Frost. (1993). Prevalence of psychiatric disorders in a community population of older adolescents. *Journal of the American Academy of Child and Adolescent Psychiatry* 32, 369–77.

Ross, C. A., G. Anderson, W. P. Fleisher, and G. R. Norton. (1992). Dissociative experiences among psychiatric inpatients. *General Hospital Psychiatry* 14, 350–54.

Ross, C. A., J. Kronson, S. Koensgen, K. Barkman, P. Clark, and G. Rockman. (1992). Dissociative comorbidity in 100 chemically dependent patients. *Hospital and Community Psychiatry* 43, 840–42.

Ross, C. A., S. D. Miller, P. Reagor, L. Bjornson, G. A. Fraser, and G. Anderson. (1990). Schneiderian symptoms in multiple personality disorder and schizophrenia. *Comprehensive Psychiatry* 31, 111–18.

Ross, C. A., and G. R. Norton. (1988). Multiple personality disorder patients with a prior diagnosis of schizophrenia. *Dissociation: Progress in the Dissociative Disorders* 1, 39–42.

Ross, C. A., G. R. Norton, and K. Wozney. (1989). Multiple personality disorder: An analysis of 236 cases. *Canadian Journal of Psychiatry* 34, 413–18.

Schenck, C. H., D. M. Milner, T. D. Hurwitz, and S. R. Bundlie. (1989). Dissociative disorders presenting as somnambulism: Polysomnographic, video and clinical documentation (8 cases). *Dissociation: Progress in the Dissociative Disorders* 2, 194–204.

Spitzer, C., K. Effler, and H. J. Freyberger. (2000). Posttraumatische Belastungsstoerung, Dissoziation und selbstverletzendes Verhalten bei Borderline-Patienten. Posttraumatic stress disorder, dissociation, and self-destructive behavior in borderline patients. *Zeitschrift für Psychosomatische Medizin und Psychotherapie* 46, 273–85.

Stein, M. B., J. R. Walker, and D. R. Forde. (2000). Gender differences in susceptibility to posttraumatic stress disorder. *Behaviour Research and Therapy* 38, 619–28.

Steinglass, P., and E. Gerrity. (1990). Natural disasters and post-traumatic stress disorder: Short-term versus long-term recovery in two disaster-affected communities. *Journal of Applied Social Psychology* 20, 1746–65.

Thorpe, M. (1993). Is borderline personality disorder a post-traumatic stress disorder of early childhood? *Canadian Journal of Psychiatry* 38, 367–68.

Watson, P. B. (1989). A tormented mind: Clinical and theoretical implications of overwhelming life events. *Australian and New Zealand Journal of Psychiatry* 23, 97–102.

Williams, M. B, and J. F. Sommer Jr., eds. (1995). *Handbook of post-traumatic therapy.* Westport, CT: Greenwood Press.

Wolfe, D. A., L. Sas, and C. Wekerle. (1994). Factors associated with the development of posttraumatic stress disorder among child victims of sexual abuse. *Child Abuse & Neglect* 18, 37–50.

Young, M., J. Read, S. Barker-Collo, and R. Harrison. (2001). Evaluating and overcoming barriers to taking abuse histories. *Professional Psychology: Research and Practice* 32, 407–14.

Chapter 28

Medicalizing Menstrual Distress

Lisa Cosgrove and Paula J. Caplan

CIRCUMVENTING THE SYSTEM

For decades, various labels have been used to medicalize changes some women have premenstrually (Caplan, McCurdy-Myers, and Gans 1992). As Chrisler (1996) has noted, changes that occur premenstrually had long been called premenstrual tension (Frank 1931) before becoming reified as "premenstrual syndrome" (Dalton 1977). Subsequently, the authors of the *Diagnostic and Statistical Manual of Mental Disorders-III-R* (*DSM*; American Psychiatric Association 1987) pathologized women's experience further under the scientific-sounding label Late Luteal Phase Dysphoric Disorder (LLPDD). However, for apparently political reasons (described in Caplan 1995), in subsequent editions of the *DSM*, the label "Premenstrual Dysphoric Disorder" (PMDD) was used instead of LLPDD (APA 1994, 2000). The seriousness of the problems related to the claim that women become mentally ill premenstrually is so great that two congressional briefings on the subject were held (February 22, 2002 and Novermber 18, 2003), sponsored by U.S. congresswoman Louise Slaughter of New York and a dozen groups concerned with women's emotional and physical health.

The first time LLPDD/PMDD was included in the *DSM*, there was a great deal of controversy, and its inclusion was achieved in a disingenuous way. The American Psychiatric Association, noting a massive protest at the 1986 conference of the Association for Women in Psychology that led to petitions and letters from individuals and organizations representing more than six million people (Caplan 1995), initially suggested leaving LLPDD out of the manual. But Robert Spitzer, head psychiatrist of the 1987 edition (*DSM-III-R*), proposed what he called a compromise: The category would go in a specially created appendix "for categories requiring further study."

Since the manual's main text is supposedly comprised of categories validated by scientific research, it seemed a victory for women that the label was given only provisional status. But once the *DSM-III-R* was published, three things became clear: (1) In the appendix, LLPDD was given a five-digit code, a title, a list of symptoms, and a cutoff point (patients must have a specified number of symptoms to qualify for the label), so it looked exactly like the format of the categories in the main text. (2) The appendix had no warning to clinicians to avoid applying the label to patients. (3) The category *was* listed in the main text (under Mood Disorders), despite the *DSM* authors' claims that it was not.

Seven years later, the authors of the 1994 edition (*DSM-IV*) followed similarly extraordinary procedures to include LLPDD (now named PMDD). In the early 1990s, the LLPDD subcommittee had assembled a massive literature review, which concluded with the information that (1) very little research supported the existence of such a thing as a premenstrual mental illness; and (2) the relevant research was preliminary and methodologically flawed. What they did not mention in their conclusion was that carefully done research had virtually proven that the "disorder" in question did not exist. In a brilliant 1992 study, Sheryle Gallant and her colleagues (1992) took the symptoms listed for LLPDD and asked three groups of people to document, every day for two months, the symptoms they experienced. The groups were women who reported severe premenstrual problems, women who reported no such problems, and men. The symptom checklist responses yielded virtually no differences among the three groups.

In fact, there is widespread recognition that PMDD is not comprised of specific constellations of discrete, objective, and measurable symptoms. Researchers on both sides of the controversy—those who support the medicalization of premenstrual distress as well as those who oppose it—agree that there are major methodological problems with research on PMDD. For example, numerous investigators have criticized the existing research for being characterized by the following problems: unclear definitions, small sample sizes, lack of control groups, lack of prospective ratings of symptoms, no documentation of the timing and duration of symptoms, and failure to collect appropriate hormonal samples (see, for example, Chrisler and Caplan, 2002; Fausto-Sterling 1992; Ussher 1996; Caplan and Caplan 1994). Despite these criticisms, PMDD remains in the latest edition of the *DSM-IV-TR* and was represented to the public initially by Eli Lilly and later by other pharmaceutical companies as a "distinct medical condition." It is noteworthy that in late 2003, Eli Lilly and Company Limited in the United Kingdom sent a letter to healthcare professionals, specifying that they should no longer prescribe Prozac for treatment of PMDD, because research had shown that it was "not a well established disease entity across Europe" (Eli Lilly and Company Limited 2003). Apparently, the European Union's regulatory commission dealing with drugs had regarded the research on PMDD as failing to prove that such a disorder even existed (Moynihan 2004). It is not clear why a similar letter has not been sent by Eli Lilly to healthcare professionals elsewhere.

THE HIGH COST OF LABELING

Since the 1980s, a sociopolitical climate friendly to the view of women as emotionally labile and out of control rapidly reified PMDD. Within the past twenty years, women have been inundated with information about how to assess and manage their "premenstrual moods," and in Western culture women are urged to interpret anger, irritability, frustration, and the like as evidence of PMDD (Chrisler and Levy 1990). Women are increasingly encouraged to overlook the context in which their emotions are manifested and, instead, to regard upsets as simple by-products of (premenstrual) hormones. Insofar as it is virtually impossible to be both "feminine" and irritable, labeling one's experience as PMDD has one clear psychological advantage: one can continue to live up to idealized representations of femininity and occasionally fall short of the ideal, as long as falling short is the result of an illness (Cosgrove and Riddle 2003; Ussher, Hunter, and Browne 2000). That is, labeling one's experience as PMDD affords women the "right" to express "negative" emotions excluded by dominant definitions of femininity (e.g., irritability, anger, feeling overwhelmed). The problem is that interpreting one's distress as PMDD preserves the fantasy and fiction of idealized constructions of femininity, but it does so at an enormous cost.

More specifically, PMS discourse reinforces a rigid and stereotypic model of femininity by forcing women into constant self-surveillance. The traditional expectations of femininity are effectively hidden from view when one labels one's experience as PMS or PMDD, for this label encourages women to understand conflict as an *intrapsychic* rather than an *interpersonal* phenomenon. Many women engage in intense premenstrual bodily surveillance, and they construe their feelings, such as irritability and anger, as signs that they have lost control, that they have failed as women. Indeed, research demonstrates that labeling one's experience as PMS/PMDD encourages self-blame in women (Cosgrove and Riddle 2003; Ussher et al. 2000). As Ussher et al. (2000) point out, women describe their "PMS self" as a distinct persona—it is thought of as "bad" or problematic in some fundamental way, in contrast to a woman's "true" or non-premenstrual self. Clearly, the diagnosis PMDD, like other intra-individual explanations for emotional upset, masks the etiological role that social injustice, violence, and sexual harassment play in the development of emotional distress (see, for example, Fine 1992; Golding and Taylor 1996; 2000).

WHAT'S IN A NAME? PROZAC AND SARAFEM

For a period of time (shortly before Eli Lilly's patent on Prozac was about to expire), in print ads in all of the major women's magazines, in television spots, and on websites, women were inundated with reports of "expert knowledge" and encouraged to diagnose themselves as suffering from PMDD in order to take advantage of the "new" treatment that had been developed. "PMDD affects millions of women. . . . but the good news is that your doctor can treat PMDD symptoms with a *new* treatment called Sarafem" (Eli Lilly advertisement 2001, emphasis added). What women were not told in these ads is that the psychotropic medication produced by Eli Lilly to treat PMDD is Prozac, which had been relabeled as Sarafem and manufactured in pink and lavender capsules. Unknown to the vast majority of consumers, "fluoxetine hydrochloride" is the generic name for both Prozac and Sarafem. Moreover, the ads would not have existed without close cooperation between the American Psychiatric Association, which publishes the *Diagnostic and Statistical Manual of Mental Disorders* (2000), and the pharmaceutical company that manufactures Sarafem/Prozac (Eli Lilly). In fact, a number of PMDD subcommittee members for the *DSM-IV* received funding for their PMDD research from Eli Lilly (Steiner et al. 1995; Pearlstein et al. 2000), and the association between Eli Lilly and the *DSM* constitutes a conflict of interest. Since PMDD was included in the *DSM*, several large-scale studies have been published that have been funded by Eli Lilly (Steiner et al. 1995; Pearlstein et al. 2000). And one of the studies most frequently cited as supporting the claim that PMDD is a "unique and distinct disorder, with a rapid response to serotonin-specific agents" (Linn and Thompson 2001, 748), is a study published by Yonkers in 1997; but, as noted by the journal editor in the *Journal of the American Medical Association*, "Dr. Yonkers has ongoing research grants with Eli Lilly and Company, Pfizer, and SmithKline Beecham, and is also on the Speaker Bureau of these companies and American Home Products, where she also serves on the consulting board" (Cohen 1998, 358).

The FDA's approval of Prozac as a treatment for PMDD came at a time when Eli Lilly stood to lose a significant amount of revenue due to the imminent expiration of the patent on Prozac, which was its best-selling antidepressant. Prozac was the most-prescribed psychotropic drug in the United States in1999 (RxList 2002), "*with sales of 2.6 billion dollars in 1999*" (Gussin and Raskin 2000, emphasis added). Thus, it is relevant to note the timing and the sequence of events that led to the approval for the use of Prozac to treat PMDD.

In June 1999, just months before the patent on Prozac was about to expire, a roundtable discussion was held, and the participants included a large number of people who had received Eli Lilly funds, including PMDD subcommittee members. Shortly afterward, an article called "Is Premenstrual Dysphoric Disorder a Distinct Clinical Entity?" in the *Journal of Women's Health and Gender-Based Medicine* was presented as the state-of-the-science result of that roundtable (Endicott 1999). Presumably recalling their own description of pre-*DSM-IV* research as sparse and poor, the authors claimed that *later* evidence proved PMDD to be a real entity and Prozac to be an effective treatment. But only a very small number of the articles cited were truly post-*DSM-IV* research, and those provided no evidence that a premenstrual mental illness exists. A lengthy section of the article constituted a promotion of Selective Serotonin Reuptake Inhibitors, including fluoxetine hydrochloride (marketed as, among other things, Prozac) by reporting that they improve symptoms of women with PMDD. However, medication response should not be used to make inferences about the cause of a disorder, for psychotropic medications affect our neurochemistry; their effectiveness does not in retrospect prove that a particular disorder or disease was present (Kramer 1993). If you give SSRIs to any group of depressed or upset people, some will feel better. But the fact that some people may feel better probably results from their having taken an SSRI; a reportedly "positive" response to SSRIs *reveals nothing about the actual cause* of distress the medication is being used to treat. Since SSRIs often alleviate symptoms of depression and sometimes of anxiety, one might speculate that the people who found it helpful had been depressed and/or anxious, but the beneficial effect of the drug does not prove that a particular disorder called PMDD exists or that they had "it."

However, Eli Lilly was able to take advantage of the legal and regulatory system to increase its profits. The FDA's Psychopharmacological Drugs Advisory Committee (PDAC) met on November 3, 1999. At the meeting, representatives of Eli Lilly brought PMDD subcommittee member Jean Endicott, first author of the roundtable paper, to speak. According to the minutes, "There was consensus among [PDAC] committee members that PMDD is a recognized clinical entity that is well-defined and has accepted diagnostic criteria" (http://www.fda.gov/ohrms/dockets/ac/

acmenu.htm#Psychopharmacologic%20Drugs 1998). Interestingly, the PDAC committee had access to the same research as the European Union regulatory committee whose decision that it did not prove it was a real entity led to Eli Lilly's December 2003 letter to healthcare professionals. The PDAC voted "yes" unanimously on the question, "Has the sponsor provided evidence from more than one adequate and well controlled clinical investigation that supports the conclusion that Fluoxetine is effective for the treatment of Premenstrual Dysphoric Disorder?" It is hard to imagine what the outcome of that vote might have been without the assistance of Dr. Endicott and the roundtable article, but the pharmaceutical company achieved its goal: the extension of its patent on Prozac. Once again, there was at least the appearance of a conflict of interest, for Dr. Endicott has worked on at least one major study that was supported by Eli Lilly. The same year that Lilly's patent was extended, Dr. Endicott was a member of a research team assessing the suicidal behavior of individuals taking fluoxetine. This study was funded in part by Eli Lilly (Leon et. al. 1999). The three lead authors of that study also served as consultants to Lilly. They hypothesized that there would be no elevation in risk of suicidal behavior associated with the use of fluoxetine, and they reported that they had found support for their hypothesis. However, many years before that, internal Eli Lilly memos raising concern about Lilly's apparent suppression (or soft-pedaling) of information about increased suicidal risks and other serious negative effects of Prozac had been exhibited in a 1984 lawsuit against Eli Lilly (O'Meara 2001a).[1] Many women prescribed Sarafem do not know that it is Prozac, a powerful SSRI, and might not choose to take an SSRI if they did know. Prozac has many known negative effects, including but not limited to digestive and sleep problems and sexual dysfunction.[2] The negative effects might be acceptable to women with severe depression, but they are completely unnecessary for women whose only complaints are physical discomforts associated with the onset of menstruation or whose complaints would be classified as within the normal range of emotions if they were men.

PMDD: WHAT CLINICIANS NEED TO KNOW

The discussion of emotional problems in biomedical language and with biomedical concepts objectifies women and encourages them to monitor their affective and bodily states continually for signs of dysfunction (Cosgrove 2004; Fausto-Sterling 2000; Harding 1998; Martin 1989; Smart 1992). Empirical research shows that women who label their experience as PMS or PMDD are significantly more likely than other women to be in upsetting life situations, such as being battered, being mistreated at work, or being in troubled marriages (see, for example, Stout and Steege 1985; Golding and Taylor 1996; 2000). To classify these women as mentally disordered—to send the message that their problems are individual, psychological ones—hides the real, external sources of their troubles. Thus, the following recommendations are made:

1. Clinicians in training should be taught that, despite its inclusion in the *DSM*, the research does not prove that PMDD is a valid and reliable diagnostic category. They should also be made aware of the potential conflict of interest when *DSM* subcommittee members have received funding from the pharmaceutical companies who make the drugs that are purported to be effective treatments for anything listed in the *DSM* as disorders. Moreover, clinicians in training should be exposed to the burgeoning literature of criticism about these conflicts of interest (e.g., Angell 2000a; 2000b; 2000c; Bodenheimer 2000).

2. Teachers and trainers of therapists have an ethical responsibility to help clinical students learn how to avoid gender bias, and thus they need to make students aware of the research that demonstrates how and why the PMS label has negative consequences for women. As previously noted, although the label PMS affords women the "right" to express negative emotions, there is strong empirical evidence that understanding one's experience as PMS/PMDD encourages self-blame in women and often undermines an appreciation for the real causes and the context in which anger, sadness, and/or irritability arise. Students need to know that most research on PMS/PMDD obscures the ways women are taught to interpret and understand their experience and that this diagnosis can conceal and trivialize the violence, sexual harassment, and abuse to which many women are subjected.

3. Clinicians in training need to learn that safe interventions exist for women who experience physical symptoms (e.g., bloating, cramping, or headaches) as well as emotional distress and upset. Interventions such as self-help groups (Pirie 1988; Pirie and Smith 1992) exercise, relaxation techniques, calcium supplementation, and dietary changes, have been very effective for many women who have symptoms temporally associated with menses, and these safer options should be routinely offered (Caplan 1995).

NOTE

1. According to investigative reporter Kelly O'Meara, "In other words, Lilly consistently has denied that Prozac causes suicidal thoughts, but has a new Prozac patent to improve the original by eliminating its potential to cause suicidal thoughts" (O'Meara 2001a, 4).

2. A small number of studies has been addressed to the question of whether one or more specific or general types of antidepressants might have a connection with one or more cancers, but these have substantial methodological problems, such as being done on rodents or having very small numbers of human participants and being based on retrospective self-reports (Cotterchio et al. 2000; Harlow and Cramer 1995; Kelly, Rosenberg, and Rao 1998; Steingart and Cotterchio 1995; Brandes et al. 1992). Clearly, far more research needs to be done before any conclusions can be drawn about whether there is an association between some antidepressants and cancer, and assistance of experts in medical research is crucial in understanding the outcomes and implications of these studies; but women and prescribing providers should be privy to the research that has been done.

REFERENCES

American Psychiatric Association. (2000). *Diagnostic and statistical manual of mental disorders-IV-TR*. Washington, DC.

——. (1994). *Diagnostic and statistical manual of mental disorders-IV*. Washington, DC.

——. (1987). *Diagnostic and statistical manual of mental disorders-III-R*. Washington, DC.

——. (1980). *Diagnostic and statistical manual of mental disorders-III*. Washington, DC.

Angell, Marcia. (2000a). The pharmaceutical industry—to whom is it accountable? *New England Journal of Medicine* 342 (25), 1902–4.

——. (2000b). Is academic medicine for sale? *New England Journal of Medicine* 342 (20), 1516–18.

——. (2000c). Disclosure of authors' conflicts of interest: A follow-up. *New England Journal of Medicine* 342 (8), 586–87.

Bodenheimer, T. (2000). Uneasy alliance: Clinical investigators and the pharmaceutical industry. *New England Journal of Medicine* 342, 1539–44.

Brandes, L. J., R. J. Arron, R. P. Bogdanovic, J. Tong, C. L. F. Zaborniak, G. R. Hogg, R. C. Warrington et al. (1992). Stimulation of malignant growth in rodents by antidepressant drugs at clinically relevant doses. *Cancer Research* 52, 796–800.

Caplan, P. J. (1995). *They say you're crazy: How the world's most powerful psychiatrists decide who's normal*. Reading, MA: Addison-Wesley.

Caplan, P., and J. Caplan. (1994). *Thinking critically about research on sex and gender*. New York: HarperCollins.

Caplan, P., J. McCurdy-Myers, and M. Gans. (1992). Should PMS be called a psychiatric abnormality? *Feminism & Psychology* 2, 27–44.

Chrisler, J. C. (1996). PMS as a culture-bound syndrome. Pp. 107–21 in J. C. Chrisler, C. Golden, and P. D. Rozee, eds. *Lectures on the psychology of women*. New York: McGraw-Hill.

Chrisler, Joan C., and Paula J. Caplan. (2002). The strange case of Dr. Jekyll and Ms. Hyde: How PMS became a cultural phenomenon and a psychiatric disorder. *Annual Review of Sex Research* 13, 274-306.

Chrisler, J. C., and K. B. Levy. (1990). The media construct a menstrual monster: A content analysis of PMS articles in the popular press. *Women & Health* 16, 89–104.

Cohen, L. S. (1998). Sertraline for Premenstrual Dysphoric Disorder (Letter to the editor and reply). *Journal of the American Medical Association*, 357–58.

Cosgrove, L. (2004). The aftermath of pregnancy loss: A feminist critique of the literature and implications for treatment. *Women & Therapy* 27, 107–22.

Cosgrove, L., and B. Riddle. (2003). Constructions of femininity and experiences of menstrual distress. *Women & Health* 38, 37–58.

Cotterchio, M., N. Kreiger, G. Darlington, and A. Steingart. (2000). Antidepressant medication and breast cancer risk. *American Journal of Epidemiology* 151, 951–57.

Dalton, K. (1977). *The premenstrual syndrome and progesterone therapy.* Chicago: Yearbook Medical.

Eli Lilly and Company Limited. (2003). Letter to healthcare professionals. December.

Endicott J., J. Amsterdam, E. Eriksson, E. Frank, E. Freeman, R. Hirschfeld, F. Ling et al. (1999). Is Premenstrual Dysphoric Disorder a distinct clinical entity? *Journal of Women's Health and Gender-Based Medicine* 8, 663–79.

Fausto-Sterling, A. (2000). *Sexing the body: Gender politics and the construction of sexuality.* New York: Basic Books.

———. (1992). *Myths of gender: Biological theories about women and men.* New York: Basic Books.

Fine, M. (1992). *Disruptive voices: The possibilities of feminist research.* Ann Arbor: University of Michigan Press.

Frank, R. T. (1931). The hormonal causes of premenstrual tension. *Archives of Neurology and Psychiatry* 26, 1053–57.

Gallant, S., D. Popiel, D. Hoffman, P. Chakraborty, and J. Hamilton. (1992). Using daily ratings to confirm Premenstrual Syndrome/Late Luteal Phase Dysphoric Disorder, Part II. What makes a 'real' difference? *Psychosomatic Medicine* 54, 167–81.

Golding, J. M., and D. Taylor. (2000). Prevalence of sexual assault in women experiencing severe PMS. *Journal of Psychosomatic Obstetrics and Gynecology* 21, 69–80.

———. (1996). Sexual assault and premenstrual distress in two general population samples. *Journal of Women's Health* 5, 143–52.

Gussin, B., and J. D. Raskin. (2000). Anti antidepressants? Drugs, depression, and the medical model. *Ethical Human Sciences and Services* 2, 161–79.

Harding, J. (1998). *Sex acts practices of femininity and masculinity.* London: Sage.

Harlow, B. L., and D. W. Cramer. (1995). Self-reported use of antidepressants or benzodiazepane tranquilizers and risk of epithelial ovarian cancer: Evidence from two case-control studies. *Cancer Causes Control* 6, 130–34.

http://www.fda.gov/ohrms/dockets/ac/acmenu.htm #Psychopharmacologic%20Drugs (1999). Pp. 1–2.

Kelly, J. P., L. Rosenberg, and R. S. Rao. (1998). Is use of antidepressants associated with the occurrence of breast cancer? *American Journal of Epidemiology* 147, S69.

Kramer, P. (1993). *Listening to Prozac.* New York: Penguin Books.

Leon, A. C., M. B. Keller, M. G. Warshaw, M. D. Mueller, D. A. Solomon, W. C. Coryell, and J. Endicott. (1999). Prospective study of Fluoxetine treatment and suicidal behavior in affectively ill subjects. *American Journal of Psychiatry* 156, 195–201.

Linn, J., and D. Thompson. (2001). Treating premenstrual dysphoric agents. *Journal of Women's Health and Gender-Based Medicine*, 10, 745–50.

Martin, E. (1989). *The woman in the body: A cultural analysis of reproduction.* Boston, MA: Beacon Press.

Moynihan, Ray. (2004) Controversial disease dropped from Prozac product information. *British Medical Journal* 328, 365.

O'Meara, Kelly. (2002). Prescription drugs may trigger killing. *Insight Magazine* (*Washington Times*). September 2.

———. (2001a). Misleading medicine. *Insight Magazine* (*Washington Times*). April 30.

———. (2001b). A prescription for violence. *Insight Magazine* (*Washington Times*), May 21.

———. (1999). Doping kids. *Insight Magazine* (*Washington Times*). June 28.

Pearlstein, T. B., U. Halbreich, E. D. Batzer, C. S. Brown, J. Endicott, E. Frank, E. W. Freeman, et al. (2000). Psychosocial functioning in women with premenstrual dysphoric disorder before and after treatment with sertraline or placebo. *Journal of Clinical Psychiatry* 61, 101–9.

Pirie, Marion. (1988). The promotion of PMS: A sociological investigation of women and the illness role. Unpublished doctoral dissertation. Toronto: York University.

Pirie, Marion, and Lorrie Halliday Smith. (1992). Coping with PMS: A women's health center has success with a life skills model. *The Canadian Nurse* (December), 24–25 and 46.

RxList. (2002). http://www.rxlist.com (accessed April 25, 2002).

Smart, C., ed. (1992). *Regulating womanhood: Historical essays on marriage, motherhood and sexuality.* London and New York: Routledge.

Steiner, M., S. Steinberg, D. Stewart, D. Carter, C. Berger, R. Reid, D. Grover, and D. Streiner. (1995). Fluoxetine in the treatment of premenstrual dysphoria. *The New England Journal of Medicine* 332, 1529–34.

Steingart, A., and M. Cotterchio. (1995). Do antidepressants cause, promote, or inhibit cancer? *Journal of Clinical Epidemiology* 48, 3796–3800.

Stout, A. L., and J. F. Steege. (1985). Psychological assessment of women seeking treatment for premenstrual syndrome. *Journal of Psychosomatic Research* 29, 621–29.

Ussher, J. M. (1996). Premenstrual syndrome: Reconciling disciplinary divides through the adoption of a material-discursive epistemological standpoint. *Annual Review of Sex Research* 7, 218–51.

Ussher, J. M., M. Hunter, and S. Browne. (2000). Good, bad, or dangerous to know? Representations of femininity in women's narratives about PMS. Pp. 87–99 in C. Squire, ed. *Culture in psychology.* New York: Sage.

Yonkers, K. A. (1997). Antidepressants in the treatment of pre-menstrual dysphoric disorder. *Journal of Clinical Psychiatry* 58, 4–10.

Part V

MOVING AHEAD

Chapter 29

A New View of Women's Sexual Problems[1]

The Working Group on A New View of Women's Sexual Problems[2]

INTRODUCTION

In recent years, publicity about new treatments for men's erection problems has focused attention on women's sexuality and provoked a competitive, commercial hunt for "the female Viagra." But women's sexual problems differ from men's in basic ways which are not being examined or addressed.

We believe that a fundamental barrier to understanding women's sexuality is the medical classification scheme in current use, developed by the American Psychiatric Association (APA) for its *Diagnostic and Statistical Manual of Disorders* (*DSM*) in 1980, and revised in 1987 and 1994.[3] It divides (both men's and) women's sexual problems into four categories of sexual "dysfunction": sexual desire disorders, sexual arousal disorders, orgasmic disorders, and sexual pain disorders. These "dysfunctions" are disturbances in an assumed universal physiological sexual response pattern ("normal function") originally described by Masters and Johnson in the 1960s.[4] This universal pattern begins, in theory, with sexual drive and proceeds sequentially through the stages of desire, arousal, and orgasm.

In recent decades, the shortcomings of the framework, as it applies to women, have been amply documented.[5] The three most serious distortions produced by a framework that reduces sexual problems to disorders of physiological function, comparable to breathing or digestive disorders, are:

(1) *A false notion of sexual equivalency between men and women.* Because the early researchers emphasized similarities in men's and women's physiological responses during sexual activities, they concluded that sexual disorders must also be similar. Few investigators asked women to describe their experiences from their own points of view. When such studies were done, it

became apparent that women and men differ in many crucial ways. Women's accounts do not fit neatly into the Masters and Johnson model; for example, women generally do not separate "desire" from "arousal," women care less about physical than subjective arousal, and women's sexual complaints frequently focus on "difficulties" that are absent from the *DSM*.[6]

Furthermore, an emphasis on genital and physiological similarities between men and women ignores the implications of inequalities related to gender, social class, ethnicity, sexual orientation, etc. Social, political, and economic conditions, including widespread sexual violence, limit women's access to sexual health, pleasure, and satisfaction in many parts of the world. Women's social environments thus can prevent the expression of biological capacities, a reality entirely ignored by the strictly physiological framing of sexual dysfunctions.

(2) *The erasure of the relational context of sexuality.* The American Psychiatric Association's *DSM* approach bypasses relational aspects of women's sexuality, which often lie at the root of sexual satisfactions and problems—e.g., desires for intimacy, wishes to please a partner, or, in some cases, wishes to avoid offending, losing, or angering a partner. The *DSM* takes an exclusively individual approach to sex, and assumes that if the sexual parts work, there is no problem; and if the parts don't work, there is a problem. But many women do not define their sexual difficulties this way. The *DSM*'s reduction of "normal sexual function" to physiology implies, incorrectly, that one can measure and treat genital and physical difficulties without regard to the relationship in which sex occurs.

(3) *The leveling of differences among women.* All women are not the same, and their sexual needs, satisfactions, and problems do not fit neatly into categories of desire, arousal, orgasm, or pain. Women differ in their values, approaches to sexuality, social and cultural backgrounds, and current situations, and these differences cannot be smoothed over into an identical notion of "dysfunction," or an identical, one-size-fits-all treatment.

Because there are no magic bullets for the sociocultural, political, psychological, social or relational bases of women's sexual problems, pharmaceutical companies are supporting research and public relations programs focused on fixing the body, especially the genitals. The infusion of industry funding into sex research and the incessant media publicity about "breakthrough" treatments have put physical problems in the spotlight and isolated them from broader contexts. Factors that are far more often sources of women's sexual complaints—relational and cultural conflicts, for example, or sexual ignorance or fear—are downplayed and dismissed. Lumped into the catchall category of "psychogenic causes," such factors go unstudied and unaddressed. Women with these problems are being excluded from clinical trials on new drugs, and yet, if current marketing patterns with men are indicative, such drugs will be aggressively advertised for all women's sexual dissatisfactions.

A corrective approach is desperately needed. We propose a new and more useful classification of women's sexual problems, one that gives appropriate priority to individual distress and inhibition arising within a broader framework of cultural and relational factors. We challenge the cultural assumptions embedded in the *DSM* and the reductionist research and marketing program of the pharmaceutical industry. We call for research and services driven not by commercial interests but by women's own needs and sexual realities.

SEXUAL HEALTH AND SEXUAL RIGHTS: INTERNATIONAL VIEWS

To move away from the *DSM*'s genital and mechanical blueprint of women's sexual problems, we turned for guidance to international documents. In 1974 the World Health Organization held a unique conference on the training needs for sexual health workers. The report noted: "A growing body of knowledge indicates that problems in human sexuality are more pervasive and more important to the well-being and health of individuals in many cultures than has previously been recognized." The report emphasized the importance of taking a positive approach to human sexuality and the enhancement of relationships. It offered a broad definition of "sexual health" as "the integration of the somatic, emotional, intellectual, and social aspects of sexual being."[7]

In 1999, the World Association of Sexology meeting in Hong Kong adopted a Declaration of Sexual Rights.[8] "In order to assure that human beings and societies develop healthy sexuality," the Declaration stated, "the following sexual rights must be recognized, promoted, respected, and defended":

- The right to sexual freedom, excluding all forms of sexual coercion, exploitation and abuse;
- The right to sexual autonomy and safety of the sexual body;
- The right to sexual pleasure, which is a source of physical, psychological, intellectual and spiritual well-being;
- The right to sexual information . . . generated through unencumbered yet scientifically ethical inquiry;
- The right to comprehensive sexuality education;
- The right to sexual health care, which should be available for prevention and treatment of all sexual concerns, problems, and disorders.

WOMEN'S SEXUAL PROBLEMS: A NEW CLASSIFICATION

Sexual problems, which The Working Group on A New View of Women's Sexual Problems defines as discontent or dissatisfaction with any emotional, physical, or relational aspect of sexual experience, may arise in one or more of the following interrelated aspects of women's sexual lives.

I. *Sexual problems due to sociocultural, political, or economic factors*
    A. Ignorance and anxiety due to inadequate sex education, lack of access to health services, or other social constraints:
        1. Lack of vocabulary to describe subjective or physical experience.
        2. Lack of information about human sexual biology and life-stage changes.
        3. Lack of information about how gender roles influence men's and women's sexual expectations, beliefs, and behaviors.
        4. Inadequate access to information and services for contraception and abortion, STD prevention and treatment, sexual trauma, and domestic violence.
    B. Sexual avoidance or distress due to perceived inability to meet cultural norms regarding correct or ideal sexuality, including:
        1. Anxiety or shame about one's body, sexual attractiveness, or sexual responses.
        2. Confusion or shame about one's sexual orientation or identity, or about sexual fantasies and desires.
    C. Inhibitions due to conflict between the sexual norms of one's subculture or culture of origin and those of the dominant culture.
    D. Lack of interest, fatigue, or lack of time due to family and work obligations.
II. *Sexual problems relating to partner and relationship*
    A. Inhibition, avoidance, or distress arising from betrayal, dislike, or fear of partner, partner's abuse or couple's unequal power, or arising from partner's negative patterns of communication.
    B. Discrepancies in desire for sexual activity or in preferences for various sexual activities.
    C. Ignorance or inhibition about communicating preferences or initiating, pacing, or shaping sexual activities.
    D. Loss of sexual interest and reciprocity as a result of conflicts over commonplace issues such as money, schedules, or relatives, or resulting from traumatic experiences, e.g., infertility or the death of a child.
    E. Inhibitions in arousal or spontaneity due to partner's health status or sexual problems.

III. *Sexual problems due to psychological factors*
   A. Sexual aversion, mistrust, or inhibition of sexual pleasure due to:
      1. Past experiences of physical, sexual, or emotional abuse.
      2. General personality problems with attachment, rejection, cooperation, or entitlement.
      3. Depression or anxiety.
   B. Sexual inhibition due to fear of sexual acts or of their possible consequences, e.g., pain during intercourse, pregnancy, sexually transmitted disease, loss of partner, loss of reputation.
IV. *Sexual problems due to medical factors*
   Pain or lack of physical response during sexual activity despite a supportive and safe interpersonal situation, adequate sexual knowledge, and positive sexual attitudes. Such problems can arise from:
   A. Numerous local or systemic medical conditions affecting neurological, neurovascular, circulatory, endocrine or other systems of the body.
   B. Pregnancy, sexually transmitted diseases, or other sex-related conditions.
   C. Side effects of many drugs, medications, or medical treatments.
   D. Iatrogenic conditions.

CONCLUSION

This document is designed for researchers desiring to investigate women's sexual problems, for educators teaching about women and sexuality, for medical and nonmedical clinicians planning to help women with their sexual lives, and for a public that needs a framework for understanding a rapidly changing and centrally important area of life.

For further information about the Campaign for "A New View of Women's Sexual Problems," to obtain additional copies of this document, or to make a financial contribution, please contact:

Dr. Leonore Tiefer, 163 Third Ave., PMB #183, New York, NY 10003
email: LTiefer@Mindspring.com

Dr. Carol Tavris, 1847 Nichols Canyon Road, Los Angeles, CA 90046
email: CTavris@compuserve.com

NOTES

Editors' note: The Working Group on A New View of Women's Sexual Problems wrote the 2000 manifesto that is reprinted here. Its primary foci were the far too

238   <i>The Working Group on A New View of Women's Sexual Problems</i>

frequent pathologizing and misunderstanding of women's sexual concerns and the increasingly active role played by the pharmaceutical industry in interpreting women's sexuality. Critiquing the presentation of women's sexuality as presented in the *Diagnostic and Statistical Manual of Mental Disorders*, which they consider to be based too much on the picture of physiological functioning portrayed by Masters and Johnson and on inaccurate understanding of the realities of women's psychology and location in society, they propose that, in trying to understand women's sexual concerns, we consider the entire context of sexuality for women. This includes the realities of women's physiology but also, importantly, the vast and layered interpersonal and wider social context that shapes their sexuality. We consider this manifesto important because, although the *DSM* does include room for consideration of psychological factors, the guidelines and standards are left too much to the subjective judgment of the individual therapist, and the sexuality-related diagnoses are rooted in what the Working Group on the New View of Women's Sexuality calls the problematic "cultural assumptions" made by the *DSM* authors. The authors of this manifesto have articulated a clear and important framework for considering how to classify and address women's sexual concerns. Since this chapter was first written, Working Group Convener Leonore Tiefer, Ph.D., has inaugurated an educational campaign designed to inform the public about the dangers of medicalizing women's sexuality and sexual problems.

1. This paper appears on the website www.fsd-alert.org and is also available in E. Kaschak and L. Tiefer, eds. *A new view of women's sexual problems* (New York: Haworth, 2001), 1–8, and is reprinted here with the kind permission of The Working Group on A New View of Women's Sexual Problems.

2. The Working Group on A New View of Women's Sexual Problems includes: Linda Alperstein, M.S.W., Associate Clinical Professor of Psychiatry, University of California at San Francisco and Psychotherapy Practice, San Francisco, CA; Carol Ellison, Ph.D., Psychotherapy Practice, Oakland, CA; Jennifer R. Fishman, B.A., Doctoral Candidate, Department of Social and Behavioral Science, University of California at San Francisco; Marny Hall, Ph.D., Author, Psychotherapy Practice, San Francisco, CA; Lisa Handwerker, Ph.D., M.P.H., Institute for the Study of Social Change, University of California at Berkeley; Heather Hartley, Ph.D., Assistant Professor of Sociology, Portland State University, OR; Ellyn Kaschak, Ph.D., Professor of Psychology, San Jose State University, CA; Peggy J. Kleinplatz, Ph.D., School of Psychology, University of Ottawa, Ontario, Canada; Meika Loe, M.A., Doctoral Candidate, Women's Studies emphasis, Sociology, University of California at Santa Barbara; Laura Mamo, B. A., Doctoral Candidate, Department of Sociology and Behavioral Science, University of California at San Francisco; Carol Tavris, Ph.D., Social Psychologist and independent scholar, Los Angeles, CA; Leonore Tiefer, Ph.D., Associate Clinical Professor of Psychiatry, New York University, School of Medicine and Albert Einstein College of Medicine.

3. American Psychiatric Association, *Diagnostic and atatistical manual of mental disorders-III, III-R, and IV.* Washington, DC: American Psychiatric Association, 1980, 1987, 1994.

4. W. H. Masters and V. E. Johnson, *Human sexual response* (Boston: Little, Brown, & Co., 1966); W. H. Masters, and V. E. Johnson, *Human sexual inadequacy* (Boston: Little, Brown, & Co., 1970).

5. See, for example, L. Tiefer, "Historical, scientific, clinical and feminist criticisms of 'the Human Sexual Response Cycle' model," *Annual Review of Sex Research* 2 (1991), 1–23; R. Basson "The female sexual response revisited," *J. Society Obstetrics and Gynaecology of Canada* 22 (2000), 383–87.

6. E. Frank, C. Anderson, and D. Rubinstein, "Frequency of sexual dysfunction in 'normal' couples," *New England Journal of Medicine* 299 (1978), 111–15; S. Hite, *The Hite Report: A nationwide study on female sexuality* (New York: Macmillan, 1976); C. Ellison, *Women's sexualities: Generations of women share intimate secrets of sexual self-acceptance* (Oakland, CA: New Harbinger, 2000).

7. World Health Organization Technical Report, series No. 572 (1975). Full text available on the Robert Koch Institute sexuality website, www.rki.de/GESUND/ARCIIIV/IIOME.HTM.

8. Full text available on the website listed in footnote 7 and also on the World Association of Sexology website, www.tc.umn.edu/~coleman001/was/wdecla/htm. It is published in E. M. L. Ng, J. J. Borras-Valls, M. Perez-Conchillo, and E. Coleman, eds., *Sexuality in the new millenium* (Bologna: Editrice Compositori, 2000).

Chapter 30

Resisting Diagnosis

Gloria Anthony[1]

As a longtime feminist, I have been interested in the effects of oppression, but some years ago I became aware of the importance of resistance to oppression. This is a story of the way some therapists have resisted the oppressive system that required us to give all patients psychiatric diagnoses.

I moved to a new city in 1990 and began working in a local clinic. Immediately I was told that when we registered a new client, the first thing we had to do was record a diagnosis on the bottom of the form, including terms from all *Diagnostic and Statistical Manual of Mental Disorders* axes that we considered pertinent. Having worked in psychiatry for several decades, I was familiar with some of the controversies about diagnostic labels and knew about some damage to which these diagnoses had led. So I refused to do it. I just did not record diagnoses for anyone I saw at the clinic, even though I would get memos every once in a while from my boss, saying, "You have not completed your diagnoses." I just put the memos in the wastebasket. In addition, some wonderful colleagues and I organized presentations to the clinic staff in which we critiqued the *DSM* and used information from various disciplines to try to educate our colleagues and bosses about the problems that psychiatric diagnoses created.

Not long ago, the clinic began using a new system of intake and statistical management. On their new form, clinicians are asked to identify psychosocial problems that the patient is having, including problems with their primary support group (family and caregivers); problems related to the social environment/network, including discrimination, racism, ageism, sexual orientation, educational problems, occupational problems, housing problems, economic problems, problems with axis to and provision of healthcare services (i.e., inadequate, unavailable healthcare services), and cultural insensitivity; problems related to interaction to the legal system/crime; physical health problems; and other psychosocial and environmental problems, including migration, cultural factors, and exposure to disasters and other hostilities. Immediately, therapists began to take note of the factors that are actually responsible for the emotional states of the people who come to our clinic, rather than of individual, intrapsychic ones.

Another part of the new intake and statistical form is a section for identifying the patient's presenting problems, not their diagnoses. We have maintained for a long time that if you discuss with your clients their concerns, you don't need a label for them. You can just describe what is happening. The categories of presenting problems that we use are not called "disorders" but rather "difficulties," "problems," or "troubles" and include those "from the environment" (such as abuse or neglect), thus clearly relating the problem to something outside the individual and not to something individual and intrapsychic in origin. Under physical difficulties, one listing is "problems related to eating," and this is described as including intense worry about the amount of food ingested and/or purged. Several of us have quite purposely implemented resistance with regard to the naming of problems related to eating. We have persistently refused to use the term "eating disorder" and politely remind those who do use it that other, preferable terms are available (see Cohen, chapter 24 in this volume). Constant vigilance is required in this work, and having a core group of resisters in our clinic is very important. Our aim is to make more salient to the therapists with whom we work the fact that everyone has problems, and those problems vary in degree, but when we participate in using terms like "disorder" and "mental illness," we draw a clear line between people to whom we apply those labels and other people. The presence of those terms on people's charts can result in their losing their children, their jobs, their income, and other horrendous things that can result from being given a diagnostic label. We have seen this happen many times to the people who have turned to therapists for help.

I have conducted some in-depth research about the ways that marginalized people have been mistreated. When I interviewed a woman from Trinidad, I specifically asked her about mistreatment, to which she responded that she had been mistreated. Then I asked her, "What about resistance?" She said, "To survive is to resist." Resistance is profoundly important. And in our clinic, our resistance to psychiatrically diagnosing human beings goes on.

NOTES

1. This is a pseudonym for the author, who would have liked to use her real name, but who knew that, given the ongoing power of advocates of the most traditional forms of labeling, including the author's employers, it would not be safe to do so.

Chapter 31

The Importance of Critical Inquiry

Lisa Cosgrove

[T]he *DSM* has become the pre-eminent organizing rubric not only for diagnosing patients in the mental heath system, but also for textbooks of psychiatry and psychology, for deciding on insurance reimbursements, and for
much government-funded mental heath research. This reliance on a single
point of view, which has come to have the status of law, should raise concern, no matter what its content. Such apparent unanimity seals off opportunities for intellectual debate and dialogue from which new ideas flow
and deeper insights are generated.

R. T. Hare-Mustin and J. Marecek, "Abnornal Psychology
and the Politics of Madness," 112

Critiques are not lethal to psychology and indeed have the potential to transform and invigorate our discipline (Gergen 2001). In fact, within the last few
years an increasing number of educators and psychologists have emphasized
the importance of active learning and the development of critical thinking
skills (Caplan and Caplan 1994; Dunlap 1998; Keely, Ali, and Gebing 1998;
McCade 1995; Sheldon 1999; Wade 1995). We hope readers will feel that
their critical thinking skills have been enhanced by reflecting on the issues
and questions raised in this book. We also hope that readers will have enjoyed
the opportunity to think more fully about their personal and ideological assumptions as they relate to psychiatric diagnosis. Our aim in editing this book
has been to add to the growing body of work that is intended to encourage
therapists to engage in critical inquiry and reflection. Critique can impede
both intra- and interdisciplinary dialogue if it is presented as a zero-sum activity, where one theory or way of thinking must triumph over another (see
also, Gergen 1994). But the questions raised and issues discussed in this book
are intended to encourage dialogue, not to foreclose it. Incorporating a social

justice model within the psychology classroom—and within the field more generally—requires intellectual debate and an open and honest assessment of the values that ground the psychological truths we choose to uphold. Thus, our aim has been to demonstrate that what are presented as absolutes in the enterprise of psychiatric diagnosis are neither neutral, objective, universal, nor innocuous, and therefore, it is not ethical for practitioners to assume that diagnoses are always useful. Ethical practitioners need to be aware that use of diagnostic labels can have harmful consequences.

The assumption that the categories that are commonly used, including but not limited to those contained in the *DSM*, naturally exist and simply awaited discovery is not warranted. In addition, as demonstrated in the chapters of this book, that assumption tends to sustain unjust social relations. The authors of the chapters of this book have emphasized the importance of examining the relationship among the "trinity of power/knowledge/rhetoric" (Maranhao, quoted here from Lowe 1999, 75). For example, the *DSM*'s shift to a medicalized paradigm and discourse coincides with the shift to conservatism in national politics that began in the 1980s (Hare-Mustin and Marecek 1997). Hence, it is essential to pay close attention to the terms and beliefs that we use to understand emotional distress, as Gergen (1994) has noted. Describing the ways that terminology works, Gergen writes that it "sustain[s] and support[s] certain ways of doing things and prevent[s] others from emerging"(Gergen 1994, 147). And so we must ask:

> What kind of social patterns does the existing vocabulary of psychological deficit facilitate (or prevent)? How do the terms of the mental health professions—terms such as . . . "cognitive dysfunction," "depression," "post-traumatic stress disorder," . . . and so on—function within the culture more generally? Do they lend themselves to desirable forms of human relationship . . . [and] are there more promising alternatives? (Gergen 1994, 147)

These questions elude easy answers, and, as noted in our introductory chapter, "we must be suspicious of anything that looks like a too simple and easy answer" (Parker et al. 1995, 14). In an attempt to encourage "thinking outside the box," I offer the following for further thinking about how our biopsychiatric discourse functions and about the politics and ethics of psychiatric diagnosis. These activities can be used in academic, clinical, consultative, or other contexts. If used in an academic setting, for instance, they could take the form of in-class discussions or debates, or they could be used to structure individual papers or group projects.

1. *Obtain a copy of* The DSM Casebook *(Spitzer et. al. 2002), read a case titled "Dolls," and critique it, keeping in mind that the diagnosis a therapist assigns a client directly influences his/her treatment recommendations. In*

that case description, Rocky is an eight-year-old boy whose parents are concerned about him because "he wants to be a girl" (Spitzer et al. 2002, 263). He is described in the following way:

> Rocky prefers to play with girls [and] . . . refuses to engage in rough play with boys and physical fighting. . . . Rocky has never been interested in toy cars, trucks, or trains, but is an avid player with dolls (baby, Barbie, and family dolls) and enjoys playing with kitchen toys. . . . He loves dancing, preferably in dresses. He is very interested in jewelry, has plastic necklaces, and pretends at times to wear earrings. . . . Although somewhat reluctant, he is able to describe much of what his parents have related about his toy and game preferences. He says that he does not want to be a boy because he is afraid he will have to play with soldiers or play army with other boys when he grows bigger" (Spitzer et al. 2000, 364).

The DSM Casebook authors believe that "there should be little question about the diagnosis in this case" (Spitzer et al. 2000, 365), and thus Rocky has been diagnosed with Gender Identity Disorder (GID). What kind of treatment recommendations will most likely be made as a result of this diagnosis? Do you find these treatment recommendations helpful? Why or why not? What implicit assumptions and beliefs (e.g., about gender, sexuality, the military, etc.) ground your response to this question? How do you think Rocky might begin to see himself as a result of this diagnosis? After reading chapter 15 in this book by William R. Metcalfe and Paula J. Caplan, what concerns and criticisms do you have about using the diagnosis GID to understand Rocky's behavior? What kinds of relationships with his parents and sister are facilitated, and what kinds of relationships are impeded by using the discourse of the medical model (i.e., by using the discourse of GID) to understand Rocky's behavior?

2. *Interview faculty members in an academic department other than psychology, psychiatry, or social work (e.g., philosophy, sociology, economics, etc.) who are doing research on a topic related to mental health issues.* How might their particular perspectives and the perspectives of their disciplines shed light on mental health issues? Questions to consider include: Are their hypotheses/research questions similar to or different from the kinds of hypotheses/questions asked by clinicians and clinical researchers? What kinds of epistemological and methodological assumptions underlie their research? Do they consider their research to be social action research? Why/why not? What are some of the benefits of doing transdisciplinary research?

3. *In the village of Geel in Belgium, people with psychiatric illness and mental retardation have lived in townspeople's homes since the 1400s* (Goldstein and Godemont 2003). *This alternative mental health approach has inspired other communities to initiate similar programs. Provide a*

detailed history of this community and compare and contrast this approach to traditional medical-model approaches. Questions to consider include: What role, if any, does diagnosis play in Geel? What are the beliefs about emotional distress, community, subjectivity, and our moral and ethical obligations to each other that underlie Geel's community-based approach? What could we learn from the people of Geel? Can you imagine an approach like this working here? Why or why not?

4. *Do some research about a group that has an explicitly activist, alternative approach to mental health. If possible, also try to interview a member of that group.* (There are several websites and groups listed in the introduction of this book.) What is different, problematic, and/or helpful about this group? What did you learn? What exactly makes them activist or alternative? Would you use this on your "resource list" for clients? Why or why not?

5. *Discuss the following statement.* "Psychoanalysis can potentially be employed to either support or oppose the status quo . . . the latent possibility that psychoanalysis would be useful in exposing socially destructive myths, internalized by citizens during the socialization process, remains a tantalizing but as yet elusive and unfulfilled promise" (Prilleltensky 1994, 68). As you respond to this statement, think about how psychoanalytic concepts continue to influence the diagnoses we give to clients. That is, how do psychoanalytic constructs function diagnostically?

6. *Compare and contrast Peter Kramer's book,* Listening to Prozac *(1993), with Peter and Ginger Breggin's book,* Talking Back to Prozac *(1994).* Identify the underlying assumptions each author makes about mental illness and depression. With which position do you most closely identify? Why? How was reading both books helpful?

7. *Write a creative dialogue between the* DSM *authors and any of the authors of this book.* Make sure that your dialogue addresses how complex and controversial it is to define and diagnose mental illness.

8. *Develop a list of recommendations that would help mental health professionals pay attention to the social and political context of psychological problems.* As Paula J. Caplan noted, "the misinterpretation of behavior as pathology also results quite often from the labeling of social problems as individual psychological problems" (1995, 80). What are some examples of the kind of pathologizing to which Caplan is referring? Do you believe that the DSM task force has too much leeway about what is classified as a mental illness?

9. *Imagine that you have been asked to serve on a* DSM-V *committee and that your specific task is to critique and revise the* DSM-IV-TR*'s definition of a mental disorder, which is:*

"[E]ach of the mental disorders is conceptualized as a clinically significant behavioral or psychological syndrome that occurs in the individual and is associated with present distress (e.g., a painful symptom) or disability (i.e., impairment in one or more areas of functioning) or with a significantly increased risk of suffering, death, pain, disability, or an important loss of freedom. In addition, this syndrome or pattern must not be merely an expectable and culturally sanctioned response to a particular event, for example, the death of a loved one. Whatever its original cause, it must currently be considered a manifestation of a behavioral, psychological, or biological dysfunction in the individual. Neither deviant behavior (e.g., political, religious, or sexual) nor conflicts that are primarily between the individual and society are mental disorders unless the deviance or conflict is a symptom of a dysfunction in the individual, as described above" (American Psychiatric Association 2000, xxxi). What changes would you make so that the definition is adequate for addressing the relationship between social injustice and psychological distress (see, for example, Hare-Mustin and Marecek 1997)?

REFERENCES

American Psychiatric Association. (2000). *Diagnostic and statistical manual of mental Disorders-IV-TR*. Washington, DC.

Breggin, P. R., and G. R. Breggin. (1994). *Talking back to Prozac*. New York: St. Martin's Press.

Caplan, P. (1995). *They say you're crazy: How the world's most powerful psychiatrists decide who's normal*. Reading, MA: Addison-Wesley.

Caplan, P., and J. Caplan. (1994). *Thinking critically about research on sex and gender*. New York: HarperCollins.

Dunlap, M. R. (1998). Methods of supporting students' critical reflection in courses incorporating service learning. *Teaching of Psychology* 25, 208–10.

Gergen, K. J. (2001). Psychological science in a postmodern world. *American Psychologist* 56, 803–13.

———. (1994). *Realities and relationships: Soundings in social construction*. Cambridge, MA: Harvard University Press.

Goldstein, J. L., and M.M.L. Godemont. (2003). The legend and lessons of Geel, Belgium: A 1500-year-old legend, a 21st century model. *Community Mental Health Journal* 39, 441–58.

Hare-Mustin, R. T., and J. Marecek. (1997). Abnormal psychology and the politics of madness. Pp. 104–20 in D. Fox and I. Prilleltensky, eds. *Critical psychology: An introduction*. Thousand Oaks, CA: Sage.

Keeley, S. M., R. Ali, and T. Gebing. (1998). Beyond the sponge model: Encouraging students' questioning skills in abnormal psychology. *Teaching of Psychology* 25, 270–74.

Kramer, P. (1993). *Listening to Prozac*. New York: Penguin Books.

Lowe, R. (1999). Between the 'No Longer' and the 'Not Yet': Postmodernism as a context for critical therapeutic work. Pp. 71–85 in Ian Parker, ed. *Deconstructing psychotherapy*. Thousand Oaks, CA: Sage.

McCade, S. A. (1995). Case study pedagogy to advance critical thinking. *Teaching of Psychology* 22, 9–10.

Parker, I., E. Georgaca, D. Harper, T. McLaughlin, and M. Stowell-Smith. (1995). *Deconstructing psychopathology*. Thousand Oaks, CA: Sage.

Prilleltensky, I. (1994). *The morals and politics of psychology: Psychological discourse and the status quo*. New York: State University of New York Press.

Sheldon, J. P. (1999). A secondary agenda in classroom activities: Having students confront their biases and assumptions. *Teaching of Psychology* 26, 209–11.

Spitzer, R. L., M. Gibbon, A. E. Skodol, J. B. Williams, and M. B. First, eds. *DSM-IV-TR casebook: A learning companion to the Diagnostic and Statistical Manual of Mental Disorders, fourth edition, text revision*.

Wade, C. (1995). Using writing to help develop and assess critical thinking. *Teaching of Psychology* 22, 24–28.

Chapter 32

Some Future Contenders[1]

Paula J. Caplan and Wesley E. Profit

Shortly before this book went to press, proposals for two new diagnostic categories hit the media. "Compulsive Shopping" was proposed by a pharmaceutical giant; "Relational Disorder" was initiated by a psychiatrist leading the *DSM* project. These proposals reflect many of the same problems and raise many of the same types of concerns as many categories that have long been considered official. *Washington Post* investigative reporter Shankar Vedantam has said that in the current debate "inside and outside psychiatry," doctors are grappling with the question of what should be called social problems and what should be called medical ailments (Vedantam 2002, A01). But even if these two new categories are never included in the psychiatric manual, like other invented labels such as "Road Rage" and "Codependency," they may come into wide use.[2]

Writing in the *Wall Street Journal*, Anne Marie Chaker reported that Forest Laboratories, Inc., had funded three studies "that test whether its antidepressants may help reduce the amount of time people spend obsessing about shopping or prowling the stores" and that "early results suggest that [Forest Laboratories' drug, Celexa] has some benefits" (Chaker 2002, D1). It is extremely problematic that all three studies were funded by the pharmaceutical company that sells Celexa, a clear conflict of interest. One wonders whether it is relevant that the Food and Drug Administration's (FDA) approval of any drug is granted only for purposes of treating a particular disease or other entity, but if it is approved for a second disease or disorder, then the drug company's patent on the drug is extended. FDA approval paves the way for potentially millions more dollars for the pharmaceutical company, because the patent extension prevents other drug companies from selling the same preparation and because the company achieves an economy of scale with each subsequent use for a drug.

Consider first those people whose lives are seriously affected because they spend so much time, money, and energy shopping. It doesn't take an expert to understand that, if Celexa, an antidepressant, reduces problematic shopping, it is likely that the shopping was a symptom of depression, and thus what is important is to address the real sources of the depression—not the shopping—especially in light of the risk of suicide both in depressed people and as a result of a negative reaction to this kind of drug (O'Meara 2001; Shogren 2004). The label "Compulsive Shopping Disorder" trivializes and minimizes the person's depression.

Furthermore, it is difficult to imagine that women would not be disproportionately described as suffering from Compulsive Shopping, even if they enjoy shopping, can afford it, and get pleasure from using the things they buy or from seeing others enjoy their gifts. It is common knowledge that many men and women will say, "You must have Premenstrual Dysphoric Disorder!" to a woman who is angry, depressed, or even just anxious. Even if they only say, "You must be PMS-ing," it is now likely that the women so described, or accused, will end up taking psychotropic drugs. The most worrying portent is that some years ago, a man accused of killing his wife offered as his defense that she was a compulsive shopper.

And what is meant by "compulsive shopping"? Poor people, especially those who live from paycheck to paycheck, shop at least once a week after they are paid. If they are day laborers, they probably shop every day. How is this "shopping" to be distinguished from Compulsive Shopping Disorder? Poor people or people with limited incomes may certainly go into debt because of the shopping they do, of the kinds just described, but that would not be due to anything that one could conceivably call a mental disorder. Furthermore, what is to be done with women or men who take seriously the idea of getting the best bargain for their money and consequently spend considerable time in stores, sometimes making several trips, before they ever make a purchase.

The proposal for Relational Disorder (RD) came from *DSM-IV* editor, psychiatrist Michael First, and psychiatrist David Reiss. The American Psychiatric Association is reported to be circulating a monograph containing the recommendation that RD be included in the *DSM-V;* this proposed category is described as applicable to couple and parent-child relationships in which, they say, neither party is mentally ill, but the relationship is (Vedantam 2002, A01). In a *Washington Post* story, it was reported that advocates say the "illness" could be "treated possibly with drugs" (Vedantam 2002, A01). In any relationship, there are usually some troubles, and these would provide strong impetus for the RD label to be applied to almost any relationship. Indeed, Vedantam's statement that creation of this new category could "result in tens of thousands of families being diagnosed with a psychiatric disorder" would seem to be an extremely low estimate. It was reported that in the first six months after the FDA approved fluoxetine hydrochloride to treat the unproven entity called Premenstrual Dysphoric Disorder (PMDD), 2.5 million prescriptions for the drug were written. PMDD is a category that can be applied only to women, and only women of menstruating age, but anyone of any age could presumably be diagnosed (along with their parent, child, or partner) with RD. The market for drugs prescribed for RD would skyrocket, and it is alarming that so many children would be considered for medication. It seems likely that the RD label would encourage the FDA to approve more psychotropic drugs for use with children, a direction that has recently been set with the FDA's approval of Prozac for children who are at least eight years old (and thus, of course, for adolescents, with the federal government supposedly alarmed about drug problems among youth) (FDA approves Prozac for kids, 2003).

Imagine a future in which a couple diagnosed with RD come to a psychiatrist's office. In keeping with the criteria for RD, the psychiatrist has declared that neither individual is mentally ill but the relationship is. The psychiatrist opens a bottle of a psychotropic medication and takes out a pill that is being used in drug trials for RD. If neither member of the couple is mentally ill but the relationship is, where does the psychiatrist put the pill?

Of course people have relationships that cause them pain, anguish, and depression, but what seems likely to happen if RD is used? Some couples have problems because one of them is depressed, violent, or emotionally constricted and virtually incapable of intimacy. For years, such couples have been in couple therapy, but when one party is *clearly* the source of the couple's problems, it is unlikely to be helpful and likely to be dangerous to have them in therapy together. It is risky because, if the therapist clearly "takes the side of" only one member of the couple, makes comments that are based on acceptance of that person's view as accurate and valid, the other member will naturally feel so hurt, invalidated, and angry at feeling "ganged up on" that there is no point in trying to work with them.

Most disturbing are those instances in which the person with whom the therapist sides is the one who is violent, cold, or depressed, and the therapist consciously or unconsciously does this because the emotionally healthy person is more resilient, slower to feel attacked and betrayed than is the partner. In a society that continues to be sexist, it remains the case that whatever the source of problems between a couple, women are more likely than men to be blamed because women are still considered the appropriate caretakers and healers of relationships (Caplan 2000).

If both members of a couple have truly serious psychological problems, then they, too, would not fit the description of RD, but the availability of that label would lead to its being used, even by well-meaning therapists who might consider it a way to avoid blaming or pathologizing each individual. The problem with classifying such couples as relationally disordered is that the serious problems of each might be downplayed or ignored. And, as Vedantam points out, "troubled relationships with siblings could be the next large group" to be considered diagnosable with RD (2002, A01). One wonders what could follow—teacher-child relationships, next-door neighbors, internet correspondents? Some psychiatrists have already asked, "What about troubled relationships between managers and employees, or even troubled relationships between individuals and the state?" (Vedantam 2002, A01). Taking it one step further, Dr. Bedirham Ustun of the World Health Organization observed: "You can take road rage as a relational disorder. It's a relationship between the person and traffic" (Vedantam 2002, A01). Thus, the future holds the alarming potential for every relationship to be distorted by the view that it is disordered.

NOTES

1. In the past, a publication that was part of the set of books connected with the *DSM* included a portion called "Some Future Contenders," describing categories being considered for the next edition of the manual.

2. Calling "Road Rage" a disorder should require one to distinguish between an irresistible impulse and an impulse that was not resisted. It is doubtful that this can be done in any objective or scientific manner. As for the term "Codependency," it is being used as soon as a therapist or a layperson hears that the individual in question lives with an alcoholic, drug abuser, or anyone else with a major problem. The label "Codependency" is rarely diagnosed thoughtfully, is often used in reference to women or children who—either for economic reasons, reasons of physical dependency, or from fear of being considered a bad wife or child—cannot leave the person who has the major problem, and is often used in a victim-blaming way has not stopped either therapists or laypeople from using the term (Kokin and Walker 1989).

REFERENCES

Caplan, Paula J. (2000). *Don't blame mother: Mending the mother-daughter relationship*. New York: Routledge.

Chaker, Anne Marie. (2003). For anti-depressant makers, shopaholics are new market. *Wall Street Journal*, January 2, D1.

FDA approves Prozac for kids. (2003). *Washington Post*, January 6, www.washington post.com/wp-dyn/articles/A8525-2003Jan3.html.

Kokin, Morris, with Ian Walker. (1989). *Women married to alcoholics*. New York: William Morrow.

O'Meara, Kelly P. (2001). Misleading medicine. *Insight Magazine* (*Washington Times*), April 30.

Shogren, Elizabeth. (2004). FDA sat on report linking suicide, drugs. *Los Angeles Times*, April 7.

Vedantam, Shankar. (2002). Doctors consider diagnosis for "ill" relationship. *Washington Post*, September 1, p. A01.

Index

Abbey, A., 203
ableism, xiv
abnormality, xx
abuse, xv. *See also* violence
Adjustment Disorder, 99, 101
advertising, xviii
age, xiv, xxii
ageism, xiv, xvi, 89–96, 246
Agoraphobia, 177–80
Ahn, W., 197
amenorrhea, 194, 197–98
American Home Products, 224
American Psychological Association's National Task Force on Women and Depression, 183
Americans with Disabilities Act, 49
Andreasen, Nancy, 30–31
Angell, Marcia, xiv
anorexia, 130, 189–90, 193–98
antidepressant drugs, xiv, xviii
Antisocial Personality Disorder, 85
Anxiety Disorders Work Group (ADWG), 34–35
Armstrong, Louise, 63–65
assessment, psychological and psychiatric, xv, xxix
Association for Women in Psychology, 221

Attention Deficit Disorder (ADD), 50, 52
auditory processing deficit, 109–11

Becker, Dana, 213
Bell, Carl, 84
Betz, E., 194
biology, xiv
Bipolar Disorder, 93
Blascovich, B. L., 173
Body Dysmorphic Disorder (BDD), 190
Bone, Michael, 64
Borderline Personality Disorder (BPD), 103–7, 127–28, 207, 209–10, 215–16; overdiagnosis of, 213; Treatment Unit, 105
Bowden, Jerome, 55
Bowers, L., 198
Breggin, Ginger, 246
Breggin, Peter, 246
British Columbia Continuing Legal Education Society seminar, 62
Brown, A., 184
bulimia, 130, 189–90

Canadian Mental Health Association, Women and Mental Health Committee of, xxii, xxiii

Caplan, Paula J., xix, 103, 210, 245
Carter, Samuel, 202
Catastrophic Stress Disorder (CSD),
    27–28
Celexa, 249–50
Chaker, Anne-Marie, 249
Chatham-Carpenter, A., 174
Chesler, Phyllis, 175
child custody, xv, xix, xxix, xxx
children, 250–51; learning disabilities
    in, 99–107; psychiatric policing of,
    99–107; sexual abuse of, 61–65, 106,
    117, 164, 202, 208
classism, xvi. *See also* social class
clinicians: attitudes and beliefs of, 9–22;
    cognitive biases of, 10–11;
    professional identity and training of,
    12–14, 227
codependency, 249
Colliver, J. A., 214
Complex Post-traumatic Stress Disorder,
    29, 35
Comprehensive Textbook of Psychiatry,
    164
Compulsive Shopping Disorder, 249–50
conflict of interest, 227, 235, 238, 249
consent, lack of, xxii
consequences of psychiatric diagnosis,
    negative, xix–xx, 242, 244
constructs, xx
consumer advocacy groups, 19
Cosmopolitan, 205
Courtois, Christine, 166
courts, xv. *See also* legal system
Craine, L. S., 214
Crawford, Mary, 89
crises, life, xxx
critical inquiry, xvi, 242–47
critical thinking. *See* critical inquiry
critique, xx. *See also* critical inquiry
Crowe, B., 143
Crowley, Dana, 185
culture, influence of, 17–20, 72–73,
    77–78, 89–91, 95, 122, 203, 234

daughters-in-law, issue of, 142
Davidson, Jonathan, 34
Dawes, R. M., 204
death penalty, 55–58
Debs, Eugene V., xviii
Declaration of Sexual Rights, 235
deep structure of bias, xvi
DeFrancisco, V., 174
dementia, 93
Department of Child and Family
    Services, xv
dependency, 93
Dependent Personality Disorder, 204
depression, xiv, xviii, 91, 93, 141–44,
    225, 244, 250–51; Dysthymia, 129;
    in women, 183–86
diagnosis, avoidance of, 241–42
digestive problems, 226
disability, xiv
Disaesthesia Ethiopica, 81
disclosure, full, by therapists, xxii, xxx
Disorders of Extreme Stress Not
    Otherwise Specified (DESNOS), 35,
    38
Dissociative Identity Disorder (DID),
    213–16
divorce, xv
Drapetomania, 81
drug companies. *See* pharmaceutical
    companies
drugs, xx, xxi, 90, 91, 93, 117, 143–44,
    150, 180, 223, 221–28, 250–51

eating disorders, 189–91, 193–98
economic power, xx, xxiii
economic problems, xvii
education, 18
Eli Lilly Co., 222–26
employment, xix, xxi, xxix, xxx
Endicott, Jean, 225–26
entities, diagnostic categories as real,
    xxiii, 223–25, 227
ethics, xxii, xxx
expectation exhaustion, 143

experimental treatment, xxii
Expressive Language Disorder, 101

False Memory Syndrome, 163–67. *See also* False Memory Syndrome Foundation
False Memory Syndrome Foundation (FMSF), 163
Farm Women's Advancement Program (FWAP), 142
Farm Women's Bureau, 142
father-blaming, 94
femininity, xv, xvi, xvii
feminist critique of the *DSM*, 41–45
First, Michael, 250
Foa, Edna, 34
Food and Drug Administration, xiv, 249, 251
Forest Laboratories, 249
formulation, xxi
Foucault, M., xix
Franko, D. L., 195
Fraser, A., 214
Freud, Sigmund, xvi, 81, 252
Freyd, Jennifer, 165
fundamental attribution error, xxii

Gage, Carolyn, xxiii
Gallant, Sheryle, 222
Gardner, Richard, 62–65
Geel, 245–46
Gelfond, M., 179
gender, 4, 10–13, 41–45, 61–65, 127–30, 173–75, 178–80, 183, 203, 207–9, 213–17, 233–34. *See also* sexism
gender-specific age bias, 84, 94
Georgaca, Eugene, 92
Gergen, K. G., xvi, 244
Gerrard, Nikki, 128
Ginter, G. G., 93
Grinnell, Gretchen, 144
Gross Stress Reaction (GSR), 27
Guarnaccia, J., 186

Haley, Sarah, 27, 30
Halleck, Seymour L., xviii, 90–91, 93
Hall-McCorquodale, Ian, 103
Hamilton, L., 204
harassment, 128, 224
Hare-Mustin, R. T., 93
Harper, David, 92
Harriet Tubman Visits a Therapist, xxiii
Harvard Mental Health Letter, 186
health insurance, xix. *See also* insurance companies
health maintenance organizations, xxi
Henson, C. E., 214
Herman, C. P., 196
Herman, Judith, 29, 37
heterosexism xvi. *See also* sexual orientation
Hickling, Fred, 82
Histrionic Personality Disorder, xvi, xv, 201–5
Hollingshead, August B., xvii, 117
homophobia, xvi. *See also* sexual orientation
homosexuality, 121–26. *See also* sexual orientation
Horney, Karen, xvi
Hudson, J. I., 166
hyperactivity, 110
hyperkinesis, 110
hypervisibility, 90
hysteria. *See* Histrionic Personality Disorder
Hysterical Personality Disorder. *See* Histrionic Personality Disorder

independence, 185
individual, intrapsychic causes of mental disorder, xviii, 92, 141, 177–79, 180, 184, 190, 223–24, 227, 231–37
individuation, 226
Ingram, Paul, 165
injustice, 224
insanity, xx
Institute of Medicine, 99

insurance companies, xxi, xxix, 11,
17–18, 20, 209, 243
intelligence, 56
intelligence quotient (IQ), 55–58
invisibility, 90

Javed, Nayyar, 128
Johnson, V. E., 233–34, 238
*Journal of Women's Health and Gender-
Based Medicine*, 225
journals, xiv
judges. *See* legal system
justice, social, 243–44

Kaplan, Marcie, 44
Kappius, R. E., 213
Kardiner, Abram, 26–27, 81
Kessler, M., 117
Kihlstrom, John, 163–65
Kim, N. S., 197
King, Martin Luther, Jr., xviii
Kirk, Stuart, 6
Kovel, Joel, 102
Kramer, Peter, 246
Kreisman, Jerold, 105–7
Kutchins, Herb, 6

labels, number of, xxi
Lamb, S., 213
Late Luteal Phase Dysphoric Disorder
(LLPDD), 221–22. *See also*
Premenstrual Dysphoric Disorder
law. *See* legal system
lawyers, xv. *See also* legal system
learning disabilities, 109–13
legal system, xv, xix, xx, xxx, 15–16,
19, 22, 49–53, 85–86
Lifton, Robert, 30
Listening to Prozac, 246
Loftus, E. F., 165–66
Lonie, I., 215
Lopez, S. R., 186
Loring, M., 204
low-income women, 115–18
Lykes, M. B., 173

MacLean, D. G., 214
MacPherson, Gael, 113
Major Depressive Disorder, 51–52, 95,
127
Malcolm X, xviii
Malleus Maleficarum, 107
Maracek, J., 93, 209
marketing, xviii
masculinity, xiv
masochism, xiv, xvii
Masters, H., 233–34, 237
Masterson, James, 103–4
McLaughlin, Terence, 92
media, xiv, xx, 17, 21
medical care, xix
medical model, xxii, 43, 45, 208–9,
221–28, 233–37, 245–46, 249
mental disorder, definition of, xx
mental health system, xxii, xxiii, 17, 18
mental illness, medicalization of, 4, 5, 6,
18, 19, 22, 101–3, 117, 208–10, 222
mental retardation, 55–58
Metcalfe, William, 245
military, xix
Miller, Jean Baker, 190
Millon Clinical Multiaxial Inventory,
204
Minnesota Multiphasic Personality
Inventory, xv, 153
Mintz, L. B., 194
mother-blaming, xiv, 94, 103, 190–91
Muerser, K. T., 214
Multiple Personality Disorder, 216. *See
also* Dissociative Identity Disorder
Munchausen's by Proxy (MBP), 62

Nakdimen, K. A., 216
National Alliance for the Mentally Ill,
19
National Coalition for Rural Childcare,
142
National Institute of Mental Health
(NIMH), 99
neurosis, xvii
New Age, xx

New England Journal of Medicine, xiv
New View of Women's Sexual
    Problems, 233–38
normality, xx, 6, 10
Norton, G. R., 214

obesity, 189–90
Obsessive-Compulsive Disorder (OCD),
    50–53, 78
Omori, M., 195
oppression, xiv, xviii
Orr, J., 129
Ovesey, L., 181–84

Panic Disorder, 129
paraphilias, 63. *See also* sexual
    problems
Parental Alienation Syndrome (PAS),
    61–65
parenting, xxx
Parker, Ian, 92
Parsons, Talcott, 4
pedophilia, 63. *See also* sexual abuse: of
    children
Pezdek, K., 166
Pfizer, 224
pharmaceutical companies, xiv, xvii,
    17–20, 93, 225, 234, 249. *See also*
    Eli Lilly Co.; Forest Laboratories;
    Pfizer; Smith Kline Beecham
physical problems, xviii, 20
Pierce, Chester, 83
Plato, 201
PMS. *See* Premenstrual Dysphoric
    Disorder
Polivy, J., 196
Pope, Harrison, 166
Pope, Ken, 166
Post-traumatic Stress Disorder (PTSD),
    25–39, 52, 63, 207–10, 213–14,
    215–16, 244; clinical use of, 28–29;
    construction of, 29–33; in practice,
    36–38
poverty. *See* social class
Powell, B., 204

power, social, xxiii
Premenstrual Dysphoric Disorder
    (PMDD), 127, 221–27, 251
problems, externally caused, xviii, xxix,
    xxx, 130, 141, 177–80, 189–91,
    209–10, 227, 233–37, 246, 250. *See
    also* ableism; abuse; ageism;
    homophobia; problems, social;
    racism; sexism; social class; violence
problems, social, xvii, xviii, xxii; 249.
    See also problems, externally caused
Prozac, 223–28, 251
Pruitt, J. A., 213
The Psychiatric Society, 102
psychoanalysts, xvii, xxiii
psychologizing, xx
Psychopharmacological Drugs Advisory
    Committee (PDAC), 225
psychosis, xvii
psychotherapists, training of. *See*
    clinicians

race. *See* racism
racism, xiv, xvi, xxii, 71–74, 77–78,
    81–87, 94, 184, 241; history of,
    81–83; as a mental illness, question
    of, 84–87; as personality disorder,
    83–84
Reactive Disorders Committee, 27,
    29–32, 37–38
Read, J., 214
Reading Disorder, 101
Redlich, F. C., xvii, 117
regulation, lack of for psychiatric
    diagnosis, xxii
Rehabilitation Act, 49
Reich, J., 204
reification of categories, 128. *See also*
    entities
Reiss, David, 250
Relational Disorder, 249–52
relationships, 223, 233–37, 244, 249–51
reliability, xxi, xxii, 5–6, 56
religion, influence of, 77, 82, 201
research, 243

resistance to mistreatment, 241–42
Rivers, W. H., 26
Road Rage, 249, 252
Rosenberg, M., 174
Ross, C. A., 214
Rothbart, M., 204
The Rules, 205
rural women, diagnosis of, 141–44

Sarafem, 224–26
Schizoid Personality Disorder, 101
schizophrenia, xxi, 149–59, 215–16;
    biases in diagnosis of, 152–58, 214;
    as a stereotype, 149–52
Scott, C., 143
Self-Defeating Personality Disorder
    (SDPD), 29, 128
self-esteem, 171–75
sex, distribution of diagnostic labels
    by, 127–30, 132–40. *See also*
    gender
sexism, xiv, xvi, xvii, 71–74, 77–78, 94,
    127–30, 132–40, 189–91, 210,
    221–28, 241, 250–51
sexual abuse: of children, 61–65, 106,
    117, 164, 202, 208; of women, 184
Sexual Abuse Legitimacy Scale, 65–66
sexual orientation, 121, 123–24
sexual problems: frotteurism, 122–23;
    Gender Identity Disorder (GID), 122,
    145; Hypoactive Sexual Desire
    Disorder (HSDD), 121, 226; Sexual
    Disorder Not Otherwise Specified,
    123; of women, 233–37. *See also*
    paraphilias
sexual profile, 124–26. *See also* sexual
    problems
sexuality, 121–26
Shatan, Chaim, 30
Siegel, Rachel Josefowitz, 185
slavery, xxiii
sleep problems, 226
Smith, Jack, 30
Smith Kline Beecham, 224

social class, influence of, xvii, xxi,
    xxiii, 115–18, 184; and mental
    illness, xvii
social workers, xxi
society, influence of, 3–6, 116, 174–75,
    184, 190. *See also* culture; problems,
    externally caused; problems, social
Spitzer, Robert, 27, 30–31, 221
standard error, 56
standardization of tests, 57
Stone Center, 185
Stoppard, Janet, xxii
Stowell-Smith, Mark, 92
stress, xiv, xxiii
stressors, psychosocial, xxiii, 115, 149,
    178
Subich, M., 195
suicide, 27, 226
Sutton, R. G., 117

Talking Back to Prozac, 246
Tavris, Carol, 128, 130
Technology-Science-Medicine Complex
    (TSM), 17–18
textbooks, xx, 41–45
Thoreau, Henry David, xviii
Thurston, W., 143
Tobin, Patricia, 113
trauma, 25–39, 93, 116, 163, 165, 166,
    202, 204, 207–10, 213–17, 236
traumatized women, 213–17
tuberculosis, xxi
Tubman, Harriet, xxiii
Tylka, T. L., 195

Underwager, R., 165–66
Unger, Rhoda, 89
United Nations Security Council, 174
Ussher, J. M., 223
Ustun, Bedirham, 252

validity, xxii, 5–6, 150
Vedantam, Shankar, 249
Victimization Disorder, 29

Vietnam Veterans Working Group (VVWG), 27
violence, xiv, xv, xxiii; 224, 251. *See also* abuse; harassment; sexual abuse
visual perceptual disorder, 110

Wakefield, H., 165–66
Wall Street Journal, 249
Walsh, Michael, 64
Washington Post, 249
Wealthy Widow Case, 93–94
what to do, xxix–xxx, 124–26, 141–44, 158–59, 201–5, 241–42, 243–47
widowhood, 93–95

Wiley, Autumn, xx
Women and Madness, xxii
Women and Mental Health in Canada, xxiii
women's movement, Second Wave of, 61
World Association of Sexology, 235
World Health Organization, 235, 252
Wozney, K., 214
Wright, L., 165
Wynne, Lyman, 30–31

Yonkers, K. A., 224

Zellman, G. L., 117

About the Contributors

Alisha Ali, Ph.D., is Assistant Professor in the Department of Applied Psychology at New York University. Her research focuses on issues of well-being and mental health in disadvantaged populations. She has published widely on such topics as the depressogenic effects of emotional abuse, attitudes about violence against women, cross-cultural psychological research, and the mental health consequences of poverty, racism, and discrimination. She also writes in the area of feminist epistemology and social action.

Gloria Anthony is a pseudonym chosen in tribute to Gloria Steinem and Susan B. Anthony. The author used a pen name because of serious concerns about retribution, both from the clinic where she works and from the powerful advocates of the most traditional forms of labeling.

Louise Armstrong is the author of the groundbreaking book, *Kiss Daddy Goodnight: A Speakout on Incest* (1978) and *Kiss Daddy Goodnight: Ten Years Later* (1987), as well as *And They Call It Help: The Psychiatric Policing of America's Children* (1993); *Rocking the Cradle of Sexual Politics: What Happened When Women Said Incest* (1996); *Of "Sluts" and "Bastards": A Feminist Decodes the Child Welfare Debate* (1995); *The Home Front: Notes from the Family War Zone* (1983); *Solomon Says: A Speakout on Foster Care* (1989); and numerous scholarly and mainstream articles and papers. She has given many keynote addresses about issues of abuse by the mental health system, violence against women, and the psychiatric maltreatment of women and children.

Dana Becker, Ph.D., is Associate Professor at the Bryn Mawr Graduate School of Social Work and Social Research She has published articles and book chapters on women and psychodiagnosis and on family therapy with adolescents, as

263

well as *Through the Looking Glass: Women and Borderline Personality Disorder* (1997). She has been a practicing clinician for more than twenty years.

Heather E. Bullock, Ph.D., is Associate Professor of Psychology at University of California-Santa Cruz. Before joining the UCSC faculty, she was an American Psychological Association Congressional Fellow with the U.S. Senate Committee on Health, Education, Labor, and Pensions (Democratic Office). Her research is focused on the social psychological dimensions of poverty and economic (in)justice, including discrimination against low-income women and the beliefs that predict support for a wide range of welfare and antipoverty policies

Emily J. Caplan, J.D., is an attorney, licensed to practice law in the states of Massachusetts, Maryland, and the District of Columbia. She is a General Attorney at the U.S. Equal Employment Opportunity Commission in Washington, DC. Ms. Caplan was born and raised in Toronto, Canada, and attended Brown University, where she received her B.A. in political science. She received her Juris Doctor from American University, Washington College of Law, where she was a Marshall-Brennan Fellow.

Paula J. Caplan, Ph.D., is a clinical and research psychologist, Visiting Scholar at the Pembroke Center for Teaching and Research on Women at Brown University, and Adjunct Professor at Washington College of Law, American University. She is the author of ten previous books, including *The Myth of Women's Masochism* (1985/1993); *Don't Blame Mother: Mending the Mother-Daughter Relationship* (1989/2000); *Thinking Critically about Research on Sex and Gender* (coauthored with Jeremy B. Caplan 1994/1999); *Lifting a Ton of Feathers: A Woman's Guide to Surviving in the Academic World* (1993); *Gender Differences in Human Cognition* (coauthored with Jeremy B. Caplan, Mary Crawford, Janet Shibley Hyde, and John T. E. Richardson 1997); *They Say You're Crazy: How the World's Most Powerful Psychiatrists Decide Who's Normal* (1995); *You're Smarter Than They Make You Feel: How the Experts Intimidate Us and What We Can Do About It* (1994); and *Children's Learning and Attention Problems* (with Marcel Kinsbourne 1979). She has a private practice in Cambridge, MA, with specialties in court-related work and children with school problems.

Emily Cohen received her B.A. in psychology from Connecticut College, where she was a member of Psi Chi, the honorary psychology society. She is currently a graduate student in developmental psychology at Teacher's College, Columbia University.

Lisa Cosgrove, Ph.D., is a clinical and research psychologist and an Assistant Professor in the Department of Counseling and School Psychology at the University of Massachusetts at Boston. She has published numerous articles and book chapters on critical psychology, research methods, feminist therapy, and theoretical and philosophical issues related to clinical practice. Her scholarship includes work in the areas of community psychology, social policy, women and homelessness, and the aftermath of trauma. Dr. Cosgrove's research has been supported through grants from National Institute of Mental Health (to the Murray Center of the Radcliffe Institute, Harvard University) and from the University of Massachusetts. She was a 2002–2003 Fellow in the William Jointer Center for the Study of War and Social Consequences where she conducted research on the intergenerational impact of war-related Post-traumatic Stress Disorder. She also has a private practice in Natick, Massachusetts.

Vincent Fish, Ph.D., M.S.S.W., is a psychologist/clinical social worker in private practice and a lecturer in the School of Social Work and the Division of Continuing Studies, University of Wisconsin-Madison. He teaches psychopathology and has published research on the impact of childhood abuse and journal articles and book chapters about memories of childhood sexual abuse, family treatment of incest, and the politics of therapy. His practice interests include psychological trauma, children in placement, and related clinical and organizational issues.

Nikki Gerrard, Ph.D., is a community psychologist and the Coordinator of the Rural Quality of Life and Adult Counseling programs, Adult Community Mental Health Services, Saskatoon Health Region, where she also is the Chief Psychologist for the Adult Services in Mental Health. Nikki designed and implemented a farm stress program over eleven years ago and has worked extensively in rural mental health. As a community psychologist, Nikki is interested in the psyche of the community and spends a lot of her time developing community strengths, through community development, education, research, and organizing. Her latest research is entitled *What Doesn't Kill You Makes You Stronger: Determinants of Stress Resiliency in Rural People in Saskatchewan* (2004). In addition to rural mental health, Nikki's research and practice interests include women's psychology and antiracism.

Pamela Reed Gibson has a Ph.D. in clinical psychology and is Full Professor of Psychology at James Madison University, where she teaches courses relating to mental health, gender and diversity, and psychology and ecology. Her research has been in the area of environment and health, specifically multiple chemical sensitivity. She is author of *Multiple Chemical Sensitivity: A Survival Guide* (2000) and *Understanding and Accommodating Multiple Chemical Sensitivity in Independent Living* (2002).

Nayyar Javed is a psychologist who works in the Adult Community Mental Health Services in Saskatoon Health Region, Saskatchewan. She offers individual and group therapy. Nayyar has integrated antiracism and feminist analysis in her work. She has published book chapters, journal articles, newsletter articles, and short stories. Nayyar has presented papers at local, national, and international forums. She is also involved in the grass roots women's, peace, and antiracism movements.

Meadow Linder is a doctoral student in sociology at the University of Michigan and received her B.A. from Brown University. She is interested in the social processes responsible for the reproduction of inequality within and across generations and the intersection of place and health. Her current research focuses on health disparities in urban communities and the role organizations play in the production and acquisition of neighborhood capital. She has previously published on the topic of contested environmental illnesses, particularly Gulf War–related illnesses.

Maureen McHugh, Ph.D., is a Professor of Psychology at Indiana University of Pennsylvania, teaching graduate and undergraduate courses in Psychology of Women, Human Sexuality and Diversity Issues in Psychology. She received her doctorate in Social Psychology from the University of Pittsburgh in 1983. She was awarded the Christine Ladd Franklin Award from the Association for Women in Psychology (AWP) for her contributions to feminist psychology, which include a number of publications on research methods, sex differences, and gender roles. She coauthored (with Koeske and Frieze) an *American Psychologist* article on guidelines for nonsexist research in psychology, and received a Distinguished Publication Award from AWP for coediting (with Frieze) a special issue of *Psychology of Women Quarterly* on measures of gender role attitudes.

Sarah McSweeney, Psy.D., completed her clinical psychology degree at the Illinois School of Professional Psychology in Chicago in 1998. Her research there focused on faculty development and curriculum change. After completing her internship training at the Children's Hospital/Judge Baker Children's Center (JBCC) program in Boston she was hired by JBCC to direct their school-based services program. In 1999 she became a mother. She is presently in private practice in Lexington, MA, and leading dream workshops for adults when she is able.

William R. Metcalfe, M.Ed., has been a psychotherapist in private practice in Toronto, Canada, for twenty-five years. He works within the gay, lesbian, bisexual, transgendered, and heterosexual communities, helping clients struggling with self-acceptance and identity issues. Mr. Metcalfe also works extensively with individuals who have experienced extremely abusive or dysfunctional backgrounds. In the 1970s he designed and directed an innovative treatment program for disturbed youth. He is a single, gay father and has a diverse background ranging from counseling and teaching to architectural design, music, and carpentry.

Karen A. Olio is an author and psychotherapist. She has published numerous articles in journals including *American Psychologist*, *Psychotherapy*, *Journal of Psychiatry and Law*, and *Voices: The Art and Science of Psychotherapy* on treatment with adult survivors of childhood trauma. She has an independent practice and offers consultation groups in Norwalk, CT.

Jeffrey Poland has degrees in philosophy of science (Ph.D., Massachusetts Institute of Technology, 1983) and clinical psychology (M.A., Southern Connecticut State University, 1982), and he has extensive clinical experience in inpatient psychiatric rehabilitation. He is coauthor (with William Spaulding and Mary Sullivan) of *Treatment and Rehabilitation of Severe Mental Illness* (2003) and of a forthcoming book, *Crisis and Revolution: Toward a Reconceptualization of Psychopathology*, to be published with MIT Press. He has held positions at Colgate University and the University of Nebraska-Lincoln, and he currently teaches in the Department of History, Philosophy, and Social Science at the Rhode Island School of Design.

Wesley E. Profit, Ph.D., J.D., is a clinically trained psychologist who has long been interested in the problems of social change for minority and disenfranchised populations, including the impact of the mental health and criminal justice systems on poor communities. Dr. Profit has worked extensively in the criminal justice system. He is credited with establishing a comprehensive mental health program in a large prison system so that mentally disordered offenders were no longer routinely confined to the most secure facilities. As the Director of Forensic Services at a maximum security forensic facility, Dr. Profit was frequently involved with the assessment and treatment of extremely violent individuals. Dr. Profit has consulted on numerous occasions on issues of extreme and unusual violence. Recently, Dr. Profit completed a two-year intensive program of legal training.

Judith R. Rabinor, Ph.D., is a clinical psychologist and the Director of the American Eating Disorders Center. She is an Associate Professor at Adelphi

University and a consultant to The Renfrew Centers and the Federation Employment and Guidance Service, Inc., Eating Disorders Prevention Project, NoBody's Perfect. She is the editor of "The Therapist's Voice" in *Eating Disorders: The Journal of Treatment and Prevention*. She has published numerous articles and book chapters on eating and body image issues and the mother-daughter relationship and is the author of *A Starving Madness: Tales of Hunger, Hope and Healing in Psychotherapy* (2002). Judith lectures and conducts professional training nationwide on eating disorder treatment and empowering women through writing. She has a private practice in New York City and in Lido Beach, Long Island.

Bethany Riddle is a doctoral candidate in clinical psychology at Duquesne University. Her research is focused on critical feminist perspectives on medical, psychoanalytic, and philosophical conceptualizations of women and women's reproductive functioning. She has published and presented work on constructions of feminity and experiences of menstrual distress and is an active member of the Committee on Sexualities and Gender Identities of the Psychoanalytic Division (Division 39) of the American Psychological Association. She will be completing a qualitative dissertation on the relationship between technological interventions in pregnancy and normative identities.

Rachel Josefowitz Siegel, MSW, is a psychotherapist in private practice in Ithaca, New York. She has integrated a feminist and anti-bias approach into her writing and her work with clients. Her primary research and therapy interests are old women and Jewish women. She has lectured widely on both subjects and has authored numerous articles and co-edited several books. She is proud to be a Jewish mother, grandmother, and great-grandmother, approaching her eightieth birthday

The Working Group on A New View of Women's Sexual Problems is composed of a dozen feminist social scientists and clinicians convened in 2000 by **Leonore Tiefer**. The group worked on the document by email over a period of months and during an intense weekend at one member's home. The group has become the core of the Campaign for a New View of Women's Sexual Problems, which is described at www.fsd-alert.org. **Leonore Tiefer**, Ph.D., is a feminist and psychologist who has specialized in many different areas of sexuality for thirty years. Her Westview Press book, *Sex is Not a Natural Act and Other Essays*, is now in a second edition (2004), and has been translated into several languages. With Ellyn Kaschak, she coedited a collection, *A New View of Women's Sexual Problems*, in 2001. She is currently working on an anthology about Viagra.

Autumn Wiley received her B.A. with a double major in psychology and sociology and completed the Women's Studies program at Brandeis University. Her undergraduate thesis was called "The inclusion/exclusion of sex and gender bias criticism of the *DSM* in abnormal psychology textbooks." She is an associate analyst at Apt Associates, working on research evaluation of reform initiatives in higher education. She has been a social and political activist, working against sexism, racism, homophobia, and, in fact, all forms of oppression for many years.